Mediating International Crises

International crises are dangerous episodes that can be destabilizing not only to the actors directly involved but also to the entire international system. Recognizing the primacy of crises as defining moments in international relations, scholars and policy makers alike are increasingly concerned with identifying mechanisms for crisis prevention, management and resolution.

Mediating International Crises is the first comprehensive study into one such mechanism that has been used with increasing frequency in the twentieth century: mediation by a third party. This important research attempts to determine whether third-party mediation is an effective means of alleviating or managing the turbulent and violent consequences of crises. The authors examine three approaches to mediation: facilitating communication between parties, formulating possible agreements and manipulating the parties through sanctions or rewards. They explore how these mediation approaches affect crisis outcomes through their interaction with factors such as the relative power relations between disputants and the degree to which a crisis provides a window of opportunity for resolution. In addition, historical data on all major twentieth century crises and data derived from simulation experiments are brought to bear on these issues. This unique blending of historical and experimental data allows researchers to gain greater insight into the processes involved in crisis mediation.

This unique work will become essential reading for academics, policy makers, and historians examining crisis and negotiation.

Jonathan Wilkenfeld is a professor of government and politics and director of the Center for International Development and Conflict Management (CIDCM) at the University of Maryland. He specializes in foreign policy, international conflict and crisis, mediation, and the application of simulation and experimental approaches. **Kathleen J. Young** is director of the ICONS Project at the University of Maryland and is a research fellow at CIDCM. **David M. Quinn** is a doctoral candidate in the Department of Government and Politics at the University of Maryland. **Victor Asal** is an assistant professor of Political Science at the State University of New York, Albany.

Routledge advances in international relations and global politics

1 **Foreign Policy and Discourse Analysis**
France, Britain and Europe
Henrik Larsen

2 **Agency, Structure and International Politics**
From ontology to empirical enquiry
Gil Friedman and Harvey Starr

3 **The Political Economy of Regional Co-operation in the Middle East**
Ali Carkoglu, Mine Eder, Kemal Kirisci

4 **Peace Maintenance**
The evolution of international political authority
Jarat Chopra

5 **International Relations and Historical Sociology**
Breaking down boundaries
Stephen Hobden

6 **Equivalence in Comparative Politics**
Edited by Jan W. van Deth

7 **The Politics of Central Banks**
Robert Elgie and Helen Thompson

8 **Politics and Globalisation**
Knowledge, ethics and agency
Martin Shaw

9 **History and International Relations**
Thomas W. Smith

10 **Idealism and Realism in International Relations**
Robert M.A. Crawford

11 **National and International Conflicts, 1945–1995**
New empirical and theoretical approaches.
Frank Pfetsch and Christoph Rohloff

12 **Party Systems and Voter Alignments Revisited**
Edited by Lauri Karvonen and Stein Kuhnle

13 **Ethics, Justice and International Relations**
Constructing an international community
Peter Sutch

14 **Capturing Globalization**
Edited by James H. Mittelman and Norani Othman

15 **Uncertain Europe**
Building a new European security order?
Edited by Martin A. Smith and Graham Timmins

16 **Power, Postcolonialism and International Relations**
Reading race, gender and class
Edited by Geeta Chowdhry and Sheila Nair

17 **Constituting Human Rights**
Global civil society and the society of democratic states
Mervyn Frost

18 **US Economic Statecraft for Survival 1933–1991**
Of sanctions, embargoes and economic warfare
Alan P. Dobson

19 **The EU and NATO Enlargement**
Richard McAllister and Roland Dannreuther

20 **Spatializing International Politics**
Analysing activism on the internet
Jayne Rodgers

21 **Ethnonationalism in the Contemporary World**
Walker Connor and the study of Nationalism
Edited by Daniele Conversi

22 **Meaning and International Relations**
Edited by Peter Mandaville and Andrew Williams

23 **Political Loyalty and the Nation-State**
Edited by Michael Waller and Andrew Linklater

24 **Russian Foreign Policy and the CIS**
Theories, debates and actions
Nicole J. Jackson

25 **Asia and Europe**
Development and different dimensions of ASEM
Yeo Lay Hwee

26 **Global Instability and Strategic Crisis**
Neville Brown

27 **Africa in International Politics**
External involvement on the Continent
Edited by Ian Taylor and Paul Williams

28 **Global Governmentality**
Governing international spaces
Edited by Wendy Larner and William Walters

29 **Political Learning and Citizenship Education Under Conflict**
The political socialization of Israeli and Palestinian youngsters
Orit Ichilov

30 **Gender and Civil Society**
Transcending boundaries
Edited by Jude Howell and Diane Mulligan

31 **State Crises, Globalisation and National Movements in North-East Africa**
The Horn's dilemma
Edited by Asafa Jalata

32 **Diplomacy and Developing Nations**
Post-Cold War foreign policy-making structures and processes
Edited by Justin Robertson and Maurice A. East

33 **Autonomy, Self-governance and Conflict Resolution**
Innovative approaches to institutional design in divided societies
Edited by Marc Weller and Stefan Wolff

34 **Mediating International Crises**
Jonathan Wilkenfeld, Kathleen J. Young, David M. Quinn and Victor Asal

35 **Postcolonial Politics, The Internet and Everyday Life**
Pacific traversals online
M. I. Franklin

Mediating International Crises

Jonathan Wilkenfeld,
Kathleen J. Young, David M. Quinn
and Victor Asal

Routledge
Taylor & Francis Group
LONDON AND NEW YORK

First published 2005
by Routledge
2 Park Square, Milton Park, Abingdon, Oxon OX14 4RN

Simultaneously published in the USA and Canada
by Routledge
270 Madison Ave, New York, NY 10016

Routledge is an imprint of the Taylor & Francis Group

Transferred to Digital Printing 2006

Typeset in Times by Wearset Ltd, Boldon, Tyne and Wear

British Library Cataloguing in Publication Data
A catalogue record for this book is available from the British Library

Library of Congress Cataloging in Publication Data
A catalog record for this book has been requested

ISBN10: 0–415–70067–1 (hbk)
ISBN10: 0–415–40677–3 (pbk)

ISBN13: 978–0–415–70067–2 (hbk)
ISBN13: 978–0–415–40677–2 (pbk)

Contents

Illustrations

Figures

Tables

Preface and acknowledgements

This book brings together three streams of research that the authors have been involved with for many years – the International Crisis Behavior (ICB), International Communication and Negotiation Simulation (ICONS), and Crisis and Negotiation (CAN) projects. The impetus for the present study, with its specific focus on crisis, negotiation, and mediation, grows out of a long-term interdisciplinary research project led by Jonathan Wilkenfeld at the University of Maryland and his Bar Ilan (Israel)/University of Maryland computer science colleague Sarit Kraus. Wilkenfeld and Kraus have a long-standing joint interest in understanding better how humans (in Wilkenfeld's case) and intelligent agents or machines (in Kraus's case) negotiate in difficult (crisis) situations in order to reach mutually beneficial agreements. Whereas Wilkenfeld's interest is in understanding the conditions under which negotiations can end conflict and crisis without the resort to violence, Kraus's objective is to understand how intelligent agents can be endowed with negotiation skills such that they can share scarce resources or cooperate to perform tasks. In both cases, negotiations are employed in situations where time is critical to some or all of the parties, resources are scarce, and tasks may require cooperative behavior. Kraus's *Strategic Negotiation in Multiagent Environments* (2001) and the present book are the two major products of this collaboration.

In the past five years, the interest of the authors has been increasingly drawn to the potential impact of third parties, and specifically mediators, on the course and outcomes of international crises. Beginning as a small graduate seminar at the University of Maryland, and with funding from the National Science Foundation (IIS9820657, IIS0208608, and SES9905575), the authors gradually developed an experimental environment in which crisis negotiation could be evaluated in the context of various styles of mediation. Parallel to this was the incorporation of mediation variables into the coding of ICB cases, requiring a two year backcoding effort. Ultimately, we assembled the data from these two separate methodological approaches so that we could address important questions pertaining to crisis, negotiation, and mediation. While a number of papers and journal articles have been written, this book is the first place to gather and present all that we have learned thus far under one roof.

Ultimately, as we acknowledge throughout this study, we seek to break new ground by bringing together empirical work based on historical cases of crisis mediation with data generated through experimental methods. While we must take great care in interpreting these results and in not extending our generalizations too far, we hope that we convey to our readers the excitement that we feel as researchers as we confront the analytic power that such a multi-methodological approach provides. So, our mission has been two-fold: to shed light on the ways in which mediation of international crises can be effective in crisis management and conflict resolution, and to demonstrate how this type of research agenda can be enhanced by bringing to bear on it data derived from multiple sources. The careful reader will be the judge of our ultimate success.

Many people have contributed to this endeavor over the years. Wilkenfeld's two long-term collaborators, Michael Brecher and Sarit Kraus, have provided key advice, assistance, and critical judgments over the course of this project. A number of graduate students have served as coders, mediators, assistants, and collaborators over the years, and their contributions have been crucial – Amy Pate, Tara Santmire, Christopher Frain, David Andersen, Kristian Gleditsch (now assistant professor at UCSD), Bidisha Biswas, Kyle Beardsley (graduate student at UCSD), Pelin Eralp, and Chris Fettweis. And a literal army of undergraduate research assistants coded cases and assisted in the experimental simulation runs – Gary Kaufman, Clio Timmerman, John Kim, Heather McQueeney, Amy Fields, Paul Witten, Alex Kurgansky, John Sawyer, Ian McKay, Cory Black, Scott Apple, Barbara Gilmore, Gilad Wilkenfeld, Jane Schmitt, David Bellis, Ryan Frazier, Dina Goldentayer, Ed Haberman, Niel Kaneshiro, Colleen Kenning, Steven Lee, Eric So, and Samantha Watts. Several faculty members in the Department of Government and Politics at the University of Maryland have allowed us to conduct the experiments in their classes: Virginia Haufler, Bartek Kaminski, Ken Conca, and Scott Kastner. Technical assistance on various aspects of our work was provided by Beth Blake, Alex Jonas, and Tara Santmire. The Department of Government and Politics, the Center for International Development and Conflict Management, and the ICONS Project have provided support, facilities, and advice during the long process of putting this study together. Finally, each of the authors would like to thank family and friends for support and patience during this project.

1 The role of mediation in managing international crises

International crises are dangerous episodes that can be destabilizing not only to the actors directly involved but to the entire international system. Crises can present overwhelming challenges to established institutions and belief systems and can change forever the distribution of power within the international community or in a regional subsystem. Recognizing the primacy of crises as defining moments in international relations, scholars and policy makers alike are increasingly concerned with identifying mechanisms for crisis prevention, management, and resolution. In this book, we investigate one such mechanism – mediation by a third party – to determine whether it is an effective means of mitigating, or at least managing, the all-too-often turbulent and violent consequences of crises.

Historically, states have employed a wide array of mechanisms to contain, manage, and resolve their crises with other members of the international system. International Crisis Behavior (ICB) data on crises in the twentieth century finds that half of all crisis actors relied on violence either exclusively or in conjunction with other techniques to manage their crises. The remaining actors employed a variety of non-violent approaches, including negotiation, adjudication and arbitration, mediation, and non-violent military actions, in an effort to achieve their goals within a crisis. Any evaluation of the effectiveness of these various approaches must consider a number of questions: Does it prevent crisis escalation? Does it help to bring crises to an end more rapidly? Are crisis actors satisfied with the outcome of the crisis? Does a legacy of tension result following the crisis? Further, is the effectiveness of any of these approaches either undermined or exacerbated by the specific context of a crisis? All of these issues are relevant in determining the merits, and possible drawbacks, of each approach. This study explores these issues as they relate to mediation.

Mediation is by no means a rare phenomenon in international crises, or in conflict in general. For disputants, intervention by a mediator may be viewed as a necessary step to help parties move beyond profound disagreements as well as mutual mistrust and resentment. For mediators, this type of involvement in a crisis or conflict can be seen as a relatively low-cost form of intervention, a way for a third party to try to exert some influence over the trajectory of a conflict of special interest to them.

While the potential appeal of mediation to disputants and to interveners alike is apparent, the value and effectiveness of mediation in conflict and particularly in international crises is relatively under-explored. Robust case studies have provided insights into the specific mediation dynamics of individual episodes, but less work has been done to achieve a systematic understanding of the interplay of crisis factors and mediation effects. Such generalizable research is needed if we are to have greater confidence about what to expect when a mediator becomes involved in an international crisis and about what mediators can and should do in order to improve their chances of successfully managing a crisis.

Toward this goal of enhanced understanding of crisis mediation, this book examines the impact that mediation efforts have on the short-term outcomes and long-term impacts of international crises. We examine when crises are most likely to be mediated and how the outcomes of mediated crises differ from those of unmediated crises. We argue that a more complete understanding of the effects of crisis mediation requires consideration of the extent to which a mediator is involved in a crisis – are they simply facilitating communication among disputants? Or are they really directing a crisis negotiation process? The effect of a mediator will vary in accordance with the style employed by that mediator. Further, we examine how specific crisis characteristics – the relative-power relationship among disputants and the degree to which the crisis is ripe for resolution as mediation begins – affect the impact that a mediator has upon the evolution of a crisis.

To gain insights into a general framework for the analysis of crisis mediation, we employ a multi-methodological approach. Our findings are derived from two primary sources – from a comprehensive dataset of all international crises since the end of World War I, and from a series of human-based simulations of crisis negotiations. In addition, we explore in detail a number of historical episodes throughout the book to help illustrate our findings on crisis mediation.

We must be as clear as possible about the meanings of the key concepts and indicators we intend to use in this study. In the first section of this chapter, we will present definitions of four key concepts: crisis, mediation, crisis management, and conflict resolution. All of these concepts are employed widely in academia, the policy community, and in the press, but their meanings can vary widely across nations, regions, and cultures. While we do not ask that our readers accept at face value the definitions that we propose, it is our hope that these definitions will help readers to evaluate the significance of our findings for crisis management and conflict resolution in the early portions of the twenty-first century. In the final section of this chapter, we introduce and briefly discuss the framework that we have developed for analyzing how mediation affects the outcomes of international crises.

Foreign policy and international crises

Our point of departure is that interstate military-security crises were the most frequent type of hostile interaction among states in international politics in the twentieth century. And while there is some evidence that the frequency of these crises is gradually declining in the post-cold war unipolar system (see Figure 1.1), one has only to think about the 2003 war in Iraq, the tension over potential nuclear weapons in North Korea and Iran, or the nuclear standoff between India and Pakistan over Kashmir to realize that dangerous crises remain a potential disrupting force for the international system and its regional subsystems.

Our definitions of crises are those employed for more than 25 years by the International Crisis Behavior (ICB) Project (Brecher and Wilkenfeld 2000). A *foreign policy crisis*, that is, a crisis for an individual state, is a situation with three necessary and sufficient conditions deriving from a change in a state's internal or external environment. All three are perceptions held by the highest-level decision makers of the state actor concerned: a threat to one or more basic values, along with an awareness of finite time for response to the value threat, and a heightened probability of involvement in military hostilities. There were 956 foreign policy crises for individual states for the period 1918–2001.

The Brecher-Wilkenfeld definition of a crisis for a single actor differs from an early definition proposed by Hermann (1969). ICB omits any requirement of surprise, it replaces Hermann's requirement of short timespan with finite time, it recognizes that a crisis can originate with an

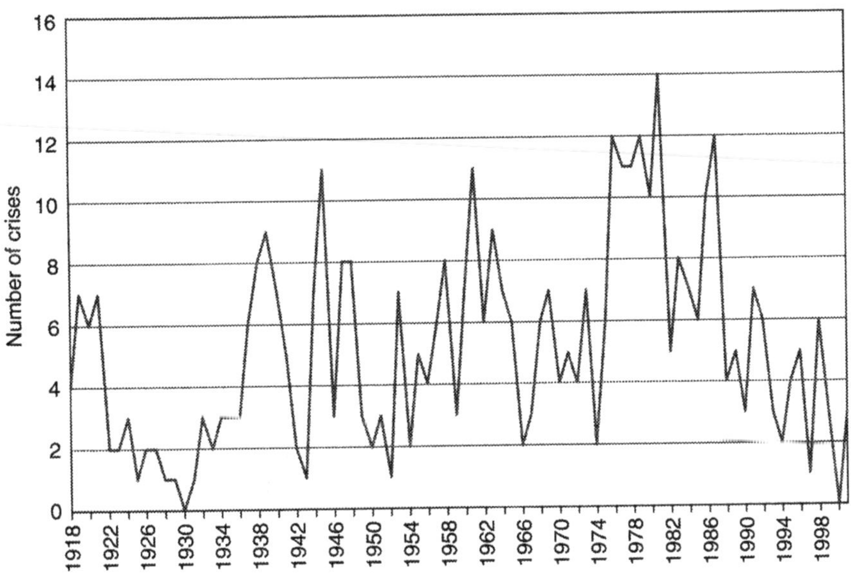

Figure 1.1 Distribution of international crises, 1918–2001

internal and not just an external event, it substitutes basic values for high priority goals, and it incorporates the notion of heightened probability of military hostilities. ICB also differs from another widely accepted definition of crisis, proposed by Snyder and Diesing (1977). While Snyder and Diesing focus on an interaction process, ICB is more concerned with perceptions and behavior. Time, whether short or finite, is critical to ICB. Forms of violence short of war are also critical to the ICB definition, and unlike Snyder and Diesing, war is included in ICB as an extreme form of crisis. Furthermore, according to Brecher and Wilkenfeld, crises can occur within the context of a war. The ICB definition of crisis draws attention to the key elements of perception, which occupies an important place in the literature on mediation, particularly regarding the issue of ripeness.

While the ICB definition of crisis at the actor level incorporates a central focus on the perceptions by the leaders of the states involved, the definition of crisis from the perspective of the international system involves a focus on disruptions to the system itself. There are two defining conditions of an *international crisis*: (1) a change in type and/or an increase in the intensity of disruptive (that is, hostile verbal or physical) interactions between two or more states, with a heightened probability of military hostilities; that, in turn, (2) destabilizes their relationship and challenges the structure of an international system – global, dominant, or subsystem.

An international crisis is set in motion by a disruptive act or event, a breakpoint or *trigger* that creates a foreign policy crisis for one or more states. Examples of crisis triggers include the German surprise attack on the Soviet Union in Stalingrad in 1942, the Vietminh offensive against Dien Bien Phu during the Indochina War in 1954 that triggered a crisis for France and later the United States and the United Kingdom, and the 1998 nuclear tests by India and Pakistan that triggered mutual crises. An international crisis ends with an act or event that signifies a qualitative reduction in conflict activity (Brecher and Wilkenfeld 2000). There were 434 international crises for the period 1918–2001.

Third-party mediation

Mediation in international conflicts and crises has been occurring since at least the early twentieth century. This phenomenon coincided with the rise of global international organizations, first the League of Nations and then the United Nations, and has become a prominent feature of the international system. However, as Sacks, Reichert, and Proffitt point out, "even though third-party intervention in dispute resolution has become a popular option for solving differences, we know little about what exactly third parties do or should do" (1999: 341). We attempt to address this deficiency in the present study.

Personal memoirs and in-depth case studies have provided some useful insights regarding mediation and mediation processes, but often these observations do not lead to generalizable understandings. A more theoretical literature on international mediation arose in the early 1960s, focused on when mediation occurs, why it occurs, how successful it is, and its implications for policy makers and future mediators. It is often prescriptive in nature. The separate, yet interrelated, literature on tactics for effective *negotiation* is also rife with assertions about what types of mediator tactics are effective in different scenarios and how mediation can and should affect negotiation processes.[1]

Bercovitch, Anagnoson, and Wille define mediation as "a process of conflict management where disputants seek the assistance of, or accept an offer of help from, an individual, group, state, or organization to settle their conflict or resolve their differences without resorting to physical force or invoking the authority of the law" (1991: 8). Bercovitch and Langley (1993) note that this behavioral definition is most useful because of its emphasis on the key components of mediation – the disputants, the third party, and the specific conflict resolution context.[2] In targeting the reach of the present study to that subset of acute conflicts characterized as crises, we recognize that in such cases mediation often takes place after violence has already occurred.

Mediation is an available resource for contending parties to use to address their conflicts non-violently or to reduce or eliminate violence once it has occurred. Mediation can either be initiated by the third party itself or by the conflicting parties. Young (1967) and Princen (1992) argue that prior to intervening in a dispute, a mediator cannot be a direct party to that dispute. However, once a mediator gets involved, its presence transforms the nature of direct negotiations among disputants. Mediation often occurs on an *ad hoc* basis but may also be prescribed by a prior agreement.

Mediation is non-binding, distinguishing a mediator from an arbitrator. Thus, as Bercovitch (1997) observes, the mediator does not possess decision making powers in relation to the final agreement reached between the two parties. Instead, the disputing parties must determine the ultimate outcome of the conflict or crisis. A mediator may also leave the negotiations at any time and is not required to assist in the implementation of an agreement, unless otherwise mandated under an international agreement or covenant. A well-known instance in which a crisis mediator agreed to assist in implementing a crisis agreement occurred during the Bosnian civil war (known as the Yugoslavia II: Bosnia crisis in the ICB dataset). As part of the Dayton Accords signed by Croatia, Yugoslavia (Serbia), and Bosnia, the United States – which had helped to mediate among these parties – was to command a force of 60,000 NATO troops to monitor the ceasefire contained in the agreement and control the airspace over Bosnia, both actions aimed at ensuring peace and stability in Bosnia.

The list of potential mediators in international conflicts and crises is extensive: single states, groups of states, international governmental organizations, regional governmental organizations, private transnational organizations, private individuals, or a combination of any of these.[3] Bercovitch (1997) notes that small states and regional governmental organizations usually are confined to mediating regional conflicts. Large states and international governmental organizations, on the other hand, can mediate conflicts across the international system. Transnational organizations – the International Committee of the Red Cross or the International Negotiation Network at the Carter Center, for example – are usually confined to humanitarian efforts and are particularly useful when disputants value secrecy, impartiality, and a normative approach to conflict resolution and/or management (Zartman and Touval 1996; Bercovitch 1997).

International crisis mediation

The theoretical literature on the topic of mediation in international relations and international conflict is clearly robust. A substantial literature on crisis negotiation and bargaining in general also exists.[4] Research that focuses on *crisis mediation*, however, is quite sparse.[5]

Analysts have generated a substantial number of case studies examining mediator involvement in individual crises (see especially Ott (1972) on Indonesia and Malaysia; Mitchell and Webb (1988) on several intra- and international conflicts; Wehr and Lederach (1996) on Central America; Princen (1992) on Camp David, Beagle Channel, and others; Zartman (1995) on multiple mediated cases; Crocker, Hampson, and Aall (1999) on multi-party mediation; Greenberg, Barton, and McGuiness (2000) on mediation and arbitration; and Schrodt and Gerner (2004) on Israel-Arab and Serbia-Croatia/Bosnia). While these analyses have generated a breadth of findings about specific episodes of mediation, they have not provided as much progress toward *general* understandings of crisis mediation. The present study hopes to make a contribution toward such development.

The dearth of systematic research on the topic of international crisis mediation is especially problematic given Dixon's observation that "mediation efforts occur between two and three times more often during crisis and hostility phases (of conflicts) than during periods of lower intensity" (1996: 678). The empirical findings of Bercovitch (1991) and Bercovitch and Jackson (2001) support this view that mediation occurs more often when conflict is intense. In addition, Zartman and Touval (1996) argue that crises, with their perceived deadlines, are most conducive to acceptance of mediation. Despite the likelihood that mediation will take place during international crises, neither the *mediation* literature nor the *crisis* literature offer a systematic analysis of crisis mediation.

That being said, a few notable studies have analyzed the effects of mediators on the processes and evolution of crises, specifically. Morgan (1994) and Dixon (1996) both find that mediation helps to defuse these dangerous situations. Morgan's framework of crisis escalation posits that the probability of an international crisis escalating to war decreases when third-party intervention takes the form of mediation. Similarly, Dixon finds that mediators in crises provide "the most consistently effective conflict management techniques for both preventing escalation and promoting peaceful settlement" (1996: 671).[6]

Much work has explored the effects that individual conditions associated with crisis situations have on the success of mediation efforts. These studies do not look at the concept of crisis explicitly, nor do they consider all conditions associated with the Brecher–Wilkenfeld definition of crisis that we use as a basis for our analyses. However, the insights that this literature has to offer are valuable to any study of crisis mediation.

Many scholars, including Wall and Lynn (1993) and Wall, Stark, and Standifer (2001), argue that the level of conflict between the disputing parties will be an important factor for determining the success of mediation. However, debate exists regarding how intense a conflict must be for mediation to be successful. Several studies have argued that mediation is more likely to be effective when conflict is moderate (Glasl 1982) or low (Carnevale and Pegnetter 1985; Bercovitch 1986) – findings that would raise doubts regarding the potential value of crisis mediation. On the other hand, Zartman and Touval (1996) argue that a conflict that has escalated to a high level of intensity is most suitable for successful mediation attempts. In fact, one can find examples of successful mediation incidents in conflicts with varying degrees of intensity. For instance, United Nations Secretary-General Kofi Annan brokered a successful agreement between the United States and Iraq during the 1997–98 UNSCOM I crisis, which resulted from Iraqi expulsion of UN weapons inspectors, without a shot being fired. On the other hand, U.S. President Bill Clinton, serving as a crisis mediator, was able to successfully orchestrate an end to hostilities during the Bosnian war via the signing of the Dayton Accords in 1995.

Another condition associated with crises is perceived time pressure.[7] It is generally concluded that time pressure produces lower demands, more concessions, and less competition during negotiations (see especially Smith, Pruitt, and Carnevale 1982; Druckman 1993, 1994a; Balakrishnan and Eliashberg 1995; Schwarzer 1998; Mosterd and Rutte 2000). Time-pressured negotiations are also thought to generate more agreements than those not associated with a real or perceived deadline. And, not surprisingly, negotiators are able to reach these agreements more quickly when time becomes a key consideration. Despite some disagreement about these stated effects of time pressure on negotiations,[8] it seems likely that mediators should be able to secure agreements in situations, like crises, marked by time constraints.

Other research reveals that time pressure by itself or in combination with other intervening variables such as mediator ability, impartiality, and interpersonal trust leads the mediator to play a more active, substantive, and pressing role in the negotiation (Brookmire and Sistrunk 1980; Carnevale and Conlon 1988; Kressel and Pruitt 1989; Conlon, Carnevale, and Murnighan 1994; Ross and Wieland 1996). The research presented here explores whether such an approach is likely to be effective in securing agreements and whether or when it is an appropriate tool for crisis management.

Crisis management and conflict resolution

Just as crises are a specific type of conflict, crisis management differs from conflict resolution.[9] The literature in this area, however, demonstrates that there is no single definition of crisis management (Snyder and Diesing 1977) or of conflict resolution (Stern and Druckman 2000), nor is there any agreement regarding what constitutes the successful achievement of either of these outcomes. Kleiboer (1998) points out that many scholars, in fact, either dispense with clear definitions of these terms, or they fail to specify distinctions between them. We believe that distinguishing between these two concepts is essential to understanding and evaluating the effectiveness of specific techniques, such as mediation.

Schroeder (1974), Gilbert and Lauren (1980), and others have argued that crisis management is an oxymoron, that many crises are inherently unmanageable. We disagree and support the position of those who believe that despite the unpredictable nature of crises, steps can be taken to affect crisis dynamics and outcome. In other words, crises *can* be managed. Evans and Newnham define management of international crises as "the attempt to control events during a crisis to prevent systematic violence from occurring" (1998: 104); this designation is derived from the more widely studied concept of conflict management, defined by Maoz as "a set of actions designed to limit or control the level and scope of violence in a given conflict, while striving to accomplish a set of objectives at the national, dyadic, or international level" (2004: 13). From this viewpoint, crisis management is usually thought of as a problem faced by top-tier decision makers wherein they must discover the optimal combination of coercion and accommodation vis-à-vis other states, towards the goal of avoiding war while still maximizing gains and minimizing losses (Snyder and Diesing 1977). The earliest works on conflict management viewed its purpose as either first and foremost winning by maximizing one's interests (see Kintner and Schwarz 1965; Bell 1971; Garnett 1975) or avoiding risk by defusing the situation (see Lipson 1966; George, Hall, and Simons 1971; Craig and George 1983). Only later did it become generally agreed that conflict or crisis management predominantly involved finding a balance between both of these pursuits. Another way to think of conflict management is to adopt George's framework (1984, 1991) as an attempt to balance coercive diplomacy and strategic military moves with risk control in order to avoid war.

For the purposes of this study, the primary and distinct mission of crisis management is termination of the immediate crisis before it escalates or spreads. Several scholars – including Burton (1987, 1990), Kelman (1992), Kolb and Babbitt (1995), Rupesinghe (1996), and Kleiboer (1998, 2002) – note that this type of effort is aimed at settlement of the immediate issues under dispute and/or violent interactions between the parties. For Kolb and Babbitt, management implies a "temporary respite in an otherwise ongoing conflict" (1995: 80), while Kleiboer (1998) describes management as an effort to neutralize the destructive consequences of a conflict. This conception of crisis management is similar to what Young (1967) terms "crisis control." Thought of in this way, crisis management can include any of the following activities: deterrence moves and reactions to them, arbitration, repression of the conflict, containment of the conflict, arms reductions, or any solution that involves the disputants simply arriving at a consensus based on compromise, with or without the assistance of a mediator (Burton 1990). As such, third parties can play a crucial role in crisis management by slowing down the pace of events occurring between the conflicting parties (Kleiboer 1998), ensuring constant communication with these parties, and trying to get them to be more flexible regarding their thoughts and actions (Mitchell 1981).

Crisis management differs from conflict resolution most fundamentally in the scope of objectives pursued. As Burton (1972, 1987, 1990), Zartman (1988, 1997), Kolb and Babbitt (1995), and Rupesinghe (1996) argue, the goal of conflict resolution is to move beyond temporary settlements and towards eliminating the roots of the conflict between the parties – often an extremely difficult and labor- and time-intensive pursuit. Susskind and Babbitt (1992) note that the challenge of conflict resolution is to get the parties to redefine or restructure their relations in such a way that their respective goals no longer conflict or to get them to believe that they each can achieve their goals despite one another, not at the cost of the other.

According to the scholarly work on conflict resolution such as that of Kleiboer (1998), temporary settlements should only be viewed as intermediate stages *en route* to an eradication of the roots of the conflict. Bercovitch (1992), in fact, argues that ceasefires and other temporary settlements are indicators of only partial mediation success.[10] Alternatively, when the mediation process results in formal outcomes that resolve "most" of the issues in dispute, allow for stable interactions between parties, and generate opportunities for more positive future interactions between parties, then it can be viewed as fully successful. The success of attempts to resolve conflicts may also be judged in terms of the implementability and permanence of an outcome (Bercovitch 1992) or how satisfied all parties are with the results of the mediation effort (Shmueli and Vranesky 1996).

Many conflict analysts prescribe resolution, rather than management, as the ultimate and more desirable outcome. Resolution is a lofty and fundamentally admirable goal, but it is not always feasible under the volatile conditions associated with crises. In the short-term, management rather than resolution is usually the least expensive (Milburn 1972), most realistic (Touval 1982; Kleiboer 1998), and often most important (Young 1967) goal for crisis actors and the larger international community alike.

Crisis management and conflict resolution are, of course, related but are distinct goals and pursuits. If the goal is crisis management, success may be defined as the securing of "any written or unwritten mutually agreeable arrangements between parties that at least temporarily resolve or remove from contention one or more, but not necessarily all, of the issues underlying the dispute" (Dixon 1996: 656). As such, securing a ceasefire or de-escalation of a crisis should be considered a successful instance of crisis management (Wehr and Lederach 1996). It is often the case that crisis management is a necessary step that must be taken before trying to find a more deep-seated solution to the conflict in which the crisis occurs, via the mechanism of conflict resolution. In many long-term, protracted conflict situations, a succession of crises may be managed, followed by a final successful instance of conflict resolution.

Analytical framework for this study

As we have noted, the effect of mediation on crisis processes and outcomes has largely been understudied in a systematic fashion, with some notable exceptions. The primary objective of this book, then, is to present an examination of this important phenomenon of international politics. However, crisis mediation does not occur within a vacuum. What other factors are thought to have an effect on crisis processes and outcomes? Past scholarly work on crisis has pointed to a large variety of factors: the structure of the international system or subsystem, state-level bureaucratic and organizational processes, cost-benefit calculations and psychological factors (stress, bias, cognitive constraints, etc.) associated with crisis decision makers, other forms of third-party intervention, the role of violence in crisis management, and whether or not the crisis has an ethnic dimension, involves a conflict between democratic states, or is part of a longer protracted conflict between two or more states.[11]

In this book, we focus on three factors thought to possess a causal or interactive relationship with crises in general and crisis mediation more specifically: the style of mediation that characterizes a third party's efforts, the relative power distribution among the disputants involved, and the degree to which a crisis is ripe for resolution. To this end, we have developed a framework with which to analyze how mediation affects crisis outcomes by accounting for these three essential process attributes, as illustrated in Figure 1.2.

Though we will present a more thorough discussion of these three crucial factors in Chapters 4 through 6, a brief introduction to these concepts is in order here. The specific crisis outcome measures with which our analysis is concerned will be discussed in-depth in subsequent chapters.

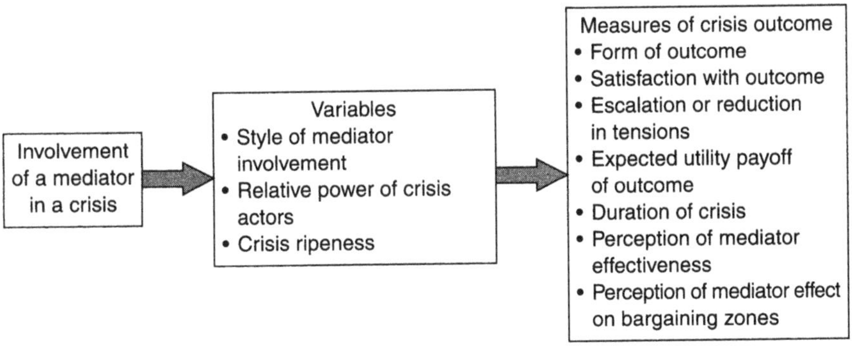

Figure 1.2 Mediation and crisis negotiation processes

A mediator can engage in a wide variety of activities while pursuing the goal of managing a crisis and/or resolving a conflict. For descriptive and analytical purposes, scholars have developed conceptual schemas to guide their thinking regarding the substance of these activities. Mediator actions are classified according to their overarching strategic purposes and/or contributions to negotiation processes, and these categories comprise what are known as distinct, yet interrelated, *styles* or *levels* of mediation. Mediation style is the primary variable of analysis in this analytical framework, and we propose that this factor has a critical effect on negotiation and crisis processes that has often been ignored in systematic studies of international mediation.

For this book, we adopt what has become the most widely used typology of mediation style in the study of international mediation, originally developed by Touval and Zartman (1985) – facilitation/communication, formulation, and manipulation. Each style differs in terms of what the mediator can contribute to the negotiation process, and therefore it is also helpful to conceptualize the styles as different "levels" of mediator substantive involvement. This typology most accurately depicts the varying repertoires of actions that different real-world mediators have at their disposal in specific situations. Although mediators will often adopt several styles during one episode of intervention, arguments have been made as to which style will be more effective at managing crises and/or resolving conflicts. An in-depth discussion of the characteristics of each of these styles, their effects on negotiation processes and crisis outcomes, and their advantages and limitations can be found in Chapter 4.

While this study is ultimately an analysis of the effect of mediation style on different crisis outcomes, we understand that there are several other variables that will affect both the likelihood of a crisis being managed and the effectiveness of different mediation styles in facilitating that management. The nature of the power relations between crisis actors is one of these key intervening variables. Realist scholars have long posited that power relations between individual states and within the international system as a whole have a profound effect on the foreign policies of states, whether or not they will go to war with each other, and what chance they have of winning a war. In this study, we are interested in the degree to which power relations between actors in crises inhibit or augment efforts to terminate these crises. While many analysts of power relations have focused solely on the overall power possessed by states as a determinant of behavior and success of action, we contend that power related to the specific issue(s) being contested in the crisis also plays an important role. Both aggregate and issue-specific power, then, will determine whether the relations between crisis actors are marked by power parity or disparity. Most importantly, we investigate whether the success of mediation is impacted by whether two crisis actors are equal in terms of power (Wall and Lynn 1993; Dixon 1996; Wall, Stark, and Standifer 2001) and, more specifically, whether different mediation styles have varying relationships with relative disputant power (Bercovitch 1986; Bercovitch, Anagnoson, and Wille 1991; Morgan 1994; Bercovitch and Houston 1996, 2000). In Chapter 5, we present a more detailed discussion of the concept of power and its effect on crisis outcomes, the success of mediation, and the impact of specific mediation styles.

In addition to the power relations between parties and the characteristics of mediation, a third vital factor that will affect the likelihood of specific crisis outcomes is the degree of ripeness that a crisis exhibits, which describes a condition in which a specific conflict or crisis is amenable to resolution. Definitions of ripeness abound, but we feel that focusing on the idea of *zone of agreement* allows one to more fully comprehend the mechanisms at work not only in crisis management or resolution but also in the conduct of mediation. The breadth of the zone of agreement between crisis actors will likely have a substantial effect on the likelihood of specific crisis outcomes and the ability of mediation as a whole and specific mediation styles to assist in bringing about these outcomes. Keeping in mind that mediators have as their goal the termination of the conflict/crisis, we posit that their activities as a whole and the different styles they can adopt while intervening will have a profound effect on the nature of this zone of agreement. Not only that, the nature of mediation and mediator style will affect which specific type of outcome the crisis actor(s) achieve. These ideas regarding zones of agreement as an indicator of ripeness are fleshed out and expanded upon in Chapter 6.

This book is not the authors' first foray into this area of study. Our past research on crisis mediation has generated significant insights regarding the nature and effectiveness of this phenomenon as a function of mediation style (Wilkenfeld *et al.* 2003), the relative power of the crisis actors (Young *et al.* 2002, 2004), and the breadth of the zone of agreement between crisis actors engaged in negotiations to resolve the crisis (Asal *et al.* 2002). While these works have examined the impact of the three variables outlined in Figure 1.2 separately, a more recent study served as a first attempt at an integrated analysis of these components (Quinn *et al.* 2003). We have also examined the impact of various styles of mediation relative to other factors affecting crisis outcomes, including integrative and cost-maximization strategies (Beardsley *et al.* 2004). This book serves as the definitive summation of our ideas on the topic of mediation in international crises. It also expands upon our past work by presenting a broader and more in-depth analysis of international crises. Not only are we utilizing a larger amount of information collected on this topic, but we are also analyzing this information in new ways not attempted in our previous work, via more extensive statistical analyses of expanded data sets collected on actual international crises and experimental simulations based on a crisis scenario, as well as a short case-study developed in Chapter 3.

Notes

1 For extended treatments of negotiation methods in international conflict, see especially Fisher *et al.* (1997) and Starkey, Boyer, and Wilkenfeld (2005).

2 A popular and slightly different definition of mediation is used by the United Nation in its *Handbook on the Peaceful Settlement of Disputes between States*: "a method of peaceful settlement of an international dispute where a third-party intervenes to reconcile the claims of the contending parties and to advance his own proposals aimed at a mutually acceptable compromise solution" (United Nations 1992: 40).

3 While high-level officials often represent single states as mediators, Kriesberg describes an additional type of mediator, what he terms the quasi-mediator. Quasi-mediators can be "members of factions or even of political parties within the governing coalitions of one of the adversaries ... unofficial persons who have close ties with officials and act as agents for them ... (or) nonofficial groups without close ties to any government representatives" (1996: 226). Lower-level officials can also act as quasi-mediators.

4 See especially Young (1968), Snyder and Diesing (1977), Lockhart (1979), Leng (1983, 1988, 1993, 2000), Morrow (1989), Fearon (1994), Morgan (1994), Lebow (1996), and Peterson (1996).

5 Furthermore, much of the work on crisis mediation does not focus on international conflict and instead can be found in the contexts of litigation, family disputes and divorce, organizational decision-making, and workplace negotiations among others. A substantial literature on hostage crisis negotiations also exists (see especially Rogan *et al.* 1997).

6 Dixon's definition of mediation, however, is somewhat unique within the conflict management literature: According to his categorization, efforts by third parties to facilitate communication between disputants do not qualify as mediation, but binding arbitration *does* qualify as mediation.

7 For reviews of the literature on time pressure and negotiation, see Pruitt (1981), Carnevale, O'Connor, and McCusker (1993), and Stuhlmacher, Gillespie, and Champagne (1998).

8 Some scholars have argued that time pressure can enhance demands and competitiveness, depending on the context of the conflict and negotiations (see Pruitt 1981 and Carnevale and Lawler 1986).

9 For a recent and comprehensive discussion and analysis of conflict/crisis management and conflict resolution, including what distinguishes these two pursuits, see Maoz *et al.* (2004).

10 Others arguing that ceasefires are not indicators of conflict resolution success include Burton (1969, 1972, 1987, 1990), Fisher (1972), Kelman (1992), Rothman (1992), Jabri (1996), Bercovitch and Regan (1997), and Jones (2000).

11 See, among many others, Allison (1971), Holsti (1972, 1989), Snyder and Diesing (1977), Lebow (1981), Leng and Singer (1988), Maoz (1990), Brecher (1993), and Leng (1993).

2 A multi-method exploration of crisis mediation

In the past, the authors of this book have utilized multiple methods of inquiry to study international crises. In the present study, we merge cross-national aggregate approaches with data derived from experimental techniques in an effort to develop a rich set of findings on how mediation impacts on crisis management and conflict resolution. We believe it is useful to briefly discuss the ways in which we went about collecting and analyzing the aggregate and experimental data for this study. In so doing, we hope to clarify the manner in which our own research design has developed. We also hope to provide some guidance to other social scientists who wish to explore the utility of these methods, either alone or combined, in pursuing additional research questions, related to international crisis mediation or otherwise. We do not discuss here the methodological specifics of our statistical analyses; instead, we set aside space in each analytical chapter (3 through 6) to discuss in-depth details such as what variables were used in each analysis, which specific statistical tests were used for each analysis, and any further pertinent methodological information regarding these analyses.

The International Crisis Behavior Project

Since 1977, researchers associated with the International Crisis Behavior (ICB) Project have been collecting and analyzing data on the causes and consequences of all international military-security crises (Brecher, Wilkenfeld, and Moser 1988; Wilkenfeld, Brecher, and Moser 1988; Brecher and Wilkenfeld 1989, 2000; Brecher 1993). With data currently spanning the period 1918–2001, ICB has identified 434 crises during this period involving 956 crisis actors. (See ICB Online at www.cidcm.umd.edu/icb and Chapter 1 of this book for a discussion of the ICB definitions of crisis at both the actor and system levels of analysis.) Users of the data have explored a vast array of research questions pertaining to conflict and crisis, including the ethnic dimension, the effect of different political regimes (notably the question of whether democracies are more peaceful than authoritarian regimes), the impact of the polar structure of the international system, third-party intervention, and the role of violence in crisis management. Information has been compiled on roughly 150 variables at both the level of the international crisis in general, as well as for individual crisis actors. This rich database also includes detailed summaries of each of the crises, and a listing of sources that were used to code each case.[1]

Central to many of these ICB-based analyses has been the question of how third-party intervention – by nation states, international and regional organizations, non-governmental organizations, and individuals – has impacted the *manner* in which such crises are resolved, as well as the *consequences* of such intervention for both crisis management and conflict resolution. However, mediation per se was not a central focus of ICB when the project was launched in the mid-1970s, in part because mediation had not yet been fully recognized as a central feature of crisis management in the international system. Between the mid-1970s and the mid-1980s, several important and highly publicized instances of crisis mediation by third parties occurred, particularly in the Middle East: Henry Kissinger's shuttle diplomacy which was instrumental in bringing about ceasefires between Israel and Egypt, and then Israel and Syria, in the aftermath of the October 1973 war; Jimmy Carter's mediation of the Israeli-Egyptian conflict in 1979 at Camp David; and mediation by Philip Habib (along with UN assistance) of the 1982 civil war in Lebanon, which involved Lebanon, Syria, and Israel. These incidents began to alert scholars to the possibility that international crisis mediation was becoming a fixture of the international system. Furthermore, with the end of the cold war, many international observers began to sense that not only was the nature of conflict changing, but that there was an even greater propensity among a variety of actors in the system to become involved as mediators in the management and resolution of crises. As such, an organized collection of data on international crisis mediation became a legitimate and important endeavor.

In 2000, the authors of this book established the Crisis and Negotiation (CAN) Project at the University of Maryland, focusing initially on experimental approaches to the study of crisis management (see discussion of experimental methodology below). This research grew out of a decade of work by Wilkenfeld and Kraus regarding the development of a strategic model of negotiation and the creation of decision-support systems to facilitate experimental work with human subjects participating in crisis negotiation experiments (see Kraus, Wilkenfeld, and Zlotkin 1995; Wilkenfeld *et al.* 1995; Santmire *et al.* 1998; Wilkenfeld 2002). As that group began to generate an array of interesting experimental findings on crisis negotiation in general, and on mediation in particular (Wilkenfeld *et al.* 2003; Wilkenfeld *et al.* 2004), we found ourselves constantly seeking verification of these findings. We discovered that systematic data on *crisis* mediation did not exist, either in ICB or elsewhere (e.g., the Militarized Interstate Disputes dataset, Bercovitch's International Conflict Management dataset, etc.). Thus, a determination was made in 2001 that we would collect such data for the entire updated version of the ICB dataset. After two years, over 25 coders, and countless hours dedicated to training, coding, and debriefing, the task was completed in mid-2003.

International crisis mediation variables

Before coding could proceed on a set of mediation variables, we needed to develop a checklist for the coders so that they could determine whether mediation had in fact occurred in a crisis, and to distinguish it from other forms of third-party intervention. This checklist was culled from prominent definitions of mediation in the literature (see Chapter 1), as well as from some of the criteria established in the relatively few quantitative studies of mediation, as reviewed by Bercovitch (1997). It was determined that all of the following conditions must be true/present for ICB coders to determine that mediation had occurred:

- intervention by a third party in a new or on-going negotiation process
- mediation is either offered by the mediator and accepted by the disputing parties, or requested by the disputing parties and accepted by the mediator
- mediator is not a direct party to crisis
- all disputing parties accept mediator's involvement
- disputing parties determine the outcome of the crisis; the mediator does not have decision making powers (i.e., is not an arbitrator)
- mediation is a non-violent form of intervention
- mediator's presence is voluntary; that is, mediator can leave the negotiations
- mediator is not required to assist in implementing agreements, but can offer or agree to do so.

Once it was determined that mediation had occurred in a given crisis, coders collected data on a set of 18 variables at the system or international crisis level of analysis, and on two variables at the actor level. The following section includes brief descriptions of these variables, including the general questions that the coders were asked to answer when approaching and researching each variable for each individual crisis.

System-level mediation variables

1 **MEDIATE**: Did mediation occur at some point in this international crisis between onset (trigger date) and termination (termination date)?
2 **MEDNUM**: How many mediators were there? Was there a single mediator or mediation team, or were there multiple instances of mediation by different actors or teams during the course of the crisis?

3 **MEDWHO**: Who was the primary mediator? Coding is for the mediator who was the most "active" in this crisis. "Active" is defined temporally. (*Note*: All subsequent variables were coded in relation to the primary mediator defined by this variable.)

4 **MEDTIME**: When did mediation begin? Was there on-going mediation involving the crisis actors prior to the onset of the crisis, or did mediation begin once the crisis had begun?

5 **MEDSTART**: On what date did mediation begin?

6 **MEDEND**: On what date during the crisis did mediation end?

7 **MEDENDCO**: If mediation continued after the crisis ended, when did this mediation end completely?

8 **MEDGOAL**: What was the goal of the mediator in this crisis? Distinction to be made between *crisis management* (attempting to control events during a crisis to prevent significant and systematic violence from occurring or escalating, including ceasefires), and *conflict resolution* (attempting to get the parties in conflict to redefine their relationship in such a way as to perceive either that they can realize their goals without conflict or that they can redefine their relationship so that their goals no longer conflict).

9 **MEDFACL**: Was a facilitative style of mediation used? Facilitation tactics include any of the following (adapted from Bercovitch 1997): made contact with parties, gained the trust and confidence of the parties, arranged for interactions between the parties, identified underlying issues and interests, clarified the situation, supplied missing information, transmitted messages between parties, fact-finding, offered positive evaluations, allowed the interests of all parties to be discussed.

10 **MEDFORM**: Was a formulative style of mediation used? Formulation tactics include any of the following (see Bercovitch 1997): controlled the pace and formality of the meetings, controlled the physical environment, ensured privacy of mediation, highlighted common interests, controlled timing, helped devise a framework for an acceptable outcome, helped parties save face, kept the process focused on the issues, made substantive suggestions and proposals, suggested concessions parties could make.

11 **MEDMANIP**: Was a manipulative style of mediation used? Manipulation tactics include the following (see Bercovitch 1997): kept parties at the table, changed parties' expectations, took responsibility for concessions, made parties aware of the costs of non-agreement, supplied and filtered information, helped negotiators to undo a commitment, rewarded concessions made by the parties, pressed the parties to show flexibility, promised resources, threatened withdrawal of resources, offered to verify compliance with the agreement, added incentives, threatened punishments, threatened to withdraw mediation.

12 **MEDSTYLE**: What was the highest level of mediation style used in

the crisis? "Highest level" is defined in terms of degree of substantive involvement. Thus, facilitation is the lowest possible level of mediation, and manipulation is the highest.

13 **MEDSTEFCT**: Which style of mediation had the greatest effect on the outcome of the crisis? "Effect" is defined in terms of most crucial influence on the crisis processes and/or outcomes, regardless of whether this influence was ultimately negative or positive in nature. The most crucial style (i.e., the style with the greatest effect) need not be the highest style (i.e., the most substantively intrusive form used). For example, a mediator may employ both manipulation and formulation; while manipulation is the *highest* form of mediation used in this instance, it is possible that the formulation tactics had a greater effect on the crisis as a whole. Hence, the case would be coded "formulation" for this variable.

14 **MEDEFCT**: What was the effectiveness of mediation on crisis abatement? "Effectiveness" is understood here in terms of easing tensions during the crisis or otherwise contributing to the termination of the crisis.

15 **MEDPACE**: What was the impact of mediation on the pace of crisis abatement?

16 **MEDCOMP**: What was the mix of crisis actors expressing a willingness to compromise before mediation occurred? Willingness to compromise refers to one or more of the following: willingness to compromise on an issue, willingness to concede on an issue of interest to the party(ies) that it is in dispute with, recognition of the rights or valid interests of the party(ies) that it is in dispute with, or any combination of the above. This variable acts as an aggregate of the data collected for the actor-level variable MEDWILCOM for each case.

17 **MEDPREF**: What proportion of all crisis actors stated that mediation had some effect (favorable or unfavorable) on the negotiations? The perception of the effect of mediation on the negotiations refers to the evaluation of mediation efforts as to whether or not these efforts had any effect on the negotiations from the point of view of the individual actors. This variable acts as an aggregation of the data collected for the actor-level variable MEDVIEW for each case.

18 **MEDEFNEG**: Out of all crisis actors who stated that mediation had some effect on the negotiations, what proportion felt that mediation had a favorable effect on the negotiations? Only consider the satisfaction values of crisis actors who did *not* view mediation neutrally or as irrelevant. Thus, perception of the effect of mediation in this case refers to the evaluation of mediation efforts as to their favorability from the point of view of the individual crisis actors who felt that mediation had *some* effect on the negotiations. This variable acts as an aggregate of the data collected for the actor-level variable MEDVIEW for each case.

Actor-level mediation variables

1 **MEDWILCOM**: Was the actor willing to compromise before mediation occurred?
2 **MEDVIEW**: What was the actor's view of the effect of mediation on the negotiations?

Coding procedures for the mediation variables

With minor exceptions, the coding procedures for the mediation variables were the same as those developed for the ICB Project in general. Coding for several cases was completed by graduate students with specialties in international conflict, crisis, or mediation in the Department of Government and Politics at the University of Maryland, College Park. However, most cases were coded by exceptional undergraduate students drawn from classes that authors of this book had taught on international conflict, crisis, or negotiation. All coders – graduate and undergraduate students alike – underwent a rigorous training process to help ensure the reliability of the data that they collected for this project.

Once ICB staff was satisfied that coders were properly trained, they were each assigned to work on a subset of the 434 previously identified ICB cases. Coders essentially "reopened" these coded cases and, using the same sources that had been used when these crises were first examined, determined the values for the new mediation variables.[2] Although pairs of coders were assigned to each crisis to ensure reliability (as checked by inter-coder reliability scores), the coders worked independently during the research stage.

Upon completion of the coding, Wilkenfeld and Quinn debriefed each pair of coders on the cases to which they were assigned. In these debriefings, areas of disagreement between the coders were explored and resolved. In the event that such a resolution was not possible after extensive discussion, a third coder was assigned to reexamine the case. Once the final coding was agreed upon, a summary of the mediation activity was incorporated into existing ICB case summaries. (See ICB Online at www.cidcm.umd.edu/icb for updated case summaries.) The coding of new ICB cases – that is, those that have occurred after 2001 – will incorporate coding of the mediation variables into the primary coding effort, and thus will be handled at the same time as the coding of all other ICB variables.

Of the 434 international crises that occurred between 1918 and 2001, 128 experienced some form of mediation.[3] Appendix A presents a listing of those 128 ICB cases in which mediation occurred, and reports key variables such as the primary mediator, goal of mediation, highest form of mediation, and effect of mediation on crisis abatement. This book endeavors to determine the dynamics and impact of mediation in the 30 percent of international crises in which it was employed. Readers may find it useful to access ICB Online to gain a comprehensive picture of the entire International Crisis Behavior dataset and the place that the mediation variables occupy within it. The browse function was created to facilitate easy access to the ICB variables, summaries, and codebooks, and the user can also take advantage of a powerful search engine to navigate the dataset in search of specific crises by period, region, issue area, actors, mediators, and a variety of other search criteria. Indeed, readers may use this interactive tool to discover patterns of crisis behavior and outcomes involving mediation that have not been included in the present study and which warrant further consideration.

Experimental research design

Analyses designed to provide insights into the nature and dynamics of crisis mediation will entail the consideration of aggregate ICB data on mediated and unmediated twentieth century crises. But analysis of these data alone cannot provide a sufficient understanding of how mediation might change the trajectory of crisis negotiations. An experimental method is particularly appropriate for gathering information on aspects of the relationship between mediation and crisis outcomes for which "real-world" data is difficult, if not impossible, to collect. For instance, through an experimental approach, we were able to gain direct feedback about negotiators' reactions to crisis outcomes and mediation efforts, and we were able to more accurately assess the evolution of particular negotiation episodes over time. In addition, the experimental environment allowed us to evaluate more finely the temporal features of crisis negotiations and how mediation affects the pace of such negotiations. Finally, our particular research design allowed us to compare the objective worth – that is, the expected utility – of outcomes agreed upon by different negotiators in similar settings to examine which factors lead to variation in the utility of outcome. Given the unique and nuanced insights that could be generated by such an approach, we developed an experimental research design to improve our understanding of the nature of the relationship between mediation and crisis dynamics.

Although it is frequently used in the behavioral and natural sciences, the experimental method has been less utilized in the social sciences (political science, sociology, economics, etc.). This begs the question: Is the experimental method a valid and/or useful means of conducting social science research? We agree with the argument made by McDermott in her review of the literature on experimental methods:

> ... experimentation can be particularly useful under certain circumstances: when existing methods of inquiry have produced inconsistent or contradictory results; when empirical validation of formal models is required; when investigators want to triangulate in on specific

> processes that have already been examined in a more general way using other methodologies; and when evidence is needed to support strong causal claims. Experiments can combine with other methods to provide what Campbell (1969) described as a "fish scale model of omniscience," whereby each methodological layer serves to illuminate and support other component parts.
>
> (McDermott 2002: 32)

Others support the use of experimentation in political science, specifically, because of its unique leverage in shedding light on certain aspects of political behavior and its utility in confirming results from other methods. McGraw (1993) sees experimentation as a methodology "on the rise" in political science because it can provide unique insights into the nature of causal relationships when appropriately employed. Kinder and Palfrey (1993) argue that experimentation should be integrated into political science as a way to "supplement, not replace, traditional empirical methods" (1993: 1) to help enlighten analysts' understanding of *how* and *why* a relationship exists (see also Campbell and Stanley 1963; Brody 1969; Laponce 1972; Wilkenfeld 2002). Rightly, quality experimental research remains reliant upon the theories and empirical data that generate initial hypotheses, but it also allows for the continued evolution and the "better articulation" of existing theories (Franklin 1996).

While experimentation in the social sciences can refer to a variety of different approaches from field experiments to computer-based modeling – such as Hughes's International Futures Simulation (1999) – our efforts have concentrated on a controlled laboratory, simulated crisis negotiation environment. Following the earlier advice given by advocates of experimentation in social science, we created this environment with the intention of testing a variety of hypotheses related to the relationship between mediation and crisis outcomes. The experiment that we have developed allow us to compare the outcomes of crisis negotiations – both mediated and unmediated – and analyze the impact of varying styles of mediation.

McDermott (2002) also argues that experiments have a key advantage over other means of conducting research. She contends that the experimental method minimizes bias by "introducing standardized procedures, measures, and analyses," enforcing the random assignment of "subjects ... to ensure that no unrelated or spurious factors vary consistently within a given population," and allowing for the construction of "control conditions" (McDermott 2002: 33–4) to minimize and assess the extent to which placebo effects have influenced outcomes.[4] Thus, by using a standardized simulation scenario (outlined in detail below) and assigning participant roles randomly, we were able to obtain data that is comparable across iterations of the experiment, since we can be confident that these data are not artifacts of unrelated external environmental conditions or irrelevant characteristics of the negotiators themselves. Perhaps more importantly, the controlled nature of our experiments allows for isolation of the effects of particular characteristics of crisis negotiations on outcomes. For these reasons, we believe that an experimental research design is an especially effective means of focusing research on all three key variables that are of concern to us – the style of mediation used, the relative power of the crisis actors, and whether or not and to what extent a crisis is ripe for resolution, as described in Chapter 1.

The experimental research design at the core of our analysis of crisis mediation is structured around human-based simulations of crisis negotiations, in which participants role-play as a representative of a country involved in an interstate military-security crisis. Each iteration of the simulation involved two participants, or one negotiation dyad. All participants were immersed in an identical crisis setting – a border crisis between Ecuador and Peru – and all had the same resources available to them – background information about the crisis and the states involved, a computer-based decision-support system (DSS) that helped them evaluate potential outcomes of the crisis, and a web-based communication system through which they negotiated with their adversary. (More details on these resources are provided in the following sections.) These simulated crisis negotiations were designed to occur in real-time, and each negotiation dyad had a maximum of two hours to resolve the crisis. Simulations were conducted in a controlled setting, in on-campus computer laboratories under the direct supervision of members of the Crisis and Negotiation research team. All subjects were undergraduate students at the University of Maryland.[5]

The use of college students as subjects or participants in experimental-based research raises issues regarding external validity of the research design, as noted by Mintz and Geva (1993), Mintz *et al.* (1997), Kanazawa (1999), and Green and Gerber (2002). Specifically, as Beer (1993) reports, many authors argue that it is problematic for political scientists to draw inferences about the activities of decision makers or public officials from a population of undergraduates. Scholars in other fields of inquiry recognize the shortcomings of this type of research as well. Sears (1986) has found that the reliance on students in psychology research produces a bias in the understanding of human behavior, yet Stevens and Ash (2001) find that the vast majority of top-level social psychology research continues to rely on student-based experiments. Kanazawa (1999) asserts that student-as-subject research is *not* problematic so long as the generalizations that researchers draw from such experiments are about theories, not the empirical findings. We adopt a more cautious attitude and agree with Druckman, who argues that simulations are useful tools for "arbitrating between competing hypotheses" (1994b: 447). We contend that in the context of our "careful experimental design" (Stern and Druckman 2000: 49), our pool of students as experimental participants provides us with a reliable depiction of how government officials might react to crises and to the efforts of a mediator, a premise that is supported by consistencies between ICB-based analyses and examinations based on the experiment-generated data.

The experimental process

All simulations for this study centered on a common scenario and were conducted in a uniform style, with only minor modifications to both the scenario and to the simulation process as needed to investigate in more detail each of the main variables in our analysis – mediation style, relative power, and ripeness. In this chapter, we describe the basic scenario and simulation process that was used in the experiments, while in subsequent chapters (Chapters 5 and 6) we explain in more detail modifications that were made to this structure to allow for a rigorous examination of the relationship between crisis mediation and relative power and between crisis mediation and ripeness.

The scenario: a crisis over territorial claims

The experiments reported on in this study utilize a scenario loosely based on the Ecuador/Peru Border Dispute of 1981 – one of the 434 ICB crises that occurred between 1918 and 2001. This crisis was part of an on-going protracted conflict between Ecuador and Peru, which lasted from 1935 until 1998 and included five international crises. The actual crisis involved an historical instance of successful mediation by a group of states at the request of the Organization of American States; the mediation effort was initiated after military clashes along the borders of these two states triggered an international crisis.

The research team developed a five-page scenario explaining to simulation participants the history of relations between Ecuador and Peru as well as the details of the crisis at hand. The scenario also reveals to participants the concerns and the relative strengths and weaknesses of each state and explores the possible outcomes to this crisis. This scenario was provided to each participant prior to the beginning of the simulation, and students were discouraged from doing any additional research on the issue, so as to help ensure that all were starting from the same set of background information. A copy of this scenario is included as Appendix B.

As the scenario describes, the disagreement at the heart of this crisis and the protracted conflict between these two states is over which state controls which portions of territory along the poorly defined 800-plus mile border between Ecuador and Peru. (See Figure 2.1 for a map of this region.) Conflicts over this territory date back to the nineteenth century and continued into the twentieth century. A short-lived crisis occurred between Ecuador and Peru over this issue in 1935, but the long-standing dispute was not resolved after this crisis was terminated. A period of

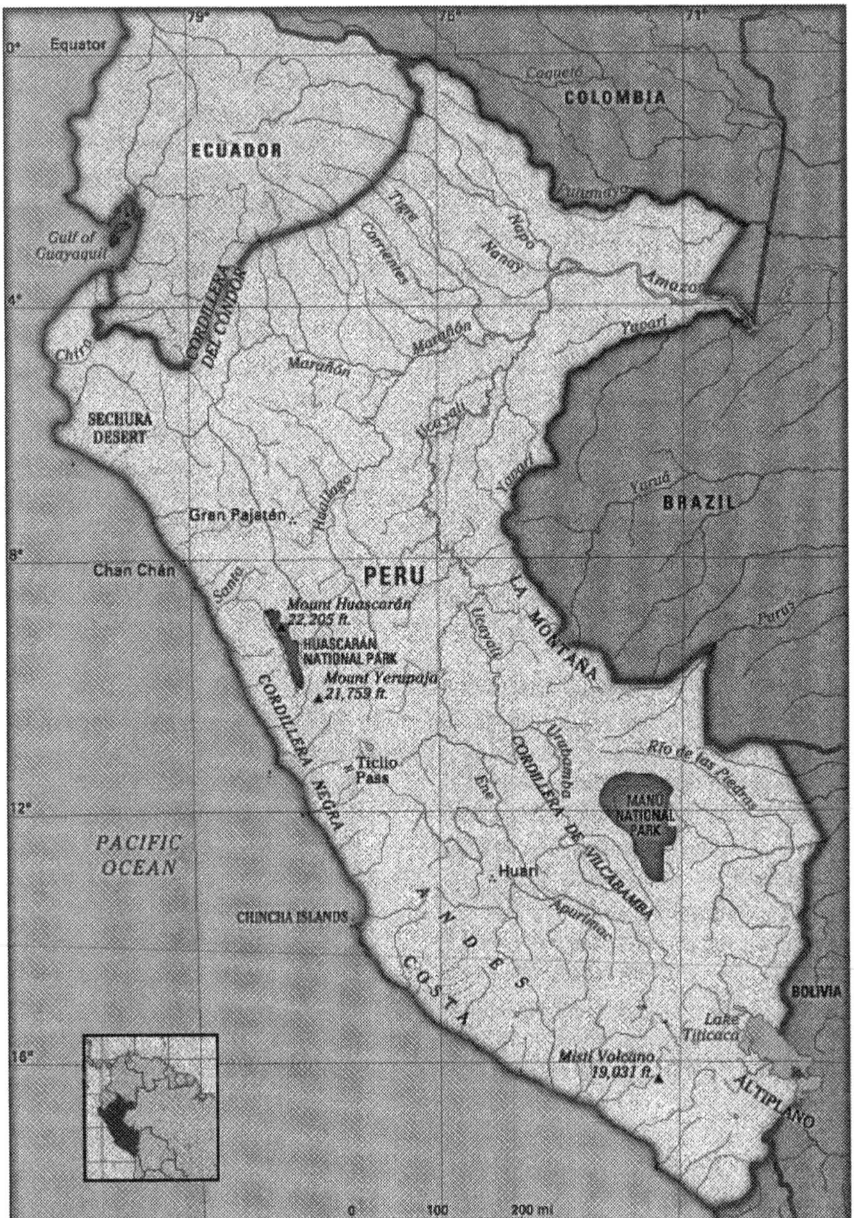

Figure 2.1 Map of Ecuador and Peru

particularly violent flare-ups over this issue began in 1938 and eventually led to a second crisis between these two states in 1941. This time, the international community intervened. On January 29, 1942, Ecuador and Peru signed the Rio Protocol delineating the border division. Peru was given a larger chunk of the territory than Ecuador, and the agreement called for demarcation of the border. The regional powers of Argentina, Brazil, Chile, and the United States served as the guarantors of this agreement.

The Rio Protocol did not permanently resolve the dispute between these states. In 1960, Ecuadorian leaders renounced the agreement and rejected the borders established by the treaty; Peru refused to recognize this move by Ecuador and dismissed Ecuador's calls for a renegotiation of the border. The guarantor states of the Rio Protocol agreed with Peru that the agreement between the states had been a fair one and was to continue to serve as the basis for the border between Ecuador and Peru.

As the crisis emerged in 1981, then, the Rio Protocol was still internationally recognized as valid and legitimate, and the land sought by Ecuador in the border region was considered to be under the sovereign control of Peru. Peru had the upper hand in the context of this crisis (i.e., over the specific issue at hand). Peru also had an advantage in terms of capabilities (i.e., aggregate power): Peru's territory is more than four times the size of its northern neighbor, it has about double the population of Ecuador, it has a larger governmental budget than Ecuador, and it spends more annually on defense than does Ecuador.

This historical case was considered to be an appropriate basis for a test of mediation dynamics because it was, in fact, mediated, and because it shares characteristics with many ICB cases. It involved a territorial dispute between two contiguous actors, it exhibited a level of violence characterized by minor clashes between actors, it demonstrated the classic characteristics of power asymmetry between crisis actors, and it occurred within an on-going protracted conflict (see Wilkenfeld and Brecher 2000). For a more complete discussion of this crisis and the four other crises that comprise the protracted conflict between Ecuador and Peru, see Simmons (1999) and Brecher and Wilkenfeld (2000).

Participants were informed via the scenario of the possible outcomes of this crisis. The mutually exclusive outcomes possible in the experimental setting are:

- an agreement for the status quo to persist;
- an agreement to a ceasefire (with no agreement on the territorial issue);
- an agreement on a ceasefire *and* a land division;
- an agreement to refer the dispute to binding arbitration, or;
- a military operation launched by either Peru or Ecuador against the other.

The simulation was divided into twelve ten-minute time periods. Negotiations which lasted the entire time period without negotiators reaching an agreement or without one of them launching war resulted in a status quo outcome. During the negotiations, either Ecuador or Peru could close its borders to people and goods from the other state, and each could decide whether to mobilize or demobilize its troops in the disputed territory. In addition, Peru had the option of granting to Ecuador much desired access to the Amazon River.

From Spring 2001 through Fall 2003, 456 students enrolled in international relations courses at the University of Maryland participated in the Ecuador/Peru simulated crisis negotiations as experimental subjects.[6] Half of the students in the 228 negotiation dyads negotiated on behalf Peru, while the others represented Ecuador. Students were randomly assigned to their roles as they arrived at the computer laboratory to participate in the simulation. For the vast majority of these students, involvement in the simulation was a requirement for their course; in some of the early iterations of the experiments, however, participation was voluntary and a nominal cash amount ($10) was offered as an incentive to participate. We observed no variation in the performance of those who participated voluntarily from the rest of the participants.

In all iterations of the simulation, an incentive was offered to those participants each semester who did the "best job" of negotiating for their country, as measured by which participants secured outcomes associated with the highest utility-point value for the country they represented (see below). Incentives varied across semesters, depending upon professors' preferences. In some semesters, students were offered extra-credit points for their course, while in other semesters they were offered a cash award of $10 to $25. Both "incentive packages" proved to be effective. Simulation monitors and instructors alike observed that students took the experiment seriously and were vested in the outcome of their particular negotiation.

Simulation tools

Negotiators for Peru and Ecuador communicated with one another through a specially developed computer-based communication system. These were not face-to-face negotiations, and subjects did not know with whom they were negotiating at any given time. In the earliest simulations, this communication "package" was somewhat analogous to a private chat room. In later simulations, we utilized a communications interface developed by the ICONS Project at the University of Maryland. Both of these communication platforms provided participants with the ability to communicate with their adversary, to take unilateral actions (such as closing their borders), to propose specific agreements (such as a division of the disputed territory), and to agree to a proposal submitted by the other. All participants in the simulations underwent a hands-on training session in which they familiarized themselves with the communication package, as well as the decision-support system, prior to their involvement in the simulation.

Each negotiator in the 228 simulations had access to a computer-based decision-support system (DSS) that displayed utility-point values associated with each of the possible outcomes of the negotiation for his/her country. As Starke and Rangaswamy (1999) explain, DSSs are part of the larger category of tools known as negotiation-support systems that have emerged in recent years, designed to take advantage of new technologies to improve the performance of leaders and managers engaged in negotiation processes. Decision-support systems, in particular, are constructed

> to help one or more negotiating parties to privately organize information, develop prenegotiation strategies, or evaluate and propose mid-negotiation offers ... They assist individuals in forming subjective representations of negotiation situations and in generating prescriptions about what to do during a negotiation. In other words, these DSS aid negotiators in overcoming their cognitive limitations...
>
> (Starke and Rangaswamy 1999: 3–4)

Decision-support systems are an invaluable tool for experimental research in negotiation settings for a number of reasons. By providing participants with a pre-constructed DSS, researchers can help to ensure that each participant shares a common understanding of the relative value of different actions within the negotiation context and different possible outcomes. This provides an additional control to the experimental setting. In addition, the DSS used in these experiments provides researchers with a specific measure of the relative value of every possible outcome of the crisis, measured in terms of expected utility. As such, we can make direct comparisons about the relative values of the outcomes achieved under different experimental conditions in order to gain a better understanding of how different conditions – for instance, mediation style, relative power, and ripeness – affect the value of outcomes achieved. (For a general overview of the role of decision-support systems in experimental research, see Wilkenfeld *et al.* (1995) and Kersten and Noronha (1999)).

The DSS structure used in these experiments was designed specifically for student use in simulated negotiations. Following the selection of the Ecuador-Peru scenario for the simulations in this research program, we developed a DSS customized to the parameters of this scenario.[7] This required determining a utility-point value for each possible outcome of the crisis for both Ecuador and Peru, as well as a determination of how that utility payoff would be affected by changes in the border status of either country, by whether a country had its troops mobilized, and by whether Peru had granted Ecuador access to the Amazon River, as well as by the passage of time. Utility-point values were determined through an evaluation of the conditions, priorities, interests, and resources of both Ecuador and Peru in the context of this crisis, taking into consideration both the tangible effects (such as more or less territory) and intangible effects (such as lost international prestige or increased support at home) that would be associated with the outcomes.

The DSS constructed for student participants revealed to them the relative value for their own country (and only their own country) of any outcome they were considering offering or accepting, as well as how outcomes would be affected by changed conditions within the context of the crisis. Figure 2.2a displays the user-interface for the Ecuador-Peru DSS. At any point in the crisis negotiation, a negotiator could select any number of possible permutations of outcomes and explore the relative values of those permutations by selecting the appropriate check boxes on their screen. Figure 2.2b displays the "output" screen of the DSS, in which payoffs associated with each specified outcome are displayed to participants.

The mediators in experiments

The key question driving this research is how mediation in general, and specific mediation styles in particular, affect outcomes under varying conditions of power relations and ripeness. As such, the introduction of a mediator into the simulation design is vital. Approximately one-third of the negotiations that we conducted involved no mediator. The remaining two-thirds of the simulations involved a mediator who represented the group of states (Argentina, Brazil, Chile, and the United States) that acted as the guarantor of the border designation between Ecuador and Peru.

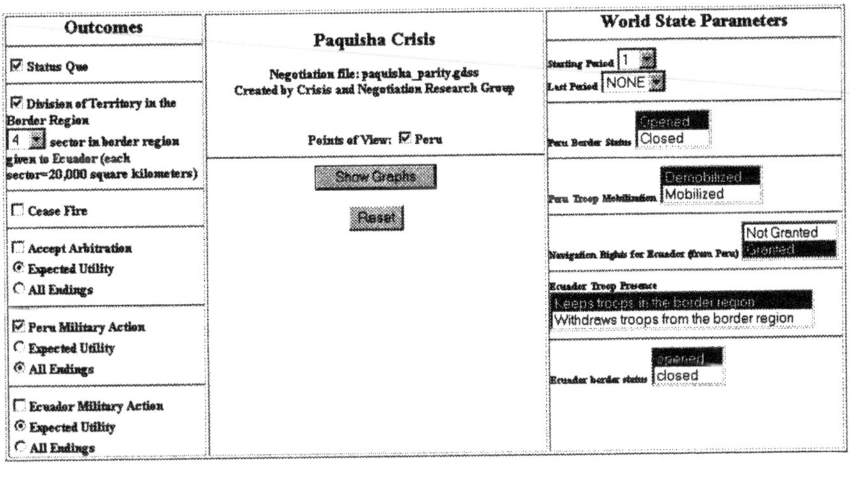

Figure 2.2a Ecuador-Peru DSS input screen

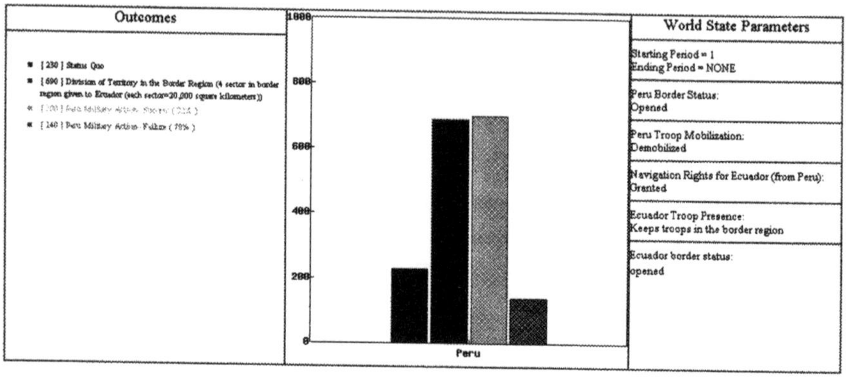

Figure 2.2b Ecuador-Peru DSS output screen

In the real-world 1981 crisis, neither Ecuador nor Peru explicitly requested mediation. The leaders of these states had previously agreed (in the 1942 Rio Protocol) that, should any disagreement arise between the two states regarding the border designation, the Organization of American States (OAS) could call upon the guarantor states to mediate between the disputants. The OAS took this action in 1981, and participants involved in mediated simulations were informed that the same had happened in the experimental setting. When subjects were presented with the scenario and trained to use the software, they were told only that their negotiations may or may not have a mediator. These subjects did not know whether their negotiations would be mediated until they arrived at the computer lab to participate in the simulation.

Each mediator was tasked with preventing an escalation of this crisis by securing an agreement between the representatives of the two states. The range of actions and tools available to each type of mediator differed distinctly, consistent with the descriptions of the different styles of mediation explored in Chapter 4. All mediated simulations reported on in this book were conducted with mediators who adopted one or the other of the two styles that occupy the extreme ends of the spectrum of substantive involvement open to these interveners – facilitation and manipulation. In this book, findings related to formulation, which lies between facilitation and manipulation on the spectrum of mediator involvement, are derived solely from analysis of ICB data.

Graduate and undergraduate political science research assistants at the University of Maryland served as the mediators in these simulations. All of these students had taken an advanced course focusing on international crises and/or negotiation. Each mediator was presented with an extensive overview of the concept of mediation and the different styles that mediators can adopt; as a guideline, we used the descriptions of these phenomena as delineated mainly by Burton (1984, 1990), Touval and Zartman (1985), Keashly and Fisher (1996) and Bercovitch (1997). Mediators were then trained in mediation in general and both facilitative and manipulative styles of mediation.

After undergoing training, mediators were assigned one particular style of mediation that they would adopt each time they mediated a negotiation. This assignment was made in consultation with the experimental staff. Each mediator in training was also able to participate in a practice run at least once before working in an actual experimental setting. All simulations were monitored to ensure reliability within mediation style prior to – and during – the actual experiments.

Mediators communicated with negotiators using the same communication software as the representatives of Peru and Ecuador, and they could direct comments or questions to either or both negotiators. Mediators were privy to every message sent between the negotiators in a given simulation. While mediators were provided with ample background material on the Ecuador-Peru crisis, they did not have access to a DSS for either Peru or Ecuador and did not know the precise utility value associated with any particular agreement. Their efforts at resolving the crisis were primarily informed by what negotiators were willing to share with individual mediators – a condition consistent with the situation often faced by mediators in "real-world" negotiations.

Conclusion

In the latter half of this chapter, we presented a general synopsis of the experimental approach that we use to study crisis mediation. We discussed the real-world crisis that was used as the foundation of our simulations. We also described some general features of our experimental scenario. Finally, we provided information on how we trained subjects and mediators, and how we conducted the experiments, generally. As noted, however, additional information about our methodology will be presented throughout the book, where appropriate.

As discussed in Chapter 1, the content of this book represents a comprehensive summation of our study of crisis mediation. The analyses presented in Chapters 4, 5, and 6 are based on the most complete set of experimental data that we have collected. Therefore, these data are culled from the most diverse set of variations of our experimental research design. For that reason, it will be important to note the parameters of each variation of this research design, and we discuss these in more detail in Chapters 4 through 6. Each of these chapters also contains added details regarding the data used specifically for the analyses contained within these chapters.

In addition, since we have not yet presented an in-depth discussion of the three central variables in our theoretical framework (mediation style, power relations, and zone of agreement), we leave the more detailed discussion of our experimental methodology as it relates to these variables to Chapters 4 through 6. In particular, Chapter 4 contains a more thorough description of how we trained mediators in different mediation styles (facilitation and manipulation), what these mediators were permitted and forbidden to do when adopting one or the other style, and how the presence of these different mediation styles in the simulated negotiations had differing effects on the simulation, as well as on the negotiators and their utility values. The analyses in Chapter 4 were based on simulations in which Ecuador and Peru were unequal powers. In Chapter 5, we present findings from simulations based on a revised scenario in which power parity exists between the crisis actors and compare these results to those found in the power-disparity simulations. More details on how we modified the experimental design to account for this change in the power relations between actors are provided in Chapter 5. In Chapter 6, we investigate the possible causal mechanism that allows mediation to be effective in crisis negotiations by examining the impact that mediation efforts have on the extent of crisis ripeness.[8] In order to examine ripeness, we had to be able to operationalize this concept in the context of our simulations, as described in Chapter 6.

As we have emphasized throughout, our methodological point of departure for the analyses to follow is that the merging of an in-depth historical analysis of crisis cases over an extended period of time, with an experimental design involving negotiators and mediators, optimizes the breadth of hypotheses that we can explore. This hybrid approach is particularly appropriate in situations where there is an extended historical record, but where it is not possible to accurately ascertain the beliefs, motives, and psychological predispositions of decision makers, and where careful experimental designs can help fill the voids in our understanding of the dynamics of aspects of international behavior. In Chapter 3, we turn to an overview of the historical record of crises in the twentieth century.

Notes

1 For details on ICB coding procedures, coder training, variables, and analyses of key crisis concepts, see Brecher and Wilkenfeld (2000).

2 For some cases, new sources were located and used, and in a few instances this resulted in some minor recoding of other ICB variables.

3 In addition to the 128 cases of mediation, three additional cases were identified in which mediation was requested by the parties but was not provided, and 29 cases in which mediation was offered but not accepted by one or more of the parties.

4 Placebo effects refer to the measurable effects that factors extraneous to the environmental manipulations fashioned by the researcher have on outcomes.

5 All experiments were approved by the University of Maryland's Institutional Review Board. All participants were notified that they were involved in a

research study and signed consent forms allowing for the use of the data generated from the simulations in which they participated.

6 This figure references the *total* number of subjects who participated in the simulations that are analyzed throughout this book. See the appropriate succeeding chapters (Chapters 4 through 6) for the specific number of subjects that participated in each variation of the simulations.

7 The DSS for this simulation, created by Kathleen Young, David Quinn, and Christopher Frain, is available at www.bsos.umd.edu/gvpt/can/appendix_3.htm.

8 It is important to note here that the data collected on zones of agreement between negotiators came from simulations that utilized the "base" scenario described in this chapter as well. Hence, these simulations were marked by power disparity between Ecuador and Peru.

3 Patterns of crisis mediation in the international system

In this chapter, we lay the groundwork for the analyses to follow by presenting a systematic overview of the historical record of international crises and mediation in the twentieth century. The survey of crises presented in this chapter relies on data generated by the International Crisis Behavior (ICB) Project, covering the period from the end of World War I and well into what we call the post-cold war unipolar system – that is, from 1918 to 2001. As noted in Chapter 2, there were 434 international crises during this period, with 956 foreign policy crises for individual states. Subsequent analyses utilizing historical and experimental methods are presented in later chapters to help sharpen our understanding of the dynamics associated with crisis mediation.

Readers familiar with the ICB Project and dataset should note two major additions to that comprehensive information source since the publication of the second edition of *A Study of Crisis* (Brecher and Wilkenfeld 2000). First, the data presented here have been updated through 2001, adding 22 new crises and identifying two new protracted conflicts – Yugoslavia (including the Yugoslavia I: Croatia-Slovenia (1991), Yugoslavia II: Bosnia (1992), and Kosovo (1999) crises) and Iraq Regime (including the Iraq No-Fly Zone (1992), Desert Strike (1996), UNSCOM I (1997), and UNSCOM II: Operation Desert Fox (1999) crises).[1]

In addition, a two-year effort was undertaken to code all ICB cases for a set of variables specifically addressing the question of whether mediation occurred, and if so, how that mediation played out. (See an extended discussion of the coding procedures for mediation variables in Chapter 2 above.) This data collection effort has revealed that mediation occurred in 128 crises, or 30 percent of all ICB cases. Interestingly, mediation was *offered* but rejected by one or more crisis actors in an additional 29 crises, constituting an additional 7 percent of all cases. Data on the 128 mediated cases provide the core for the analyses reported in this chapter and in later chapters of this book. See Appendix A for a listing of all mediated crises for the 1918–2001 period.

Several central questions will be addressed in the course of our overview of crisis mediation.

- Under what conditions are crises likely to be mediated?
- What actors and organizations are most likely to become involved as mediators?
- What are the goals of the mediators?
- What effect does mediation have on crisis outcomes?

Under what conditions are crises likely to be mediated?

In this section, we examine a number of factors that impact the probability that mediation will be employed as a crisis management tool. We first analyze bivariate relationships between each of these factors and the likelihood of mediation occurring in a crisis. The first set of factors, consisting of the polarity of the international system, the level of the international system primarily affected by the crisis, and the geographic characteristics of the crisis, address system-wide attributes. The second set – conflict setting, power relations among crisis actors, and the relevance of ethnic conflict – pertain to the relationship among adversaries. Taken together, these factors address both the systemic and relational contexts for crisis mediation. This section concludes with a multivariate analysis of the likelihood of crisis mediation; the model used in this analysis examines the effects of both systemic and relational factors. We begin, though, with a discussion of past scholarly work regarding factors that are believed to be associated with mediation incidence in the international system.

In order for mediation to occur, all parties to the conflict must consent to the involvement of a mediator as a third party in the dispute. The decision to request or accept a mediator is most likely to occur when one or several of the following conditions are present: the conflict is long and complex; the parties have reached a mutual hurting stalemate; their bilateral conflict management efforts have failed; and/or they each possess the desire to cooperate (Bercovitch 1992, 1997). Additionally, if parties reach a stalemate and are entrenched in positional bargaining stances, mediation can serve to eliminate the dilemma faced by disputants of whether to make concessions or to opt for conflict escalation (Zartman and Touval 1996).

Traditional approaches to mediation assume that disputants desire mediation out of humanitarian interests in resolving the conflict (Bercovitch 1992, 1997). However, most scholars point to individual interests as the primary motivating factor in accepting intervention by a mediator – the individual expectations of those involved in the conflict that a potential mediator will be effective in helping each party to secure a more favorable outcome than would otherwise be possible (Touval and Zartman 1985). Mediators can bolster the benefit an actor accrues from a conflict or crisis by helping each side "get their way;" that is, they can lead one (or many) parties to victory in a conflict. Frequently, this desire for a more beneficial outcome involves the estimation that the mediator will influence one's adversary to reach an agreement.

Princen concurs that individual interests, rather than "shared values" or "a convergence of interests," are the driving force behind acceptance of mediation (1992: 61). Even if the idea of having its conflict mediated is not very attractive to a disputant, it may agree to mediation solely due to its perception that rejecting it would be more harmful than accepting it. For example, rejecting mediation may damage one's relationship with the prospective mediator. In addition, parties that are prepared to make concessions may also seek mediation with the hope of protecting their image; the disputant can use the mediator as a scapegoat for unpopular concessions. Furthermore, a party may also request mediation in hopes of damaging relations between its adversary and the mediator during the mediation process.

Parties may seek mediation out of the belief that a mediator will act as a guarantor of an agreement, increasing the chances that all sides will live up to the conditions of an agreement and reducing the chances of future costly conflicts. Mediation may also be sought simply to buy time in or stall a negotiation process (Touval and Zartman 1985; Zartman and Touval 1996).

It may also be the case that parties seek mediation in hopes of improving their capabilities and position relative to their adversary. Touval and Zartman (1985) and Bercovitch (1992, 1997) discuss the potential absolute gains that a disputant might receive by accepting mediation, but realists assert that a state's primary motivation is "to prevent others from achieving advances in their relative capabilities" (Grieco 1988: 498). Thus, a disputing party may refuse to cooperate with a mediator's suggestions or even accept a mediator in the first place if that party believes that the mediator will disproportionately benefit an adversary. Conversely, a disputing party may also accept mediation efforts as long as the gains it expects to receive via mediation will enhance its positions relative to its adversary.

Bercovitch (1992, 1997) highlights the possibility of more altruistic motives for desiring mediation. Without denying the relevance of self-interest, he claims that disputants may view mediation as an expression of their commitment to peaceful international conflict resolution. Additionally, he argues that adversaries may seek mediation simply out of a desire to improve their relationship with each other.

By analyzing ICB data, we are able to go beyond theoretical speculation and examine empirically which factors significantly affect the likelihood that an international crisis will be mediated. We focus on factors related to the international system in general, characteristics of the crisis actors, and the dynamics of the crisis itself.[2]

Polarity structure of the international system

One of the fundamental ways in which we view the international system is through the lens of system polarity and how that polarity in turn impacts the interactions among state actors. The polarity of the system reflects the power relations among the constituent member states. This distribution of power has a potential impact on the manner in which mediation is likely to be employed and the prospects for its effectiveness. ICB has identified five polar structures for the 83 year period under analysis:

- **Multipolarity (1918–39)**: A diffusion of military power and political decision among relatively equal units – France, Germany, Great Britain, Italy, Japan, the Soviet Union (USSR), and the United States.
- **World War II (1939–45)**.
- **Bipolarity (1945–62)**: A concentration of military power and political decision in two relatively equal actors, the United States and USSR, during this era. The two polar centers are preeminent in determining the conditions of stability, the limits of independent behavior by bloc members or unaffiliated actors, and the outcomes of major wars in the system.
- **Polycentrism (1963–89)**: A hybrid structure, with two preeminent centers of military power (here, the United States and USSR) and multiple centers of political decision making.
- **Unipolarity (1990–)**: With the collapse of the Soviet Union, the international system has evolved from "pure" polycentrism to something more akin to unipolarity, with the United States as the dominant power. Some refer to this system as hegemony (Brecher and Wilkenfeld 2000).

As mentioned, 30 percent of the 434 international crises for the entire 1918–2001 period were mediated.[3] Figure 3.1a presents the distribution of crises by year over this time period, as well as the distribution of mediated cases. For ease of interpreting trends, Figure 3.1b presents five-year moving averages for each of these measures. The moving averages converge toward the end of the twentieth century, as crises become less frequent and a higher percentage of crises experience mediation. Table 3.1 presents a tabular summary of these frequencies. These data reveal a steady increase across periods in the proportion of crises in which mediation is offered by third parties and accepted by the crisis adversaries. The exception to this temporal trend is the World War II period, with only one crisis mediation attempt (Ecuador-Peru Border II (1941)). By the post-cold war unipolar period, 46 percent of all crises were mediated, although not always successfully. The data show mediation to be an increasingly frequent tool for crisis management in the current international system structure, and that the relationship between frequency of crisis mediation and the polar structure of the international system is statistically significant ($\chi^2 = 21.5$, $p < 0.00$). While the frequency of crises in the unipolar system appears to be declining, the rate of third-party mediation is increasing. We will return to this point when we present a final multivariate analysis later in this chapter.

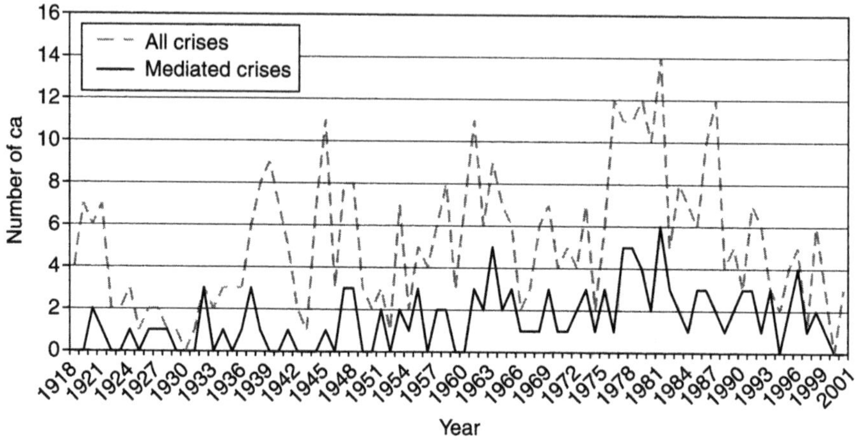

Figure 3.1a Frequency of crises and crisis mediation by year, 1918–2001

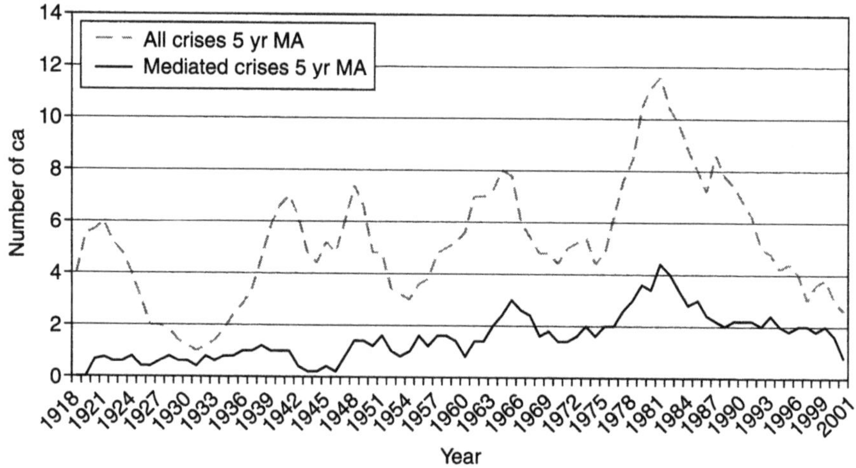

Figure 3.1b Moving five-year averages of crisis and crisis mediation, 1918–2001

International system level

A second trend for third-party mediation of crises focuses on the level of the international system primarily affected by the crisis. According to ICB, every crisis can be located in one of four system categories (Brecher and Wilkenfeld 2000):

- **Dominant system** is identified by crisis interaction among the major powers in world politics. For the period between the two world wars,

Table 3.1 Polarity and frequency of crisis mediation

Polar structure	*Mediated*	*Unmediated*	*Total*
Multipolar	16	58	74
(1918–39)	(22%)	(78%)	(17%)
World War II	1	31	32
(1939–45)	(3%)	(97%)	(7%)
Bipolar	24	64	88
(1945–62)	(27%)	(73%)	(21%)
Polycentric	67	126	193
(1963–89)	(35%)	(65%)	(45%)
Post-cold war	20	23	43
(1990–)	(46%)	(54%)	(10%)
Total	128	302	430
	(30%)	(70%)	(100%)

$\chi^2 = 21.5, p < 0.00$.

the major powers include the Europe-centered great power complex, the United States, and Japan. For 1945 through 1989, this refers to the U.S./USSR bloc system (e.g., Cuban Missiles 1962), while for unipolarity, the dominant system refers to those crises in which the United States was either a crisis actor or an involved actor (e.g., Kosovo 1999).

- **Mainly dominant system** denotes crisis interactions among great powers with spillover effects on one or more subsystems and their state actors (e.g., Suez Nationalization (1956–57), Taiwan Strait IV (1995)).
- **Mainly subsystem** crises are those in which the key crisis actors are lesser powers with a predominantly regional focus, but where there is some spillover to the dominant system as a result of participation by one or more of the major powers (e.g., Angola (1975–76), Cyprus-Turkey Missiles (1998)).
- **Subsystem** crises are characterized by geographic proximity and regular interactions among their members. Subsystem crises are those that occur within a subsystem without the direct participation of any major power (e.g., Football War (1969) involving El Salvador and Honduras, Red Sea Islands (1995) involving Eritrea and Yemen).

Table 3.2 shows that the preponderance of crises occurs at the subsystem level (283, or 66 percent of all ICB cases), and that the level of the international system at which a crisis occurs is significantly related to the likely use of mediation as a crisis management tool ($\chi^2 = 36.6, p < 0.00$). Subsystem crises are mediated at a higher than average rate (39 percent). On the other hand, only two dominant system cases (5 percent) were mediated: the failed UN mediation in the Berlin Blockade crisis (1948–49), and

Table 3.2 International system level and frequency of crisis mediation

System level	*Mediated*	*Unmediated*	*Total*
Dominant system	2 (5%)	38 (95%)	40 (9%)
Mainly dominant system	5 (12%)	35 (88%)	40 (9%)
Mainly subsystem	10 (15%)	57 (85%)	67 (16%)
Subsystem	111 (39%)	172 (61%)	283 (66%)
Total	128 (30%)	302 (70%)	430 (100%)

$\chi^2 = 36.6, p < 0.00$.

multiple mediation attempts, primarily by the United States and mostly of marginal impact, in the Kosovo crisis (1999). Mediation is thus likely to be employed in crises occurring in the periphery of the international system, and when major powers are not involved as crisis actors and are marginally concerned – 87 percent of all mediation occurred in crises at the subsystem level. Recent subsystem crises in which mediation was judged to have been the most important factor in easing tensions include the final Chad-Libya crisis (1986), Rwanda-Uganda (1990), and the crisis triggered for Sierra Leone in 1991 following cross-border raids by rebels from the National Patriotic Front of Liberia (NPFL).[4]

Geography

Geographic factors have been a central concern in research on international conflicts and crises. Joint borders are a potential source of conflict interactions, and both the Correlates of War Project (Small and Singer 1982) and the Militarized International Disputes dataset (Gochman and Maoz 1984; Jones, Bremer, and Singer 1996) show that a majority of wars and international disputes have their basis in conflicts over territory. There are two primary ways in which geography can be conceptualized as playing a role in the crisis-mediation relationship. First, we examine the distribution of instances of mediation across broad geographic regions, in an effort to discern identifiable patterns. Second, we investigate how contiguity or non-contiguity of crisis actors might impact on whether mediation is attempted.

Table 3.3 exhibits a good deal of regional variation in mediation rates, from lows of 17 percent and 24 percent for Europe and Asia, respectively. Crises in the Americas, on the other hand, were significantly more likely to involve mediation, at a rate of 44 percent. In some sub-regions (not displayed in Table 3.3), mediation is virtually non-existent. In Central Asia,

Table 3.3 Geographic region and frequency of crisis mediation

Geographic region	*Mediated*	*Unmediated*	*Total*
Asia	23 (24%)	74 (76%)	97 (23%)
Middle East	30 (36%)	53 (64%)	83 (19%)
Africa	38 (34%)	72 (66%)	110 (26%)
Europe	16 (17%)	76 (83%)	92 (21%)
Americas	21 (44%)	27 (56%)	48 (11%)
Total	128 (30%)	302 (70%)	430 (100%)

$\chi^2 = 15.8, p < 0.00.$

for example, only one of eight crises was mediated, an effort by the then-Conference on Security and Cooperation in Europe (CSCE) in the Nagornyy-Karabakh crisis (1991). Similarly, only three of 24 East Asian crises were mediated: Shanghai (1932), Marco Polo Bridge (1937), and North Korean Submarine (1996). Sub-regional variations were particularly sharp in Africa, from a low of four out of 27 cases (15 percent) for Southern Africa to a high of 11 of 18 cases (61 percent) for Central Africa; and in the Americas, with a 33 percent rate of mediation for the 34 crises in Central America versus a 67 percent rate for the 15 crises in South America. These rather extreme sub-regional variations argue against a "one-size-fits-all" approach to crisis management and conflict resolution, even with an approach like mediation, which boasts well-developed and time-tested methods and an array of international, regional, and state institutions able to take on mediation responsibilities.

Table 3.4 reports on the relationship between contiguity and mediation. Crises that involve immediate neighboring states are significantly more likely than other crises to involve mediation ($\chi^2 = 16.6$, $p < 0.00$). Clearly, the vast majority of crises – 68 percent – involve contiguous actors, and 36 percent of those contiguous cases are mediated. This contrasts with only a 15 percent mediation rate when crisis actors are distant from each other geographically. This low rate of mediation may be explained, in part, by the fact that many (although not all) of the distant cases occur at the dominant system level, which historically displays a very low mediation rate (see Table 3.2 above). But even among near neighbors, defined as crisis actors in the same region, the mediation rate is only 20 percent. So, clearly, some of the characteristics of those crises between and among contiguous states lead to mediation more frequently than in other situations.

Table 3.4 Geographic contiguity and frequency of crisis mediation

Geographic relationship of crisis actors	*Mediated*	*Unmediated*	*Total*
Contiguous	105 (36%)	188 (64%)	293 (68%)
Near-neighbor	11 (20%)	44 (80%)	55 (13%)
Distant	12 (15%)	70 (85%)	82 (19%)
Total	128 (30%)	302 (70%)	430 (100%)

$\chi^2 = 16.6, p < 0.00$.

Conflict setting

International crises can be classified according to those that unfold in the context of an on-going protracted conflict (or PC) versus those that occur as more isolated eruptions of intense discord. A protracted conflict has been defined as "hostile interactions which extend over long periods of time with sporadic outbreaks of open warfare fluctuating in frequency and intensity" (Azar, Jureidini, and McLauren 1978: 50). ICB identifies 33 protracted conflicts for the 1918–2001 period. ICB further distinguishes between PCs and long-war protracted conflicts, the latter including crises occurring in the midst of long wars such as World War II, Greece-Turkey, and Indochina. Some PCs began and ended during the 1918–2001 period, such as East-West, Ecuador-Peru, and Angola. Other PCs, most notably Arab-Israel, India-Pakistan, Greece-Turkey, Honduras-Nicaragua, and Taiwan Strait, continue to simmer as of 2005. And two new protracted conflicts have emerged in the post-cold war unipolar system: Yugoslavia, which began in 1991 with the Croatia-Slovenia crisis, and Iraq Regime, which began with the 1992 No-Fly Zone crisis. It is assumed that the unique nature of PCs – notably their duration and the large number of contentious issues embedded within the conflicts – affects many dimensions of the crisis environment, including the extent to which mediation is likely to become a component of crisis management.

The results of the analysis presented in Table 3.5 show that a relationship, significant at the $p < 0.01$ level, exists between the conflict setting of a crisis and the likely introduction of mediation efforts in that crisis. These data reveal only a marginally greater propensity for mediation to be employed in protracted conflicts as compared with non-protracted conflicts. The results are striking, however, when we isolate long-war PCs, such as World War II and Indochina, for which the rate of mediation is considerably lower than for either PCs or non-PCs. This is not unexpected, since crisis management in the midst of on-going wars is difficult to

Table 3.5 Conflict setting and frequency of crisis mediation

Conflict setting of crisis	*Mediated*	*Unmediated*	*Total*
Non-protracted conflict	49 (29%)	121 (71%)	170 (40%)
Protracted conflict	67 (35%)	122 (65%)	189 (44%)
Long-war protracted conflict	12 (17%)	59 (83%)	71 (16%)
Total	128 (30%)	302 (70%)	430 (100%)

$\chi^2 = 8.6, p < 0.01$.

achieve. But overall, and excluding long-war PCs, it does not appear that the PC status of a crisis is a strong determinant of whether or not that crisis will be mediated.

Power relations

International relations theorists have long been concerned with how the power relations among adversaries affect behavior. Our interest is whether disparity or equality in power among crisis adversaries is likely to impact on whether or not mediation efforts are undertaken. For purposes of this analysis, the operationalization of power consists of a state's possession of several types of resources: population, economic, diplomatic, geographic, and military. Crises are classified as to whether there is low or no power discrepancy among the adversaries (power symmetry), or whether there is a high-level of power discrepancy among them (power asymmetry).

The results reported in Table 3.6 show that, while crises among states of unequal power are more common in the international system – 74 percent – crises characterized by power symmetry among the crisis actors are far more likely to experience mediation than are crises characterized by power disparity – 46 percent versus 27 percent. That is, third parties are much more likely to intervene to manage or resolve international crises when the adversaries are relatively equally matched on a composite measure of power than when one of the sides to the conflict is clearly more powerful than the other(s). This outcome may be the result of the reluctance of third parties to get involved, or the unwillingness of one or another of the parties in an asymmetric power relationship – presumably the more powerful side – to seek or accept mediation. The more powerful of the adversaries may calculate that it can dictate the terms of an eventual agreement more easily from its position of strength and that mediation can only detract from the value of the ultimate agreement. Yet there are exceptions, perhaps the most notable being the mediation by Algeria that

Table 3.6 Power relations among crisis actors and frequency of crisis mediation

Power relations	*Mediated*	*Unmediated*	*Total*
Power symmetry	45 (46%)	52 (54%)	97 (26%)
Power asymmetry	74 (27%)	196 (73%)	270 (74%)
Total*	119 (30%)	248 (70%)	367 (100%)

$\chi^2 = 11.74, p < 0.00.$

Note

*This analysis excludes the 63 ICB cases that involve only one state as a crisis actor.

ultimately brought the Iran hostage crisis to an end in 1981, even in the face of adversaries possessing vastly different power capabilities. More typical were the mediation efforts of Henry Kissinger on behalf of the U.S. government that brought the Israel-Egypt and Israel-Syria October War crises to an end in 1973–74. We return to the question of how the relative power of crisis actors moderates mediation effects later in this study, using both ICB and experimental data.

Ethnicity

Ethnicity in the context of crisis analysis refers to the role of ethnic conflict in the hostility between crisis adversaries. Interstate ethnic conflict takes one of two forms: secessionist, when an ethnic group aspires and acts to secede from a state in which it is a minority community (e.g., Abkhazians in the Georgia-Abkhazia crisis (1992–93) involving Georgia and Russia); and irredentist, when a state claims part of another state's territory on grounds of ethnic affinity with its population and/or its historical association with the territory (e.g., Italy's claim to Trieste in its 1953 crisis with Yugoslavia). It is assumed that the presence of secessionist or irredentist claims as the driving force of an international crisis will affect a number of crisis dimensions, including the willingness and ability of members of the international community or its institutions to attempt to mediate the crisis and the receptiveness of crisis actors to such offers. Since 31 percent of all international crises for the period 1918–2001 had an ethno-political dimension, understanding the relationship between ethnicity in crisis and mediation is of central importance.

The presence of an ethnic dimension in crises clearly makes mediation more probable, particularly so in irredentist conflicts as they spill over into the international system (see Table 3.7). Only 24 percent of crises without an ethnic dimension attracted mediation attempts, even though they constituted 69 percent of all crises in the international system. What accounts for this sharp contrast? One argument is that ethnic conflict attracts a good

Table 3.7 Ethnic conflict and frequency of crisis mediation

Ethnic conflict in the crisis	*Mediated*	*Unmediated*	*Total*
Secessionist conflict	18 (38%)	29 (62%)	47 (11%)
Irridentist conflict	39 (45%)	47 (55%)	86 (20%)
Non-ethnic conflict	71 (24%)	226 (76%)	297 (69%)
Total	128 (30%)	302 (70%)	430 (100.0%)

$\chi^2 = 16.5$, $p < 0.00$.

deal of international attention, in part because of the keen involvement of politically active diasporas (Collier and Hoeffler 2002; Sheffer 2003), and in part because they are often the most violent of all international crises at the sub-war level. Among post-cold war mediated crises with ethnic dimensions were the Zaire Civil War crisis of 1996, in which South African President Nelson Mandela mediated under UN auspices; Zambian mediation in the Democratic Republic of Congo Civil War crisis in 1999; and multiple mediation efforts (primarily by the United States, but also by the UN, Russia, and Finland) in the Kosovo crisis of 1999. Given the increased proportion of crises with ethnic dimensions in the post-cold war era, it is important to note that such crises appear to be more receptive than others to mediation.

Multivariate analysis of crisis mediation incidence

The bivariate analyses give us a good idea of the nature and strength of the associations between crisis mediation incidence and each systemic and relational factor on its own. However, they do not tell us much about each factor's relative explanatory power in the context of all of these factors. Just because a crisis has an ethnic dimension or occurs between two contiguous actors, for instance, does not ensure that it will be mediated. A confluence of factors is always at play and will affect the likelihood of any specific crisis being mediated. By conducting a multivariate analysis, we can assess how well each factor affects this likelihood while controlling for all other factors discussed above.[5]

Methodology

To test the hypothesis related to mediation incidence, we employ two multivariate logistic regression models. Both models consider the same set of crises ($n = 430$)[6] and the same dependent variable – a dichotomous indicator of whether mediation occurred in a crisis, with 1 signifying mediation incidence. The models employ different indicators for two explanatory factors – the polarity of the international system and the geographic region in which the crisis occurs.

The indicators of system polarity and geographic region were originally multi-category, non-ordinal qualitative variables, as described earlier in this chapter. First, we recoded these indicators into several dummy variables, with each type of polarity (five dummies) and geographic region (six dummies) as separate variables. Next, we attempted to maximize the variance in and explanatory power of our overall analysis by including the separate dummies for each type of polarity and geographic region in our model (see Model 1 in Table 3.8). To avoid the "dummy variable trap" and its distortion of coefficient estimation, it was necessary to exclude one category for both polarity and geographic region so that these dummy variables would not be perfectly collinear. These excluded categories become the reference categories by which we interpret the coefficients of all other polarity and geographic region dummy variables. We use post-cold war/unipolarity as the reference category for polarity and the Americas as the reference category for geographic region. The earlier bivariate analyses demonstrated that these two categories were more likely than any others to be positively associated with crisis mediation.[7]

Since we expect that mediation will be significantly more prevalent in the post-cold war era and in the Americas than in *all other* systems and geographic regions, we also analyzed a second version of our model that utilized only one 0-1 dichotomous indicator for polarity and one for geographic locality. This version is represented by Model 2 in Table 3.8. The "1" values of these indicators represent the post-cold war period and the Americas, respectively. In this case, we are able to compare the effect that a crisis occurring during the post-cold war period has on the likelihood of mediation, compared to all other polar periods combined. In the same way, we are able to compare the effect that a crisis being located in the Americas has to all other geographic regions combined.

The results of both of these models are displayed in Table 3.8. For ease of interpretation, these results are used to generate the predicted probabilities of observing a "1" on the dependent variable.[8] It is also important to note that several of the independent variables used in one or both models are not operationalized in the same manner as in the earlier bivariate analyses (see notes in Table 3.8).

Results

We begin our analyses by examining the results of Model 1. The Likelihood Ratio Chi-squared value is quite high for this model, and the overall model is statistically significant ($p \leq 0.000$). The results indicate that nearly all of the independent variables have a statistically significant association,

Table 3.8 Multivariate logistic regression models of mediation incidence

	Model 1		*Model 2*	
Geographic region: Europe	−1.022*	(0.474)	—	—
Geographic region: Middle East	−0.574	(0.407)	—	—
Geographic region: Africa	−1.039**	(0.404)	—	—
Geographic region: Asia	−1.199**	(0.433)	—	—
Geographic region: Americas	—	—	0.886**	(0.352)
Polarity period: Multipolarity (1918–39)	−1.390***	(0.483)	—	—
Polarity period: World War II (1939–45)	−2.401*	(1.117)	—	—
Polarity period: Bipolarity (1945–62)	−0.859*	(0.425)	—	—
Polarity period: Polycentrism (1963–88)	−0.845*	(0.380)	—	—
Polarity period: Post-cold war (1989–2001)	—	—	0.948**	(0.360)
International system level	−0.575***	(0.199)	−0.739***	(0.181)
Geographic relationship of crisis actors	0.604*	(0.307)	0.518	(0.291)
Protracted conflict	0.373	(0.257)	0.435	(0.241)
Ethnicity	0.734***	(0.258)	0.655**	(0.248)
Constant	0.200	(0.490)	−1.614***	(0.313)
N	430	—	430	—
LRχ^2	73.575***	—	65.521***	—
df	12	—	6	—

*$p \leq 0.05$; **$p \leq 0.01$; ***$p \leq 0.005$

Notes

Standard errors are in parentheses. The dependent variable – "Mediation incidence" – was coded as follows: 0 (no mediation), 1 (mediation). For the independent variables, those signifying the geographic location of the crisis in Model 1 were each dichotomized, with 0 indicating the Americas as the reference category and 1 indicating the region reflected in the variable name. For Model 2, "Geographic region: Americas" was coded 0-1, with 1 indicating the Americas and 0 indicating all other geographic regions combined. In Model 1, those independent variables signifying the polarity period during which the crisis occurred were each dichotomized, with 0 indicating the post-cold war period as the reference category and 1 indicating the period reflected in the variable name. For Model 2, "Polarity period: post-cold war" was coded 0-1, with 1 indicating the post-cold war period and 0 indicating all other polarity periods combined. The other independent variables were operationalized as follows: "International system level" [0 = subsystem, 1 = mainly subsystem, 2 = mainly dominant system, 3 = dominant system]; "Geographic relationship of crisis actors" [0 = near-neighbor or distant actors, 1 = contiguous actors]; "Protracted conflict" [0 = non-protracted conflict, 1 = regular or long-war protracted conflict]; "Ethnicity" [0 = non-ethnic conflict, 1 = secessionist or irredentist conflict].

whether positive or negative, with the likelihood of a crisis being mediated. The baseline probability of crises being mediated within the context provided by Model 1 is 55 percent. This baseline was calculated by holding all dichotomous variables at their modal values and all interval and ordinal variables at their mean values.

Since it was used as the reference category for the geographic region variables, the probability of a crisis being mediated when it occurs in the Americas is equal to the baseline, or 55 percent. The negative coefficients associated with all other geographic region indicators tell us that crises occurring outside of the Americas are expected to have a lower probability of being mediated. In fact, Asian crises are nearly half as likely to be mediated – an overall likelihood of 27 percent – compared to those in the Americas. European and African crises fare slightly better, but still only have a 31 percent probability of exhibiting mediation. (As a caveat, we cannot with confidence say that the probability of Middle Eastern crises being mediated is notably different than that of crises in the Americas, since this variable is not statistically significant.) These results generally corroborate those found in the earlier bivariate analyses but reveal that Asian, not European, crises have the lowest probability of being mediated when compared to crises in the Americas and when controlling for the other factors included in the multivariate model.

The data in Model 1 reveal that crises occurring during the post-cold war/unipolar period have a 55 percent probability of being mediated. Crises occurring in all other periods have a lower probability of being mediated than those in the post-cold war period, as indicated by the negative coefficients for these period variables. The probability of mediation drops from 55 percent to 35 percent for crises in the bipolar and polycentric periods; it falls even further to 24 percent for multipolar crises.

The results for Model 1 confirm the bivariate findings reported earlier in this chapter with respect to three out of the four remaining independent variables as well. The level of the international system in which the crisis occurs, the geographic relations of the crisis actors, and the ethnic nature of a crisis, are all reliable predictors of mediation incidence. Subsystem crises have a 64 percent likelihood of being mediated, while crises exclusively between dominant actors only have a 24 percent probability of exhibiting mediation. In addition, when a crisis occurs between contiguous actors, it has a 69 percent chance of being mediated, compared to only 55 percent if it involved distant or near neighbors. Finally, the likelihood of mediation in crises with an ethnic dimension is 72 percent, while non-ethnic crises only have a 55 percent probability of being mediated. The protracted-conflict context of a crisis, which exhibits a weak impact on mediation in the bivariate analysis, is the lone insignificant independent variable.

Turning to Model 2, the Likelihood Ratio Chi-squared value is sizeable and statistically significant at $p \leqslant 0.000$, but it is lower than the corresponding value for Model 1. Hence, the overall set of relationships in this model are not as strong as that contained in Model 1. The differences between Models 1 and 2 relate specifically to the indicators we use for geographic location of the crisis and system polarity. Model 2 does not analyze the effect that each individual geographic region and polarity period has on mediation incidence in comparison to the Americas and the post-cold war period, respectively. Rather, it considers how the latter two factors compare to all other regions and periods combined, restricting the overall degree of variance contained within Model 2. Such limitations lessen the *combined overall impact* of the specific variables in this model, in contrast to Model 1. Nevertheless, we see many of the same general trends found in the results of Model 1: once again, the geographic location of the crisis, the polarity and level of the international system in which the crisis occurs, and whether the crisis has an ethnic component are important determinants of the likelihood of mediation taking place.

The baseline probability of a crisis being mediated within the context of Model 2 is 16 percent. This percentage represents the likelihood of mediation incidence if the crisis does *not* occur in the Americas or in the post-cold war era, if the crisis involves mostly great powers but spills over into one or more subsystems, or if it does not have an ethnic component. The probability of mediation increases twofold from this baseline if the crisis occurs in the Western Hemisphere or after the fall of the Soviet Union, and it nearly doubles if the crisis is related to a secessionist or irredentist conflict (the actual overall likelihood of mediation is 27 percent for crises with an ethnic element, 32 percent for crises occurring in the Americas, and 33 percent for those occurring in the post-cold war era). Furthermore, under the conditions described by Model 2, the likelihood of mediation in dominant system crises is only 3 percent; this probability increases eightfold to 24 percent for those crises that occur purely in a subsystem of the international system.

However, in Model 2, the geographic relationship of the crisis actors to one another is no longer a significant explanatory factor of mediation incidence. Finally, the indicator of whether a crisis occurs within a protracted conflict is approaching statistical significance in Model 2 ($p \leq 0.01$). As such, although protracted conflict crises have been more frequently mediated than non-PC crises, we cannot conclude with full confidence that the PC setting is a determinant of mediation incidence.

To summarize the findings from these models, the general direction of the relationship between each independent variable and the likelihood of mediation is consistent across models: Crises are more likely to be mediated if they occur in the Americas or in the post-cold war period. Mediation is also more likely to occur in crises between contiguous rather than non-contiguous actors and in crises between non-dominant powers, as opposed to great or superpowers in the international system. In addition, ethnic crises have a higher probability of being mediated than do non-ethnic crises. Finally, whether a crisis is part of a protracted conflict consistently has little to no effect on the likelihood of crisis mediation in all analyses presented.

By itself, the level of the international system in which a crisis occurs has the strongest relationship with whether or not mediation will occur. However, when other factors are introduced into the analysis, the region and polar period in which the crisis occurs become stronger predictors. As the number of dominant polar powers in the international system has decreased over time and international and regional organizations have played an increasingly significant role in international conflicts, mediation has become more prevalent and acceptable as a whole. In addition, crises in the Americas are much more likely to be mediated than those in all other regions, which is likely due to the fact that both the institutions and traditions in the region foster such intervention.[9]

Furthermore, the ethnic factor is a consistently significant predictor of crisis mediation. As Gurr argues, a "regime of managed ethnic heterogeneity" (2000: 277) has proliferated throughout the international system since the end of the cold war. This regime consists of international norms (i.e., "conflict-mitigating doctrines") and practices aimed at protecting ethnic identity and collective rights, and carried out and upheld by both domestic and international actors. Mediation aimed at managing crises related to ethnic discord is an important aspect of this emerging regime. However, the ethnicity factor generally has a weaker relationship with the likelihood of mediation than most other crisis characteristics. When we control for the effects of each region individually, ethnicity, however, is a more important determinant of mediation than both the geographic relationship of the crisis actors and the system level in which the crisis occurs.

Which actors are most likely to mediate?

The above analyses reveal systematic patterns regarding which crises will be mediated. We now turn to a consideration of the types of actors that served as mediators during the period 1918–2001, following a discussion of general mediator motives in the international system.

Mediator motives for intervening

Conventional wisdom tells us that mediators intervene out of humanitarian interests in resolving conflict. However, most scholars – including Princen (1992), Hopmann (1996), and Merrills (1998) – argue that such concerns are almost always coupled with less altruistic, more self-interested motives for originating mediation. As Carnevale and Arad (1996) argue, mediators generally have interests in the dispute and its resolution; others, like Touval (2003), argue that mediators will intervene *only* if they are trying to promote or protect their own interests in the outcome of the conflict.

Touval and Zartman (1985) provide the most comprehensive discussion of mediator motives for intervention in international conflicts. States will mediate if a conflict could negatively affect their relations with the disputing parties (e.g, if the conflict is between two allies of the mediator) in order to try and limit the potential damage that it could incur as a result of the conflict. A state may also intervene with the intention of developing closer relations with one or more of the disputants and/or extending its influence over them. States may also choose to mediate in order to avoid becoming involved in an existing conflict as a disputant (Zartman and

Touval 1996). In addition, states may be in competition with each other over who will mediate a conflict, so the motive of preventing one's rivals from intervening may be present in some cases.

In a critical work, Princen (1992) explores the distinction between direct and indirect interests of potential intermediaries. Princen agrees that all mediators possess self-interested motives for intervening in a conflict, but he argues that mediators cannot possess direct interests in the dispute (e.g., claiming sovereignty over a territory being disputed by two other parties) because such interests would make them disputants in a conflict. Instead, he argues that *principal mediators* have indirect interests in the issues of a conflict. Principal mediators can derive value (e.g., security) from the disputants, cut side deals with one or more disputants, or establish relations that will insure benefits for the mediator in the future. In contrast, the interests of *neutral mediators* are "public" in nature, in that their value extends to those who are not involved in the dispute and comes only from the disputants reaching an agreement. Examples of such public interests are general peace, stability, and order. Thus, neutral mediators can possess more altruistic motives for intervening, similar to the partially selfless motives that disputants may have for requesting mediation.

Most scholars also argue that different types of mediators possess different motives for intervening. For instance, small- and medium-sized states are often concerned about preventing a conflict from spilling over into their territory, preventing a conflict from drawing in more powerful external actors, refraining from taking sides in a dispute, promoting norms that will enhance their own security, augmenting their own influence and prestige, and increasing "their usefulness and independence in relation to their stronger allies" (Zartman and Touval 1996: 448). Serving as a mediator can help to achieve all of these goals.

Furthermore, non-state actors also possess distinct motives for engaging in mediation. Many international organizations (IOs) are expected to live up to their mandates to provide assistance in the promotion of peaceful and non-violent resolution of conflict. In addition, they may choose to mediate to pre-empt the influence of more self-interested mediators, or because they perceive that states are inherently ill-suited to mediate objectively and effectively. Finally, the charters of some international and regional organizations (such as the UN, Arab League, Organization of American States, and African Union) suggest or mandate that these organizations attempt to resolve certain conflicts. However, history has demonstrated that member states of these IOs or regional governmental organizations (RGOs) have often opted against intervention in conflicts or crises, even in the form of mediation (Zartman and Touval 1996).

Bercovitch (1992, 1997) discusses why *unofficial* individuals – so-called global diplomats having no affiliation with a government or IO (Starkey, Boyer, and Wilkenfeld 2005) – will act as mediators. Examples of such global diplomats include Pope John Paul II and former U.S. President

Jimmy Carter.[10] Bercovitch indicates five motives for these individuals initiating mediation, some similar and others distinct from the motives linked to official mediators of states, IOs, or non-governmental organizations (NGOs): 1) a desire to play an instrumental role in altering the path of an entrenched or escalating conflict; 2) a desire to observe, analyze, and influence a conflict; 3) a desire to gain access to important political leaders and subsequently open lines of communication; 4) a desire to implement certain ideas about conflict management; and 5) a desire to enhance one's own personal and/or professional reputation and credentials. Mediation by unofficial individuals is still a relatively new phenomenon, but the frequency of its use in international conflicts in general has increased in recent years.

Mediators in ICB cases

Table 3.9 presents a frequency distribution for four types of crisis mediators: international governmental organizations, regional organizations, single states, and groups of states. See Appendix A for a complete listing of mediators in all 128 cases of crisis mediation.

The data in Table 3.9 indicates that each category of actor identified by ICB plays an active role in international crisis mediation. Relevant regional organizations that have become involved in crisis mediation include the Arab League, such as during the Egypt-Sudan Border I crisis (1958); the Organization of American States (OAS), including in the Dominican Republic-Haiti II crisis (1963); and the now defunct Organization of African Unity (OAU) in the Cameroon-Nigeria I crisis (1981). It remains to be seen whether the OAU's successor, the African Union (AU), will similarly adopt the role as a regional mediator, although the Constitutive Act of the AU declares as one of its principles "the right of

Table 3.9 Types of crisis mediators

Type of mediator	*Instances of crisis mediation*	*Percentage of mediated cases*
International governmental organization *(League of Nations, UN)*	30	24
Regional governmental organization	23	18
Single state	39	32
Group of states	32	26
Total*	124	100

Note
*This table excludes one case of mediation by a private transnational organization (the Catholic Church in Beagle Channel II (1978)), two cases in which the mediator was a private individual (Yasser Arafat in the 1973 Iraq Invasion-Kuwait crisis and former U.S. President Jimmy Carter in the 1996 North Korean Nuclear crisis), and one case – North/South Yemen II (1979) – with missing data on this variable.

Member States to request intervention from the Union in order to restore peace and security" (African Union 2002). Serving as a crisis mediator would be one way in which the AU could fulfill this goal.

In addition to international and regional organizations, a wide variety of states have served as third-party mediators in the midst of international crises, including traditional powers like the United States, United Kingdom, and Russia/USSR as well as less prominent states like Niger (Chad-Libya I crisis 1971–72), Algeria (U.S. hostages in Iran crisis 1979–81), and Zaire, in conjunction with Burundi, Kenya, and Tanzania (Rwanda-Uganda crisis of 1990–91).

A more fine-grained examination of the data reveals trends over time in relation to which type of mediator was most likely to be involved in crisis intervention. For instance, the multipolar system (1918–39), which had the lowest rate of crisis mediation of all non-war systems, nevertheless showed a reasonably high rate of mediation for the League of Nations – 38 percent. The United Nations in the immediate post-World War II era (the bipolar era) served as the mediator in almost half (46 percent) of all mediated crises. However, in the subsequent polycentric era (1963–89), the UN took on the role of mediator in only 14 percent of the crises that involved mediation. These findings for the League and the UN seem to indicate that the evolution of the international system has resulted in the diminishing of the role of global international organizations in the crisis mediation process. Regional organizations, on the other hand, became significantly stronger factors in post-World War II mediation efforts and have continued to serve as mediators in about 20 percent of mediated crises in later periods. Interestingly, single states became increasingly involved in mediation attempts over time, reaching a high of 42 percent of all mediation attempts in the unipolar period. Groups of states played a significant role in the multipolar era, involved in 44 percent of the mediated crises including the Burgenland Dispute (1921), mediated by Italy, France, and the United Kingdom, and the Chaco II crisis (1932–35), involving mediation efforts by Argentina, Brazil, Chile, and Peru. Since that time, however, mediation by groups of states has become much less common; only 16 percent of mediated crises in the post-cold war era have involved groups of states working together as the third party.

What are the goals of mediation?

What goals did mediators set for themselves as they approached the mediation task? Were they interested in achieving crisis management – that is, attempting to control events during a crisis to prevent significant and systematic violence from occurring or escalating, or putting an end to violence that was already occurring? Or was conflict resolution the goal, that is, attempting to get the parties to redefine their relationship in such a way as to perceive either that they could realize their goals without conflict or

Table 3.10 Goals of crisis mediators

Goal of mediator	*Instances of crisis mediation*	*Percentage of mediated cases*
Crisis management	70	56
Conflict resolution	55	44
Total*	125	100

Note
*The intent of mediators could not be determined for three of the cases in which mediation occurred.

that they could redefine their relationship so that their goals no longer conflicted? Table 3.10 reports the ICB findings on this question.

While crisis management is somewhat more prevalent than conflict resolution as the goal of the mediators, this difference is not very sharp. Recent examples of mediation for the specific achievement of crisis management include efforts by the Conference on Security and Cooperation in Europe to mediate in the Nagornyy-Karabakh crisis (1991–92), mediation efforts by the United States in the North Korean Submarine crisis (1996), and the multiple mediation attempts during the Kosovo crisis (1999). Recent examples of mediation for the purpose of overall conflict resolution include the actions of Australia in the Cambodia Peace Conference of 1989–90 and efforts by the OAU in the Eritrea-Ethiopia crisis of 1998–2000. (An extended discussion of Eritrea-Ethiopia case is provided at the end of this chapter.)

It should be noted, however, that crisis management can be a pre-requisite for conflict resolution. When mediators are striving for conflict resolution, they must also try to manage the immediate crisis. This is demonstrated by the crises associated with the Ecuador-Peru protracted conflict. While the OAS-endorsed mediators of the 1995 Ecuador-Peru crisis strove for conflict resolution, they succeeded first as crisis managers, securing a ceasefire between the states and gaining acceptance for an observer mission to monitor the ceasefire. Mediation efforts continued after the crisis terminated, however, and in 1998, outside the context of a crisis, the mediators were able to secure an agreement that resolved the territorial and sovereignty issues at the core of this protracted conflict. These mediators, then, succeeded at both crisis management and conflict resolution. Closer examination of the ICB data reveals that single states as mediators are much more likely to limit their goals to crisis management, whereas other mediators – international and regional organizations, groups of states – split relatively evenly between crisis management and conflict resolution as the goal of mediation. See Appendix A for a listing of the primary goals of the mediators in all 128 ICB-identified cases of crisis mediation.

What effect does mediation have on crisis outcomes?

Achieving agreement

Perhaps the central question when examining the impact of mediation on crises is whether or not the intervention has led to the achievement of agreement among the parties. Regardless of whether the objective of the mediation was full conflict resolution, or narrower crisis management, agreement is usually the way the international community assesses success or failure of the mediation attempt. In all, 38 percent of all ICB cases between 1918 and 2001 ended with an agreement among disputants. Table 3.11 presents the ICB findings on how mediation relates to the chances of agreement being achieved.

Mediated crises are far more likely to terminate in agreement than are unmediated crises, 66 percent versus 26 percent. We have included here agreements of three types: formal agreements (treaty, armistice, ceasefire), semi-formal agreements (letter, oral declaration), and tacit understandings (mutual understandings by adversaries, neither stated nor written). Unmediated crises are far more likely to end without agreement, with terminations characterized by arrangements imposed by outside forces or unilateral acts by a crisis actor – such as military invasion of an adversary's territory, severance of diplomatic relations, or the quelling of riots.[11] Clearly, evidence from twentieth century diplomatic history demonstrates the utility of mediation efforts in bringing about crisis termination through agreement.

Crisis legacy

A logical follow-up question has to do with the lasting impact of crisis outcomes. One way to measure the extent to which mediation impacted the outcome of an international crisis is to assess the nature of tensions among the adversaries subsequent to crisis termination – were tensions reduced or heightened among crisis actors following the crisis episode? ICB measures

Table 3.11 Crisis mediation and achievement of agreement

	Agreement reached	*No agreement among adversaries*	*Total*
Mediated	85 (66%)	43 (34%)	128 (30%)
Unmediated	77 (26%)	225 (74%)	302 (70%)
Total	162 (38%)	268 (62%)	430 (100%)

$\chi^2 = 64.6, p < 0.00.$

Table 3.12 Crisis mediation and legacy

	Reduction of tensions	*Escalation of tensions*	*Total*
Mediated	79 (64%)	44 (36%)	123 (30%)
Unmediated	144 (49%)	149 (51%)	293 (70%)
Total*	223 (54%)	193 (46%)	416 (100%)

$\chi^2 = 7.92, p < 0.00.$

Note

*This analysis excludes cases that ended between 1996 and 2001. Insufficient time has passed to assess the legacy of those crises.

the legacy of crises in terms of whether the principal adversaries are involved in a crisis with each other during the five-year period following crisis termination. The data in Table 3.12 explore the extent to which management of crises has been effective in permanently reducing tensions among the adversaries.

Paralleling the earlier findings on the positive relationship between mediation and the achievement of agreement, Table 3.12 shows a significant positive relationship between mediation and reduction of tensions. This relationship is not as strong as that between crisis mediation and the achievement of agreements, a difference probably explained by the relatively high rate of mediator involvement in protracted conflicts (see Table 3.5), which are characterized – by definition – by repeated crisis iterations. Nevertheless, the overall picture indicates that mediation efforts on the part of various organs of the international community lead to both agreements and tension reduction.

Two other aspects of crisis outcomes were examined, but mediation had no significant effect on these measures. The first measured whether crisis actors viewed the outcome as a victory, defeat, stalemate, or compromise. This actor-level variable is aggregated at the system level into a measure of the "content of the outcome." Combinations of victory and defeat among crisis actors were considered crises with definitive outcomes, while mixes involving either compromise or stalemate by actors were considered ambiguous. There was a tendency for crises with mediation to result in ambiguous outcomes, undoubtedly because compromise is considered to be an ambiguous outcome, but this tendency was not statistically significant. A second measure is designed to assess the extent of actor satisfaction with the outcome of the crisis, again aggregating the perceptions of actors into a composite measure of the overall crisis level. The possible values were all satisfied, mostly satisfied, equally mixed, mostly dissatisfied, and all dissatisfied. Here it was not possible to discern any meaningful impact of mediation on the satisfaction of the parties to the crisis. We will return to this issue of actor satisfaction in additional ICB analyses and in the experimental design reported later in this book.

Summary of trends in crisis mediation

The preceding overview of the ICB data demonstrates that crisis mediation is a relatively frequent occurrence in the international system, more so since the end of the cold war. While mediation has its highest rate of occurrence in the Americas, high rates were also evident in the Middle East and Africa. Mediated crises are likely to involve neighboring states outside of the dominant level of the international system, and the crises often reflect an ethnic component. In addition, crises among actors of relatively equal power show a tendency toward being mediated. While there is some evidence that the probability of mediation is heightened among crises that are embedded within protracted conflicts, we cannot with full confidence say that this factor is a significant determinant of crisis mediation in the context of other important variables. Historical data also reveal that mediated crises are more likely than unmediated crises to end in agreement and to help ease tensions in the long-run among crisis actors. Furthermore, a single state or group of states is the primary mediator in more than 50 percent of mediated crises. Finally, mediators are more likely to have crisis management as their primary goal of intervention, rather than conflict resolution.

This overview sets the backdrop for a closer look at crisis mediation dynamics, specifically those factors identified in this study as key to understanding these dynamics – mediation style, relative power of crisis actors, and crisis ripeness. Before moving on to these analyses, though, we provide a review of one instance of crisis mediation to illustrate how this method of crisis management can play out.

A case analysis of crisis mediation: Ethiopia-Eritrea (1998–2000)

Ethiopia and Eritrea experienced a violent crisis over a disputed border region from May 6, 1998, to December 12, 2000. We first describe the background to this crisis, followed by a summary of the crisis events, including a description of the mediation efforts. We end this case analysis by comparing its characteristics to the ICB results discussed in this chapter.

Background and pre-crisis events

Eritrea had been the northernmost region within Ethiopia until Italy claimed Eritrea as a colony in 1890, and it remained under Italian rule

Figure 3.2 Map of Eritrea-Ethiopia

until the end of World War II. In 1896, Italy attempted to establish control over a larger section of Ethiopia, but the latter thwarted Italy's advance. Italy and Ethiopia signed the Addis Ababa peace treaty that same year. More concerned with consolidating power over the southwestern parts of his empire, Ethiopian Emperor Menelik II granted Italy control over the Eritrea region and some additional pieces of land. During the 1930s, Italy furthered its gains in the region via military conquest, and the Ethiopian province of Tigre was annexed to Eritrea. After Italy's defeat in World War II and its removal from Ethiopia, there was much disagreement among the Four Powers (Britain, France, the United States, and the Soviet Union) regarding whether Eritrea should be recognized as a separate state or whether, alternatively, it was a part of Ethiopia. They referred the case to the United Nations, which in 1950 declared that Eritrea would be granted the status of an autonomous region in a federation under Ethiopian control. An Eritrean separatist movement emerged shortly thereafter.

Eritrean nationalists argued that Eritrea had been "given up" by Ethiopia in 1896 and subsequently existed as a separate entity under colonial rule for more than 50 years; hence, they contended that Eritrea should be accorded independent status. The Ethiopian government under Haile Selassie, a vigorous anti-colonialist and pan-Africanist, rejected this claim to self-determination, arguing that the colonial legacy of Eritrea made its separate status illegitimate. The United States and leaders of many African states supported Selassie's claim. The Organization of African Unity (OAU), which generally supported a policy of preserving the integrity of existing African borders, refused to take sides in the dispute. By 1962, Selassie's government had removed all autonomous powers that had once been granted to Eritrea and had dissolved the Ethiopia-Eritrea federation, claiming that Eritrea was a part of Ethiopia. Eritrean secessionists (represented mainly by the Eritrean People's Liberation Front, the EPLF) had turned violent during the previous year, initiating what would become a thirty-year war of self-determination against the Ethiopian government.

Selassie's successor, a Marxist Ethiopian army officer named Colonel Mengitsu Haile Mairiam, forged close ties with the Soviet Union during the 1970s, much to the dismay of the West. When the Soviet empire collapsed in 1991, Mengitsu lost his ruling mandate. A coalition of domestic anti-government groups, including both the EPLF and Tigrayan nationalists – represented mostly by the Tigre People's Liberation Front, the TPLF – joined forces to overtake the Ethiopian government in 1991. In April 1993, a referendum was held in Eritrea to determine its political status. An overwhelming majority voted in favor of independence, and Eritrea officially became a separate state a few months later. The international community and the OAU accepted Eritrea's new status.

Relations between Eritrea and Ethiopia were quickly normalized following Eritrea's independence. The former EPLF members who now ruled Eritrea worked closely with the Tigrayan leadership of Ethiopia, previously their allies during the final months of the Mengitsu regime (Taras and Ganguly 2002). Both countries began guarded transitions toward democracy, embracing minorities and making strides toward increased openness in executive recruitment. By mid-1998, Ethiopia had generally progressed further along the road to democracy, enshrining protections of ethnic self-determination in its constitution and holding elections. Political competition was restricted in Eritrea, and Eritrean

President Isaias Afwerki was reluctant to hold open elections while its democratic institutions were still in their infant stages. Despite democratization efforts, it was clear that both countries had been severely traumatized by the secessionist war that preceded Eritrean independence and had ineffective and inefficient state apparatuses. In addition, they were experiencing growing internal discord from various ethnic groups seeking self-determination – Afars in Eritrea and Oromos, Somalis, and Afars in Ethiopia. Furthermore, cooperation between Eritrean and Ethiopian elites galvanized the political opposition in Ethiopia, many of whom were bitter about the loss of Eritrea.

Although the outbreak of hostilities between Ethiopia and Eritrea in 1998 came as a shock to many in the international community, signs did indicate that their working relationship had become strained in the years leading up to the crisis. As part of the deal struck between the EPLF and Tigrayan opposition leaders during the end of the Mengitsu regime, the EPLF had promised Tigrayan leaders that, once the communist authority was toppled, Ethiopia would be permitted much-desired access to the Red Sea in return for recognition of Eritrean independence. However, "once Eritrea obtained independence ... legal complexities made it impossible for Ethiopia to receive a corridor to Red Sea ports" (Taras and Ganguly 2002: 220). As a result, Ethiopia lost international trade opportunities, while Eritrea gained an advantage in this realm. In addition, while Eritrea and Ethiopia had used the same currency after the former became independent, Eritrea began using its own currency in 1997, further straining the economic, and subsequently the political, ties between the two countries. Finally, Ethiopia and Eritrea never agreed to a clearly demarcated border between their countries nor did they define the citizenship status of individuals living in this border region after Eritrea gained independence. Hence, the "'ownership' of citizens and resources along the border was open to reinterpretation according to convenience" (International Crisis Group 2003: 3).

In light of these factors and sensing growing internal opposition to his own regime, Ethiopian Prime Minister Meles Zenawi began to espouse Ethiopian nationalism, and the personal relations between Meles and Afwerki became highly strained. The stage was now set for the eruption of a crisis between the two countries in 1998.

Crisis and mediation events

A crisis was triggered for both states on May 6, 1998, when shots were exchanged between Ethiopian and Eritrean soldiers in the town of Badme, which sits along the western sector of the border between the two countries. It is unclear who initiated these hostilities, though each country blamed the other for triggering the incident. Ethiopia and Eritrea also accused each other of encroaching on its sovereignty, each arguing that

Badme was part of its territory – Ethiopia argued that it was located in Ethiopian territory, while Eritrea argued that colonial maps and treaties demonstrated that it was on Eritrean soil. In reality, Badme was administered by Ethiopia before the crisis, its residents voted in Ethiopian elections, and it used Ethiopian currency. However, the EPLF and TPLF had disagreed about the status of the region surrounding Badme since before the fall of the communist regime in Ethiopia. In addition, the border in this region "did not exist in any physical sense, and people crossed it regularly to find grazing for their herds, to trade, or to seek employment" (International Crisis Group 2003: 2).

Ethiopia, landlocked since Eritrea blocked its access to the Red Sea, immediately diverted its international trading activities from Eritrean to Djiboutian ports. A few days after the eruption of hostilities, Ethiopia and Eritrea invited a joint U.S.-Rwandan mediation team to help prevent the crisis from escalating. The mediators drew up a proposal that entailed unilateral Eritrean withdrawal from the regions it had occupied around Badme. This proposal was backed by the OAU and was presented to the two sides by the Congolese president. Ethiopia accepted this proposal; Eritrea did not, contending that the occupied areas rightfully belonged to Eritrea. Thus, this mediation effort failed to halt the crisis.[12] By late May 1998, a full-scale war between the two states had begun, fought mainly in the "trench warfare" style of World War I. Estimates of several thousand casualties were reported during the first month of fighting. The countries also accused each other of forcefully expelling their citizens from each other's territory, and the UN High Commissioner for Human Rights expressed concern regarding the expulsion of Eritrean nationals by the Ethiopian government in July 1998. The latter responded by denying the accusation.

In June 1998, however, U.S. President Bill Clinton placed numerous calls to the leaders of both countries, and a U.S. team mediated a suspension of air strikes from both sides. According to the International Crisis Group (2003), this U.S. action ultimately served to protect the capitals of each state and to limit the amount of additional devastation that could have occurred in the border region. Later that year, the OAU (led by Algeria) worked closely with a U.S. team headed by National Security Advisor Anthony Lake to draft two documents – one delineating a framework for agreement, the other a plan for implementation – based heavily on those developed by the earlier U.S.-Rwandan team (International Crisis Group 2003). The documents called for a ceasefire, a withdrawal of both sides' troops to the positions they held before the crisis had erupted, and a demarcation of the border between the two countries. The documents were presented to both sides; once again, Ethiopia accepted these proposals, but Eritrea did not. International crisis mediation efforts had failed yet again.

On February 6, 1999, the nearly eight-month-old ceasefire was broken as hostilities between Ethiopia and Eritrea were renewed in the region around Badme. Ethiopia violated the moratorium on air strikes. Three weeks later, Eritrea announced that it had withdrawn its forces and set up a new defense line west of the Badme region, due to the recent successful Ethiopian recapture of that region. As March began, Eritrea announced that it would accept the OAU-U.S. proposals. However, no moves were made on either side toward implementation of these proposals. Heavy fighting continued until July 14, 1999, when both sides accepted – albeit tentatively – the agreement and implementation plan developed by the OAU-U.S. team. At this point, the OAU was the primary mediator in the conflict, though the U.S. team headed by Lake still worked closely with the OAU and met with Ethiopian and Eritrean officials from time to time.

Despite its acceptance of the agreement and implementation plans, in August 1999 Ethiopia expressed concern over a third document developed jointly by the OAU, the U.S., and the United Nations (International Crisis Group 2003). This document delineated the technical arrangements (including detailed procedures and a timeline) for implementation of the other two plans. Specifically, it called "for the establishment of a Neutral Commission to determine the precise areas from which the two sides were to re-deploy," provided "for the deployment of inter alia military observers to verify envisaged redeployments," and called "for demilitarization and delimitation of the entire common border between the two countries" (United Nations Department of Peacekeeping Operations 2004). Eritrea accepted this document, but Ethiopia eventually rejected it. Despite this additional setback, there was a relative lull in fighting for eight months, though minor clashes continued occasionally. Another major episode of violence began on February 23, 2000 – 22 months after this crisis had begun – and, again, each side accused the other of initiating these hostilities.

Indirect peace talks facilitated by the OAU and U.S. continued throughout this period of renewed violence, and the UN sent a team led by former mediator of the Bosnian conflict Richard Holbrooke to bring the two sides together at the negotiating table (Taras and Ganguly 2002). Each of these external efforts broke down on May 5, 2000. One week later, Ethiopia "conducted a massive offensive, breaking Eritrea's defensive line in numerous places, bombing ports and airports, and thereby disrupting supply lines, including those through which humanitarian aid was flowing" (International Crisis Group 2003: 4). By this time, Ethiopia had established a presence in Eritrean territory (Taras and Ganguly 2002). On May 17, the UN Security Council adopted a resolution that imposed an arms embargo on each side, despite initial Russian resistance. Further UN resolutions were adopted that condemned the fighting and implored the two sides to reach an agreement (United Nations Department of Peacekeeping Operations 2004).

Mediation efforts led to the resumption of indirect peace talks at the end of May 2000, and by June 18, a ceasefire was signed by both sides. The

OAS brokered this cessation of hostilities, with support from the UN Security Council. The agreement "called for a peacekeeping mission to monitor it [the ceasefire], the redeployment of forces, and a demilitarized Temporary Security Zone (TSZ) completely inside what was considered to be Eritrean territory" (International Crisis Group 2003: 4). By the time this ceasefire was agreed upon, the war had battered both states economically, with Eritrea suffering more severely. Various estimates placed the number of dead in the tens or hundreds of thousands (Taras and Ganguly 2002), and an additional 650,000 people were displaced.

On July 31, 2000, a UN Security Council Resolution established the United Nations Mission in Ethiopia and Eritrea (UNMEE).[13] In mid-September 2000, UN liaisons and military observers were placed in the area, and logistical preparations for implementation of several aspects of the June 18 agreement were made. The OAU-brokered plan was finalized, and the crisis was terminated on December 12, 2000, when Eritrean President Afwerki and Ethiopian Prime Minister Meles signed a border agreement, witnessed by the OAU, the United States, the UN Secretary-General, and the European Union. This agreement, known as the Algiers accord, outlined the stipulations of the ceasefire and removal of troops from areas occupied after May 6, 1998, and it provided for the delimitation and demarcation of the border between Eritrea and Ethiopia. It also supported an investigation into the causes of the conflict and activities aimed at "addressing both sides' compensation claims" (International Crisis Group 2003: 4).

ICB trends and the Ethiopia-Eritrea crisis

While the Ethiopia-Eritrea case is only one instance of crisis mediation, it illustrates many of the trends apparent through analysis of ICB data. These analyses demonstrated that crisis mediation was more common in the post-cold war period. During this unipolar period, external mediation became a much more acceptable and frequently utilized means of conflict prevention and resolution. In fact, it was during this period specifically that the OAU abandoned its policy of non-intervention in conflicts where existing state borders were in question. This opened the door to more instances of OAU mediation. In addition, it has been argued that the UN's decision to send peacekeeping forces to monitor the implementation of the December 12, 2000, agreement was born out of a desire to demonstrate its relevance as an intervener in the post-cold war African political landscape, following failed peacekeeping efforts in Somalia, Rwanda, and Sierra Leone (Taras and Ganguly 2002).

Several other factors strongly and positively associated with the probability of mediation were present in the Ethiopia-Eritrea crisis. First, this crisis occurred purely within a subsystem of the international system. It was located in a peripheral region of the international system, and major powers were not involved as crisis actors. During the cold war, the region was of tactical importance to the two superpowers because of the economic advantages it provided in the form of access to the Red Sea. Once the cold war ended, so did most of any remaining major or superpower concern. While these powers were not willing to ally themselves with either side as crisis actors, they were willing to intervene as mediators. In this role, they could execute a high degree of influence over the outcome of the crisis without paying the much higher costs of being involved militarily. Both humanitarian and reputation concerns were motivating factors in the decision to mediate.

As noted earlier, subsystem crises are often marked by geographic proximity of actors who engage in regular interactions with each other, as demonstrated by Ethiopia and Eritrea. They are contiguous actors, and the ICB-based evidence revealed a trend toward crises of this sort having a higher probability of mediation than those between more distant actors. Crises between contiguous actors often involve border disputes such as those in the Ethiopia-Eritrea conflict. Since the possession of land as a politico-economic or symbolic resource is frequently viewed in zero-sum terms, disputes over territory are notoriously intractable. Often external mediation is the only way that such crises can be managed and/or conflicts can be resolved. For these same reasons, it is sometimes necessary for third-parties to act as guarantors of peace agreements signed in such crises, as the UN and OAU did in relation to the Ethiopia-Eritrea crisis.

The results of bivariate ICB analyses also provided evidence that the likelihood of mediation is higher in crises between relatively equal powers. With its higher degree of access to key shipping ports and its refusal to allow Ethiopia to use them, Eritrea had an economic advantage over Ethiopia. According to data collected by the UN Development Programme in 2000, Eritrea also scored slightly higher than Ethiopia on the human development scale – an index of the measure of a country's life expectancy, education and adult literacy, and GDP per capita (United Nations Development Programme 2004). However, with the exception of early victories by the Eritrean armies, it was clear that Ethiopia possessed a much higher level of military strength during the 1998–2000 crisis: it consistently delivered severe defeats to Eritrean forces during the final two years of the crisis. Viewing these factors together, then, the two states were relatively equal in terms of power. As Hopmann (1996) argues, conflicts marked by power disparity usually involve stronger parties that are resistant to third-party intervention out of the belief that they can "win" the conflict on their own. Such considerations do not exist in symmetric crises like the Ethiopia-Eritrea case. In fact, both sides requested mediation only after the crisis began.

A final factor that was found to have a significant relationship with the likelihood of crisis mediation in ICB analyses was ethnicity. Specifically, crises with an ethnic component are more often mediated than crises without this element. The Ethiopia-Eritrea crisis itself did not have an immediate ethnic aspect, and thus it does not fit with the ICB trends in relation to this variable. Stepping back from the immediate context of the crisis, however, one sees that ethnicity played a large role in the earlier conflict between these states. In the not-so-distant past, Eritrean secessionists had engaged in a 30-year war against the Ethiopian government. In addition, the crisis in many ways was a byproduct of unresolved issues related to Eritrea's successful achievement of statehood in 1993. Hence, although ethnicity did not play an immediate role in the context of the Ethiopia-Eritrea border crisis, the incident was steeped in a deep-seated ethnic conflict that had not been fully resolved.

How does the Ethiopia-Eritrea case measure up to the ICB results regarding mediators and their goals? Although the Ethiopia-Eritrea crisis involved several separate incidents of mediation by different actors – an IO (the UN), individual states (the U.S., Djibouti, the Congo), a group of states (the United States and Rwanda), and RGOs (the EU and the OAU) – the *primary* mediator of this crisis was ultimately the OAU. It was involved at the highest level of intensity for the longest period of time compared to all other mediators. The OAU commenced its mediation efforts in May 1998, and its mediation activities did not conclude until the final day of the crisis – December 12, 2000. Referring back to the results presented in Table 3.9, we see that RGOs such as the OAU are the least likely of the four main types of mediators displayed in this table to be involved as the primary mediators in international crises. That being said, the number of crises mediated by RGOs has risen since the end of World War II, and this trend has continued in the post-cold war era. As noted, the OAU played a larger role in African crises after the fall of the Soviet Union, due in large part to its decision to drop a previously held standard of non-intervention in conflicts where the sanctity of existing borders was at stake. Taras and Ganguly (2002) also point out that Ethiopia played a large role in constructing the OAU and dominated this organization for much of the time that it was fighting Eritrean secessionists. Thus, Ethiopia was not willing to challenge or alter the OAU stance on upholding the principle of border sanctity. It was not until Ethiopia's overall power in this organization decreased and the military imbalance in the Ethiopia-Eritrea conflict became severe that the OAU was willing and able to intervene in the conflict.

The Ethiopia-Eritrea case does not strongly fit the trends we found regarding the goals of crisis mediators. According to the data presented in Table 3.10, crisis mediators are more often concerned purely with crisis management than conflict resolution. When a mediator's primary goal is crisis management, it rarely engages in significant attempts to solve all underlying causes of the conflict. On the other hand, mediators who are concerned with conflict resolution promote both crisis management and long-term settlement. Crisis management was an important goal of these mediators, and in fact, there is some evidence that it was a priority during the negotiations that led up to the June 18, 2000, ceasefire (International Crisis Group 2003). However, each set of proposals for ending the crisis, beginning with the May 1998 U.S.-Rwandan plan and including the final agreement, contained stipulations for delimiting and demarcating the border between the two countries in addition to ending hostilities, proposals consistent with conflict resolution goals. The Algiers agreement included additional provisions for investigating the causes of the crisis and addressing compensation claims by each actor for losses it received in the conflict. Hence, conflict resolution was a central goal of the crisis mediators in this case example as well.

According to ICB, mediated crises are more likely than unmediated crises to end with formal agreements and to be followed by a reduction in tensions among crisis actors. Consistent with this trend, a formal agreement was signed by Ethiopia and Eritrea on December 12, 2000, ending the crisis between the two states. The mediation efforts of the OAU played a large part in achieving this agreement, not only by bringing the parties together and pushing them toward settlement, but also by formulating the actual substance of the Algiers agreement. And, since the OAU plan was based in large part on the U.S.-Rwandan proposals presented in May, 1998, some form of the Algiers accord had been guiding negotiations between the parties since a few weeks into this multiyear crisis.

As for a reduction in tensions, the ICB operationalization of this outcome is the non-recurrence of an additional crisis between parties within a five-year period following termination of the crisis under examination. Table 3.12 shows a somewhat higher propensity for mediated crises to end with a reduction in tensions than unmediated crises. We are unable to fully assess whether or not tensions have been reduced between Ethiopia and Eritrea at the time of this writing, as five years have not passed since the end of the crisis on December 12, 2000. However, serious concerns have been raised in recent years regarding the implementation of the Algiers agreement. For the first two years, both sides complied with the agreement to a large extent, and implementation was progressing in a positive direction. Then, in April 2002, the neutral Boundary Commission created by the Algiers accord released its decision regarding the delimitation of the Ethiopian-Eritrean border. Its conclusion was that Badme proper belonged to Eritrea, and the surrounding region (the Badme plains) belonged to Ethiopia. Under the provisions of the final agreement, the Commission's decision was to be "final and binding." However, Ethiopia was displeased with the decision and asked the Commission to review the issue once again. The Commission rejected this request, prompting UN Secretary-General Kofi Annan to call for adherence to the Commission's decision. Eritrea has said it would be willing to engage in "negotiation, dialogue or other process aimed at the normalization of relations, or even the amelioration of the worst human effects of the demarcation, which will cut some communities in half" (International Crisis Group 2003: 7). However, it requires that demarcation occur along the lines prescribed by the Boundary Commission before these negotiations take place. Ethiopia, on the other hand, remains insistent that the Boundary Commission's decision must be reexamined before demarcation occurs. Neither side has moved from this position since April 2002.

In addition, security in the border region has become more fragile since 2003. Illegal incursions into the TSZ have been made by troops from both sides, and some minor skirmishes between sides and killings have occurred in this region. Ethiopian troops have been more often guilty of illegal movement in the TSZ (International Crisis Group 2003). However, especially since 2003, Eritrean soldiers have been labeling UN peacekeepers as serious threats to peace, accusing them of various criminal activities. The UNMEE has claimed that its members have been harassed by Eritrean troops and that these soldiers have placed significant restrictions on the UNMEE's ability to carry out its mandated activities. At the time of this writing, the situation has regressed further: the Boundary Commission said in March 2004 that it was unable to move forward on demarcation of the border, and the UN issued an ultimatum to the two sides in May 2004, stating that the UNMEE would withdraw its activities unless both sides agreed to keep it there. Intermittent skirmishes still occur, many refugees still exist, and the security situation in the region remains tense. The African Union (the successor organization to the OAU) discussed the Eritrea-Ethiopia situation at its July 2004 meetings, encouraging the parties to uphold the Algiers accord but also noting that some restrictions on UNMEE activity in the TSZ had been relaxed in recent months. Especially noteworthy was Ethiopia's July 2004 removal of a ban on UNMEE flights from the capital of Eritrea (Asmara) to the Ethiopian capital (Addis Ababa), which it had imposed since the end of the crisis in 2000. UN Secretary-General Kofi Annan also visited both parties during the same month in an attempt to try to accelerate the resolution process. Only time will tell if these contentious issues can be resolved and a further crisis prevented. That being said, as of spring 2005, no additional crises between Ethiopia and Eritrea have emerged.

Notes

1 The Iraq Regime protracted conflict will include at least one post-2001 crisis, the Iraq War beginning in March 2003, when the next update is released.

2 It should be noted here that even though we analyze traits of the crisis actors in this study, all ICB measures that we utilize are found in the system-level dataset produced by this project, where the unit of observation is each individual crisis. Hence, all indicators of actor characteristics are system-level aggregates of these traits for all actors involved.

3 The data reported in Wilkenfeld *et al.* (2003) were based on a preliminary coding of mediation derived from information contained in the summaries of

crises, and covered the period 1918–96. The data reported here are based on an extensive recoding of all ICB cases, utilizing the sources identified when the original ICB data were collected, and hence is a more comprehensive and reliable coding of mediation. These newest mediation data, along with the entire updated ICB datasets for 1918–2002, are available at www.cidcm.umd.edu/icb.

4 Summaries of these, and all ICB cases, are available at www.cidcm.umd.edu/icb. It should be noted that these summaries include new sections detailing relevant mediation efforts.

5 It is important to note here that one ICB variable – the power relations among crisis actors – contains a large amount of missing data. Hence, in the interest of maximizing the number of and variation among cases under analysis, we exclude this factor from the multivariate analysis.

6 There were four cases – Goa II (1961), Mali-Mauritania (1962), Operation Protea (1981), and Contras IV (1989) – for which it could not be definitively determined whether mediation occurred.

7 The indicator for the geographic region of Australasia was also excluded from Model 1 because it was constant for all the cases being analyzed. No crisis in the ICB dataset has occurred in this region.

8 Per Aldrich and Nelson (1984), probabilities for significant variables can be derived using the logistic distribution function: $P(y=1)=1/(1+e^{-Z_i})$ where $Z_i = \alpha + \beta_i X_i$.

9 The Americas region has a regional organization with a strong history of mediating (the Organization of American States), a good deal of multi-state, sub-regional cooperation directed toward intervention (e.g., groups of states have mediated under the guise of the Pan-American Conference and as mandated by the Rio Protocol), and a hegemonic power (the United States) with a strong precedent of involving itself in crises where its interests are at stake.

10 In some instances, Jimmy Carter has been considered an official representative of the U.S. government as a mediator, even when he no longer served as president. At other times, there is convincing evidence that Carter acted on his own as an unofficial individual while mediating a conflict (e.g., the 1993 North Korean nuclear crisis that involved North and South Koreas and the United States as crisis actors).

11 Just under 5 percent of all ICB cases (19 of 432) end by fading away over time. These cases are also included in the no-agreement category.

12 A governmental delegation from Djibouti also attempted to mediate between the two sides early in the crisis, but its efforts failed.

13 The UNMEE was mandated to carry out the following tasks: monitor and verify the redeployment of Ethiopian and Eritrean forces, monitor and ensure compliance with the TSZ and ceasefire, chair a Military Coordination Commission consisting of both OAU and UN members that would allow the UN to communicate with Ethiopia and Eritrea on military matters in order to avoid potentially dangerous misunderstandings, assist in de-mining efforts in the TSZ and surrounding areas, and coordinate actions with (both UN and non-UN) human rights and humanitarian agencies in the TSZ and surrounding areas (International Crisis Group 2003; United Nations Department of Peacekeeping Operations 2004).

4 Mediation style

Observers and analysts of mediation and its effects often cluster all mediator activities together as one type of third-party intervention, without regard to the different ways in which mediation might be employed. One of the most notable variations among mediators is the *style* of mediation used – to what degree does the mediator try to direct the discussions of crisis actors? Is a mediator willing and/or able to propose a solution to the conflict under discussion? Is he/she able to utilize leverage to push the parties toward agreement? Or, does the mediator adopt a more "restrained" approach, serving as a go-between among the sides to a crisis? The style that a mediator employs in a given situation can have a pronounced impact on that mediator's effect on a conflict or crisis. As such, mediation style needs to be taken into consideration in any effort to better understand the potential of mediation as a tool for international crisis management.

A classification of mediation styles

As noted, much of the literature on international mediation obscures the fact that mediators can play a variety of different roles in international conflicts. Touval and Zartman (1985) argue that a true understanding of the dynamics of mediation requires systematic consideration of mediator style. Towards this goal, they have identified three basic styles that mediators can adopt in their efforts to resolve a conflict – that of the communicator/facilitator, the formulator, and the manipulator.[1] The style employed in a given crisis will reflect the preferences and capabilities of crisis actors as well as mediators and will, we argue, be a determinant of the impact of mediation on the crisis.

Facilitation

The *mediator as facilitator* (Burton 1984; Bercovitch 1992; Bercovitch and Houston 1996; Hopmann 1996) or *communicator* (Touval and Zartman 1985; Zartman and Touval 1996; Bercovitch 1997) serves as a channel of communication among disputing parties (Keashly and Fisher 1996). The mediator as facilitator may simply provide the physical space for negotiations, an activity classically conceptualized as "good offices." However, the mediator as facilitator can also organize additional logistics of the negotiation process, collect information, set the agenda regarding which issues will be discussed and in what order, and/or assist conflicting parties in understanding the messages being conveyed among parties. A facilitator can also serve as a conduit of messages between disputants, especially when face-to-face communication isn't possible or desired. Under these circumstances, the facilitator can assist efforts by all sides in a conflict to "save face" by presenting each party's concerns and stances to their fellow disputant. Hopmann (1996) discusses facilitation as a composite of several roles: the process facilitator (i.e., good offices); the facilitator of communication, compromise, and convergence (i.e., the equivalent of Touval and Zartman's *communicator* role); and the facilitator of cognitive change, attempting to induce the parties to see the problem in a new light and view each other empathetically, without making specific suggestions regarding potential solutions. The mediator as facilitator makes no *substantive* contribution to the negotiation process but, rather, is restrained to ensuring continued, and hopefully constructive, discussion and dialogue among disputants.

Thus, mediation can be limited to the facilitative role, such as that played by the OAU during the 1986 crisis associated with an attempted coup in Togo. A crisis was triggered for Togo when an attempt was made to stage a military coup against President Etienne Eyadema, who had ruled the country for more than two decades after leading his own coup against former president Nicholas Grunitzky. Eyadema accused both Ghana and Burkina Faso of supporting the rebels that opposed him. Despite denials from officials in both Ghana and Burkina Faso, Togo closed its borders with Ghana and deported nearly 300 Ghanians after charging them with illegal entry into Togo. Two months after the crisis began, the Organization of African Unity (OAU) sent a fact-finding mission to review the situation. OAU Secretary-General Ide Oumarou had discussions with the leaders of both Togo and Ghana, providing them with information related to the crisis. The OAU's mission released a report that neither rejected nor supported Togo's claims regarding the involvement of Ghana and Burkina Faso. In this mode of involvement, the OAU did little more than contact the parties and seek and report on information – tasks associated with facilitative intervention. This crisis concluded weeks after the OAU report, when Togo announced its acknowledgement that Ghana had nothing to do with the attempted coup.

Facilitation can be more active as well, as demonstrated by UN mediation efforts during the French Hostages in Mauritania crisis, triggered in September 1977. Early in 1977, Polisario guerillas had attacked Zouerate – a town in Mauritania with a large French constituency – and killed two

French citizens, while taking six others hostage.[2] France, which supplied Morocco and Mauritania with arms, asked both the UN and Algeria to assist in getting these hostages released. The guerillas were unwilling to cooperate with attempts to free these hostages, and, in October, took two more French citizens hostage. This second abduction triggered a crisis for France, which responded by putting paratroopers on alert. This alert triggered a crisis for Algeria – home to many Polisario camps and bases that could come under attack by the paratroopers. While Algeria complained to the UN Security Council that French intervention should be prevented, France sent even more troops to the Algerian-Senegalese border.

UN Secretary-General Kurt Waldheim played a significant role in this crisis as a mediator. On separate occasions, he met with Polisario representatives, the Algerian Foreign Minister, and a French ministry official. On December 15, following talks with Polisario Foreign Minister Ibrahim Hakim, Waldheim announced that Polisario intended to release all eight French hostages to his custody on December 23. This promise was kept, Waldheim escorted the hostages to Paris, and the crisis ended for France and Algeria. Waldheim never suggested specific resolutions or pressured the parties into agreement. Rather, true to the role of a facilitator, he talked to each of the crisis actors, transmitted messages among them, and assisted them greatly in their efforts to cooperate.

Some analysts maintain that the restrained intervention style of facilitation does not qualify as "true" mediation (Dixon 1996; Berridge 2002). This position is particularly common among scholars who discuss facilitation solely as a conflict resolution-promoting endeavor, labeled as third-party consultation (Fisher 1972; Fisher and Keashly 1988; Keashly and Fisher 1996) or interactive problem solving (Burton 1969, 1984; Kelman 1972, 1992). Bercovitch and Langley (1993) contend, though, that a broad definition of mediation – one that includes facilitation as a type of mediation – is more useful and appropriate when trying to gain a holistic understanding of the dynamics of international mediation. The inclusive threefold typology of mediation allows for a more direct comparison and evaluation of those situations in which crisis actors themselves arrive at solutions and in which the role of the third party is "primarily facilitative and diagnostic, but also nonevaluative, noncoercive, and nondirective over outcomes" (Keashly and Fisher 1996: 238).

Even though we adopt Touval and Zartman's typology of mediation styles, we have chosen to use *facilitation* in place of their terminology *communication*. It incorporates a range of scholarly typologies of such activity – the "facilitator" role in the context of problem-solving workshops, as conceived by Burton and Kelman; the third-party consultant role developed by Fisher and associates; and a synthesis of Hopmann's threefold categorization of facilitative activity. Bercovitch and his associates often use the terminology of "communication" and "facilitation" interchangeably (see Bercovitch 1992; Bercovitch and Houston 1996).

Formulation

The second mediation style commonly identified is *mediation as formulation*. Unlike facilitation, formulation involves a substantive contribution to negotiations by the mediator. This substantive participation involves the mediator conceiving and proposing new solutions to the disputants. Such activities are especially useful when the parties reach an impasse in the negotiation process or, according to Hopmann (1996), when the parties' emotions are running high. Zartman and Touval (1996) note that the mediator-as-formulator usually tries to redefine the issues at hand in a conflict and generally attempts to employ innovative strategies aimed at "unblock(ing) the thinking of the conflicting parties" (1996: 454). While a formulative mediator will encourage parties to move towards agreement and will try to convince them of the costliness of unilateral action (Touval and Zartman 2003), the mediator-as-formulator is not empowered to pressure the crisis actors to accept or pursue any particular outcome – a capability associated with manipulation, as described in the following section.

An example of formulative mediation in an international crisis can be found in the Vilna I crisis between Poland and Lithuania that began in July 1920. This was the first of three crises that constituted a protracted conflict between the countries. Its occurrence can be traced to the Polish-Russian War that ensued when Poland attacked Russia in April 1920, following Russia's refusal to meet Poland's demand for restoration of its 1772 border.[3] After World War I, the Allied powers fixed the Lithuania-Polish border, and Vilna was placed in Lithuanian territory. In July 1920, a year of hostilities between Bolshevik Russia and Lithuania ended, with Russia agreeing to recognize Lithuania, and Lithuania granting Russia permission to cross its territory to engage Poland. This triggered a crisis for Poland, which countered by attacking Lithuanian forces near Vilna, triggering a crisis for Lithuania. A full-scale war ensued, with Russia providing military assistance to the Lithuanians.

Poland asked the League of Nations to intervene on September 5, 1920. The Supreme Allied Council of the League of Nations began mediating the conflict less than two weeks later, and it helped devise an agreement between Poland and Lithuania that provided for a ceasefire, for Lithuania's neutrality in the Polish-Russian War, and for temporary recognition of the Ally-imparted Lithuania-Poland border. Hours after this agreement was signed on October 7, a Polish general crossed the border and subsequently occupied Vilna. The League of Nations mediated further and helped to establish arrangements for a future plebiscite that would decide whether Vilna belonged in Poland or Lithuania. Both countries accepted this agreement, ending the crisis. The League of Nations did engage in facilitative activities including bringing the parties together, passing messages between them, and engaging in fact-finding activities, but it also made substantive suggestions to the parties and assisted them in devising a framework for acceptable agreement. As such, it played the role of a formulative mediator as well, and ultimately its formulative tactics helped bring an end to the crisis.

Manipulation

Manipulative mediators also provide a substantive contribution to negotiations. In addition to formulating potential solutions, though, this mediator uses its position and its leverage to "manipulate the parties into agreement" (Touval and Zartman 1985: 12).[4] The manipulative mediator can offer incentives (i.e., carrots) to crisis actors to persuade them to adopt a specific outcome and can threaten or actually impose penalties or sanctions (i.e., sticks) on those parties that do not accept a proposed agreement. Hopmann (1996) indicates that mediators that have adopted this style can also influence the direction of negotiations by manipulating the international environment. While it is often the case that only powerful mediators can play the manipulator role, the parties to a conflict or crisis do determine, in part, the extent of a manipulator's power in the context of specific disputes (Zartman and Touval 1996). Touval and Zartman (1985) also argue that in its most active form, the mediator as manipulator can become a party to the solution, if not the dispute itself. Under these circumstances, as mediators become advocates, a mediator's perceived neutrality and objectivity might be threatened.

The 1974–75 crisis involving Turkey, Greece, and Cyprus regarding control of the island of Cyprus demonstrates the relevance of manipulative mediation as a crisis management tool. This crisis (known as Cyprus III in ICB) was one of 11 crises that have emerged, to date, as part of the ongoing Greece-Turkey protracted conflict. Approximately three-fourths of the Cypriot population is Greek, while the remaining quarter is Turkish. Portions of each of these communities advocate that Cyprus – long controlled by the Ottoman Empire and subsequently by the United Kingdom – should be an independent state in the international community. Others, however, support the idea of *enosis*, or a formal union between Cyprus and Greece, while still others contend that Cyprus would be best served by a formal partition of the Greek and Turkish regions of the island (a policy known as *taksim*).

This was the political backdrop in 1974, when Archbishop Makarios, the president of Cyprus and a well established advocate of an independent Cyprus, was overthrown in a coup led by the Cypriot National Guard and strongly believed to be engineered by Greek officials in Athens. The coup resulted in a new government in Cyprus – one which advocated a union between Cyprus and Greece. This coup triggered a crisis for Cyprus, as well as Turkey, which responded five days later by launching an invasion of the island, with 40,000 troops, to protect Turkish Cypriots on the island. This move, in turn, triggered a crisis for Greece and gained the attention

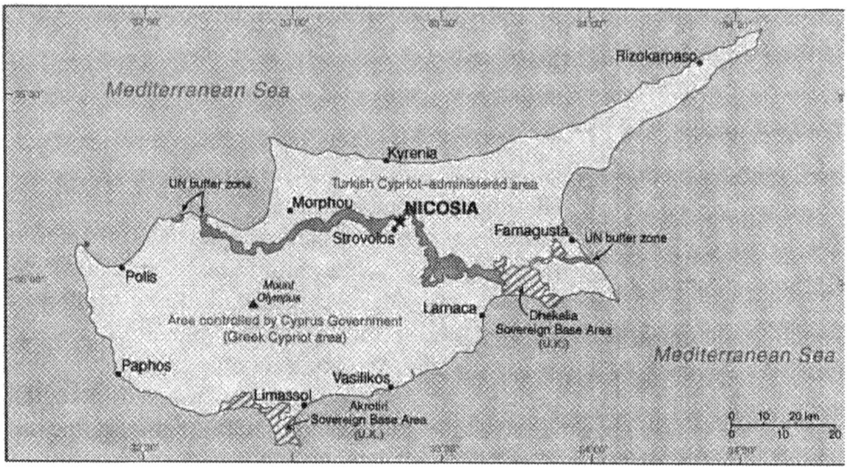

Figure 4.1 Map of Cyprus

of the international community. The United Kingdom and the United States, as well as the UN, all stepped in to mediate in the midst of this crisis, and, as Yilmaz and Gerner (2003) note, the mediators in this crisis adopted a manipulative style as they worked to push Greece and Turkey to a ceasefire and to an eventual agreement on the fate of Cyprus.

U.S. officials were critical of both Turkey's invasion of Cyprus as well as Greece's involvement in the overthrow of Makarios and were anxious to see a return to more stability in Cyprus and between Greece and Turkey. U.S. Secretary of State Henry Kissinger (who was also serving as President Richard Nixon's National Security Adviser at this time) worked with British Foreign Minister James Callaghan to coax Greek and Turkish leaders to accept an Anglo-American ceasefire plan, with Kissinger informing the crisis actors that if they did not accept the ceasefire plan, "the United States would remove all of its nuclear weapons from both sides of the Greek-Turkish border" (Kissinger 1999: 222), leaving the two states outside the protection of the U.S. nuclear umbrella.

The British government played an even more active role than did the U.S. government during this crisis, due in part to the coincident timing of the crisis and Richard Nixon's resignation as president of the United States. (He was replaced by Gerald Ford on August 9, 1974.) The ceasefire was violated, and Greece and Turkey continued to refuse to make concessions to one another about the future of Cyprus. In August 1974, Callaghan threatened to mobilize NATO against Turkey if it didn't accept a UN plan for removing Turkish troops from the disputed island and, by

August, as the crisis dragged on, the United Kingdom had begun to mobilize troops for a potential invasion of Cyprus (Yilmaz and Gerner 2003). These heavy-handed tactics did succeed in helping to slow the escalation of this crisis, but in the end did little to help bring about a lasting resolution to the Greek-Turkish conflict. This crisis ended with Turkey declaring control over the northern 40 percent of the island of Cyprus and the continuation of the protracted conflict between the states. Nonetheless, it serves as a good example of the range of tactics – and especially the arsenal of "sticks" – that a manipulative mediator can use during crisis management efforts.

Mediation style, crisis management, and conflict resolution

A number of authors view mediation as an "ongoing and fluid" process that "changes as the dispute changes and as the intermediary and the disputants gain information and skill" (Princen 1992: 65; see also Young 1967; Bercovitch 1992, 1997; Mitchell 1993; Hopmann 1996; Zartman and Touval 1996). According to this conception, mediators should not adopt *one* style in a given situation but should adapt throughout the course of a conflict or crisis. Nonetheless, many scholars have argued that certain styles will allow a mediator to more effectively pursue goals of crisis management or conflict resolution, and advocate that mediators adopt one particular style. However, analysts disagree about *which* of these styles is best suited to achieve these goals.

Jabri (1996) maintains that facilitation is the best-suited mediation style for securing long-lasting, mutually beneficial outcomes and resolving the fundamental causes of conflicts. Advocates of the mediator as facilitator style – including Fisher (1972), Carnevale and Pegnetter (1985), Burton (1990), Kelman (1992), Rothman (1992), and Keashly and Fisher (1996) – contend that disputing parties should arrive at their own solutions rather than having outcomes developed and/or imposed by a third party. Princen adds that, unlike facilitation, manipulative strategies can damage the "atmosphere of good will, trust, and joint problem solving" between the parties (1992: 58), whereas facilitation fosters sentiments thought to be associated with successful conflict resolution. Many observers encourage limiting mediation activities to facilitation during low-intensity conflicts (see Rubin 1980; Hiltrop 1985, 1989; Thoennes and Pearson 1985; Donohue 1989; Lim and Carnevale 1990). Dixon (1996) sees a wider potential impact for facilitation and concludes that this type of third-party intervention effectively promotes peaceful settlement during *crises* more consistently than do manipulative moves.

Others, though, contend that formulative mediators are better equipped than facilitators at bringing a conflict or crisis to resolution. Morgan (1994) notes that issue linkage, which is often part of a formulator's repertoire, is an especially effective tactic for mediators to employ.

Additionally, in a seminal work on bargaining and conflict, Schelling (1960) argues that mediators with more resolution-suggesting power – a power that facilitators do not have – will effectively move forward stalemated negotiations by causing parties to consider, and perhaps even accept, possible resolutions to the dispute that had not been part of their existing cognitive structures. Hence, these new suggestions are not *de facto* viewed as capitulations or concessions, and all sides are more likely to view those mediator-suggested outcomes as "successful" outcomes.

In spite of these theoretical arguments for limiting a mediator's role to facilitation or formulation, Terris and Maoz (2001) find that mediators in the international system are more likely to employ a more intrusive style like manipulation, and they present empirical data to demonstrate the effectiveness of this approach. According to examinations conducted by Bercovitch (1986) and Bercovitch and Houston (1996), manipulative strategies enjoyed roughly a 52 percent success rate in international disputes. Comparatively, these studies found that facilitation strategies succeeded in moving parties toward conflict resolution in only 32 percent of the disputes. Berridge (2002) maintains that a key function of international mediators is to build diplomatic momentum among disputants so as to avoid lulls in the negotiation process. Such lapses in progress can damage morale and commitment among negotiators and that can provide skeptics with an opportunity to publicly question the wisdom of the negotiation efforts. Berridge argues that this function requires mediators to adopt a manipulative style: "The mediator needs to employ a judicious combination of carrots and sticks, together with deadlines and press manipulation in order to sustain diplomatic momentum" (2002: 201).

Scholars are also in disagreement as to which style of mediation is more effective during crises in particular. Whereas Dixon (1996) argues that facilitative mediation is the most effective approach for crisis episodes, Morgan (1994) notes that manipulative mediators' ability to provide side payments to crisis actors makes them especially effective in helping to manage crises. According to advocates of this mediation style, manipulative mediators can change the overall stakes of a situation in order to encourage agreements even in the most dangerous and hostile environments.

In addition to the work that focuses specifically on crises, many scholars have argued that situations exhibiting specific, but not necessarily all, characteristics of crises are better suited to specific mediation styles. For example, intense conflict settings in general, have been found to be more receptive to the substantive contributions and pressuring moves of a manipulative mediator than less-intense situations (Rubin 1980; Glasl 1982; Hiltrop 1985, 1989; Lim and Carnevale 1990; Bercovitch 1997). In addition, there is a higher likelihood in general that mediators will adopt more substantively intrusive roles in situations, like crises, characterized by time pressure (Brookmire and Sistrunk 1980; Carnevale and Conlon

1988; Kressel and Pruitt 1989; Conlon, Carnevale, and Murnighan 1994; Ross and Wieland 1996).

Frequency of mediation styles in ICB

Before delving deeper into an analysis of which mediation style is best suited for crisis management, consideration needs to be given to the question of which style or styles have actually been used during international crises. Do we see variation in the approaches to crisis mediation, or – despite the disagreement among observers over which style should be best suited to crisis management – have crisis mediators adhered to one specific style in a "one-style-fits-all-crises" approach?

As discussed in Chapter 2, the International Crisis Behavior (ICB) project recently undertook a data collection effort, which resulted in the addition of a number of mediation-related variables to the ICB dataset. Included among these new data is information on the *style* of mediation used in each of the 128 crises that were mediated between 1918 and 2001. Coders identified whether or not each mediated crisis exhibited one or more of the three strategies that comprise the typology developed by Touval and Zartman (1985) – facilitation, formulation, and manipulation. Coders used a list of criteria presented by Bercovitch (1997: 137–8) and in Chapter 2 above to determine if each style was adopted.

If a crisis is mediated, the mediator will always employ one or more facilitative tactics during their attempt to assist the parties in reaching a resolution. At the very least, the mediator will contact both sides, bring them together, or simply provide a neutral space for them to negotiate their differences. Although some mediators are limited to facilitation throughout their intervention, the majority of crisis mediators utilize several styles of mediation during individual crises. However, mediators use neither formulation nor manipulation without also using facilitation. Similarly, they rarely use manipulation without also suggesting solutions to the parties. Thus, the spectrum of mediation style is, for the most part, cumulative as one moves from lesser to greater modes of substantive involvement.

Since multiple styles of mediation are often used in the same crisis, we focused analysis on the "highest" level of mediation employed during the course of the crisis. As identified in Chapter 2, unlike the variables that indicate whether or not each style occurred, each crisis has only one value for the variable measuring the highest form of mediation. Highest form is defined according to the overall behavior of a mediator in a negotiation process; the categories of this variable are ordered on the basis of increasing intensity of this contribution (0 = no mediation, 1 = facilitation, 2 = formulation, 3 = manipulation). For instance, the highest level of involvement is always coded as manipulation whenever manipulation is

Table 4.1 Mediation style in ICB cases

Highest form of mediation used	*Number of mediated crises*	*Percentage of mediated crises*
Facilitation	14	12.7
Formulation	53	48.2
Manipulation	43	39.1
Totals*	110	100.0

Note
*Due to missing data on one or more variables indicating each style of mediation, we were unable to determine the highest form of mediation used for 18 crises in the ICB dataset. Hence, the number of crises with mediation reported in this table (110) differs from the actual number found in the aggregate summary statistics presented in Chapter 3 (128).

used. Table 4.1 presents summary statistics on each style of mediation conceived as "highest" form.

As the data in Table 4.1 suggest, mediators in different crises have relied on each of the three distinct styles at differing rates. The trend, however, has been for crisis mediators to adopt a more involved style than just facilitation. In only 12.7 percent of mediated crises did the third party restrain its role to facilitation. In almost half of all mediated cases (48.2 percent), the mediator formulated and presented crisis actors with possible agreements or solutions, and in an additional 39.1 percent of cases, mediators went further and offered incentives to and/or threatened sanctions on crisis actors in an effort to persuade (or manipulate) the crisis actors to accept the proposed agreement.

The diversity of approaches used, coupled with the on-going disagreement about which approach crisis mediators *should* use, serve as the motivation for the analyses that follow in this chapter, and in Chapters 5 and 6. These examinations are designed to assess which approach to mediation is most effective during times of international crisis and what the impacts of these different mediation styles are on the evolution and outcome of crisis episodes.

Mediation style and effectiveness of crisis mediation

The analyses below seek to provide insights into the question of the impact of crisis mediation, in general, and – more specifically – how the mediation style employed by a third party affects a crisis situation. To assess the effectiveness of mediation in light of mediator style, we examine crisis outcomes. In this study, we focus on five different aspects of crisis outcomes in hope of offering a more thorough picture of the influence that mediation has on international crises. In examining these measures of outcome, we join the long line of scholars who contend that mediation will beget more favorable endings to conflicts and crises than if these hostile interactions remained unmediated.

As noted earlier, however, there is greater disagreement among scholars regarding which style of mediation is a more effective means of crisis management or conflict resolution. In addition, there is little research on which style might be more effective during crises, in particular. With one exception noted below, we generally concur with those scholars who argue that the more a mediator contributes to the crisis negotiation process in substantive terms, the more successful those mediators will be. In general, we believe that more active mediation offers more to parties in a conflict. Reformulations and suggestions offered by formulative mediators, and the sanctions and rewards offered by manipulation create new options for parties, and "a way out" that was not there without the mediator. Thus, we expect that mediators who use formulation, and to an even greater degree those who use manipulation, will more effectively resolve crises than those third parties that limit their activities to facilitation. With this in mind, the analyses in this chapter address the following hypotheses:

Hypothesis 1a: Crises in which manipulative mediation is used will be more likely to terminate in formal agreement than all other crises.

Hypothesis 1b: Crises in which formulative or facilitative mediation are used will be more likely to terminate in formal agreement than unmediated crises.

Hypothesis 1c: Crises in which formulative mediation is used will be more likely to terminate in formal agreement than crises exhibiting only facilitative mediation.

Hypothesis 2a: Crises in which manipulative mediation is used will be more likely to result in negotiators being satisfied with the crisis outcomes than all other crises.

Hypothesis 2b: Crises in which formulative or facilitative mediation are used will be more likely to result in negotiators being satisfied with the crisis outcomes than unmediated crises.

Hypothesis 2c: Crises in which formulative mediation is used will be more likely to result in negotiators being satisfied with the crisis outcomes than crises exhibiting only facilitative mediation.

Hypothesis 3a: Actors in crises exhibiting manipulative mediation will achieve outcomes with higher utility value than actors in all other crises.

Hypothesis 3b: Actors in crises exhibiting facilitative mediation will achieve outcomes with higher utility value than actors in unmediated crises.

Hypothesis 4a: Crises in which manipulative mediation is used will end more rapidly than all other crises.

Hypothesis 4b: Crises in which facilitative mediation is used will end more rapidly than unmediated crises.[5]

While manipulation is generally thought to be a highly successful mediation style (see Touval and Zartman 1985; Bercovitch 1986; Morgan 1994; Bercovitch and Houston 1996; Wilkenfeld *et al.* 2003), it is unlikely to be more effective than the less substantively intrusive forms of mediation with regard to one specific characteristic of a crisis outcome – the extent to which crisis termination resulted in a reduction in tension among the adversaries after the crisis is over.[6] ICB defines an escalation in tensions between crisis actors as the recurrence of a crisis between these actors within five years after the crisis of concern terminates; a reduction in tensions involves no such recurrence. Keeping this in mind, even if a crisis actor *objectively* achieves an outcome of higher utility and/or is satisfied with the utility it does achieve, it may re-assess these benefits after crisis termination. Thus, even though a manipulative mediator may have been successful at ending the crisis more quickly, perhaps by coercing the two parties into signing a formal agreement and thus curtailing the immediate tensions in the context of the crisis, one or more disputants may decide after the fact that the outcome forced upon them by a manipulative mediator is not satisfactory and/or that the underlying causes of the conflict have not been resolved.

According to Beardsley *et al.* such re-evaluation and dissatisfaction is especially likely when manipulators promote "artificial zones of agreement" (2004: 12) in pursuit of ending hostilities as quickly as possible. Since manipulation "only alters the relative costs of conflict and deflates each party's reservation point," it "is likely to have a lesser effect on tension reduction" because it does not necessarily lead to the outcome that is "in line with the true distribution of capabilities" (Beardsley *et al.* 2004: 12). Crisis actors are less likely to be content with outcomes in which the distribution of benefits between parties is not aligned with the actual distribution of capabilities, since they will feel that such outcomes are "unfair." Thus, we contend that formulative and facilitative mediation styles will more effectively promote post-crisis tension reduction and long-term contentment because these strategies attempt to provide for the revelation of information regarding capabilities and mutually acceptable alternatives to violence (Blainey 1973; Fearon 1995; Kraus, Wilkenfeld, and Zlotkin 1995). Formulation should be even more effective than facilitation since it tries to synchronize the focal points of the disputants on one out of all possible alternatives. Hence,

Hypothesis 5a: Crises in which formulative mediation is used but manipulation is not will be more likely to be followed by a reduction in tensions between crisis actors than all other crises.

Hypothesis 5b: Crises in which facilitative or manipulative mediation are used will be more likely to be followed by a reduction in tensions between crisis actors than unmediated crises.

Hypothesis 5c: Crises in which facilitation is the only mediation style used will be more likely to be followed by a reduction in tensions between crisis actors than crises exhibiting manipulative mediation.

In order to examine this array of hypotheses, we present analyses based on a multi-method approach outlined in Chapter 2. Hypotheses 1a though 2c (related to agreements and satisfaction) and 5a through 5c (related to tension reduction) will be tested using ICB data on mediation and crisis outcomes. Hypotheses 2a, 2b (related to satisfaction), and 3a through 4b (related to the utility value of outcomes and the duration of crises) will be tested using data derived from the controlled setting of experiments based on an Ecuador-Peru border crisis.

Mediation style in the twentieth century

We begin by examining the relationships between each mediation style and different crisis outcomes using the ICB dataset. First, we present the methodology used in the ICB-based analyses, and then we discuss the results of these analyses.

Dependent variables

To test the relationships between each mediation style and different crisis outcomes, we employ three multivariate logistic regression models – one corresponding to each outcome measure as identified in Hypotheses 1a through 2c and 5a through 5c: the achievement of a formal agreement, satisfaction with outcome, and tension reduction. Although the ICB dataset contains other measures of crisis outcomes, we focus on these because they provide some indication of the durability of crisis resolutions and the degree to which underlying issues between the parties have been resolved (Beardsley *et al.* 2004).

The first dependent variable addresses the basic form of crisis outcome. This variable does not assess the substance/content of outcomes, but their character. Formal agreements are one of seven mutually exclusive forms of crisis outcomes identified in ICB.[7] Examples of formal agreements include treaties, armistices, and ceasefires. We created a dichotomous indicator out of the ICB "form of outcome" variable, assigning the "1" value to cases ending in formal agreements and the "0" value to crises with any of these other forms of outcomes.[8]

The second measure of crisis outcome that we utilize considers crisis actors' satisfaction with the outcome. ICB contains an ordinal indicator of the combination of how satisfactory the outcome of a given crisis was to respective crisis actors. For our purposes, we re-coded this variable into a 0–1 indicator of satisfaction – those crises where all or most actors were satisfied with the crisis outcome received a score of 1, while all others were coded 0.

The final ICB crisis outcome measure is primarily concerned with the legacy of a crisis – how the nature of tensions contained in the relationship between disputants plays itself out after the crisis terminates. As discussed earlier, a reduction in tension is defined as the non-recurrence of a crisis between the adversaries within five years after the crisis of concern terminates. Thus, we created a dichotomous variable, with 1 indicating a post-crisis reduction in tensions between actors and 0 indicating an escalation in tensions.[9]

Independent variables

Each analysis employs the same three indicators of mediation style. Because mediators frequently use multiple styles of mediation, we isolate the effects of each style of mediation on the likelihood of a specific crisis outcome in order to get an idea of what each model demonstrates. Toward this end, we utilize the "highest form of mediation" variable described earlier to derive our independent variables. This variable was subsequently re-coded into four dummy variables – one corresponding to each style of mediation conceived as "highest form," and the fourth indicating the absence of mediation. For each ICB-based multivariate model analyzed below, the indicator of "no mediation" was excluded and subsequently used as the reference category.

Results

The results of each model relating mediation style to the three crisis outcomes are displayed in Table 4.2. As was the case with the mediation incidence analyses in Chapter 3, these results are discussed with reference to the predicted probabilities of observing a "1" on the dependent variable.

Formal agreement

We begin our analyses by examining how the level of mediator style affected the probability of a crisis ending in a formal agreement. The Likelihood Ratio Chi-squared value is quite high for this model (72.658), and the overall model is statistically significant at ($p \leq 0.005$). The baseline probability of crises terminating in a formal agreement in the context provided by this model is 11 percent. That is, the chance of an unmediated crisis ending with a formal agreement among disputants is only 11 percent. As was discussed in Chapter 3, this baseline is calculated by holding all

Table 4.2 Mediation styles and crisis outcomes in ICB

Highest form of mediation	*MODEL 1*		*MODEL 2*		*MODEL 3*	
	Formal agreement		*Actor satisfaction*		*Tension reduction*	
Facilitation	0.273	(0.785)	−1.361*	(0.806)	0.970*	(0.603)
Formulation	1.643***	(0.335)	0.125	(0.354)	0.575*	(0.312)
Manipulation	2.793***	(0.373)	0.388	(0.362)	0.604*	(0.344)
Constant	−2.065***	(0.182)	−0.025	(0.158)	−0.054	(0.116)
N[†]	412	—	249	—	402	—
LRχ^2	72.658***	—	5.239	—	8.006**	—
df	3	—	3	—	3	—

*$p \leq 0.10$; **$p \leq 0.05$; ***$p \leq 0.005$

Notes

Standard errors are in parentheses.

[†]The number of cases in Model 2 results from the omission of single-actor crises from this model.

dichotomous variables at their modal values and all interval and ordinal variables at their mean values.

The indicators of both formulation and manipulation are statistically significant and positively related to the likelihood of a formal agreement being achieved. When formulation is the highest style of mediation employed, the probability of parties signing a formal agreement more than triples to 40 percent. Crises in which mediators use some combination of carrots, sticks, threats, or incentives to manipulate the disputants into settlement have a 67 percent overall likelihood of terminating in a formal agreement – a six-fold increase over the probability of unmediated crises concluding in this manner. However, the likelihood of agreement in facilitated cases does not significantly differ from the chances of agreement in unmediated crises. Even though the coefficient corresponding to this variable is positive, we cannot with confidence say that crises in which facilitation is the highest form of mediation utilized have a higher probability of ending in a formal agreement than unmediated crises.

What can we conclude from this? Crises in which more substantive forms of mediation occur – formulation and manipulation – are generally more likely to end with the adversaries signing a formal agreement than those crises in which mediation efforts are limited to facilitation or mediation does not transpire at all. In addition, when mediators use manipulation, the crisis has the highest overall probability of terminating in this manner. Thus, we find evidence supporting H1a, H1c, and, in part, H1b.

The 1974 Cyprus case demonstrated the potential of manipulation to push states to a ceasefire agreement. The effect of manipulation is evident as well in the Oman-South Yemen crisis that lasted from November 1973 until March 1976. Tensions between South Yemen and Oman[10] were focused mainly on the support given by the Marxist government of South Yemen to the Popular Front for the Liberation of the Occupied Gulf (PFLOG), a group of rebels based in the Dhofar region of Oman (the most economically depressed region in the country). Iraq, China, and the Soviet Union also supported PFLOG. Tensions also existed between South Yemen and Oman regarding which state controlled the disputed Kuria Muria Islands, located off the coast of the Dhofar.

Clashes occurred in the border region between the two countries in 1972, when PFLOG rebels stationed in South Yemen launched incursions into Omani territory. However, a crisis did not begin for Oman until South Yemeni aircraft attacked several of its military posts on November 18, 1973. South Yemeni forces were also actively engaged in fighting alongside PFLOG rebels in the Dhofar region. With increasing levels of support from Britain, Iran, Jordan, Saudi Arabia, the United States, and the United Arab Emirates, the Omani sultan whom PFLOG was trying to overthrow responded in full. By the end of 1975, the rebels were driven from Dhofar completely and retreated to South Yemen.

The Arab League unsuccessfully mediated the crisis in May 1974. Kuwait intervened to mediate shortly thereafter, but its solo mediation effort also failed to end the crisis. However, Kuwait drew up a peace plan that was eventually realized when Saudi Arabia, the primary mediator in this crisis, intervened in early 1976. Saudi Arabia promised to pay the bankrupt government of South Yemen a sum of $400 million over five years. In exchange, South Yemen agreed to cease its support for PFLOG rebels. On March 10, 1976, officials from South Yemen and Saudi Arabia announced a statement of mutual friendship in accord with the above stipulations, and the Saudis oversaw a ceasefire between Oman and South Yemen the following day. Even though the rebels had suffered major defeats, it was the assurance of monetary compensation that deterred South Yemen from continuing the crisis. Without Saudi Arabia's promise of resources to South Yemen as reward for its concessions, it is unlikely that South Yemen would have ceased harboring and supporting Omani rebels (Bidwell 1983) or signed a ceasefire agreement with Oman. Saudi Arabia's ability to use its leverage pushed South Yemen to concede and sign the formal agreement that ended the crisis.

The results of our analysis do not completely support Hypothesis 1b, since it appears that mediators who employ only a facilitative style have no effect on the likelihood of formal agreement ($\alpha = 0.73$). This finding is consistent with the results observed in Beardsley *et al.* (2004) regarding the effect of mediation style on crisis outcome.[11] Interestingly, Beardsley *et al.* found evidence that facilitative mediation does have a positive and significant impact on the likelihood of a crisis ending in a formal agreement when it is the most crucial style of mediation used in a given crisis. Hence, when facilitation is used in conjunction with "higher" forms of mediation and has the largest impact of all of these styles in a particular crisis, the crisis will have a higher likelihood of ending in a formal agreement than if it was not mediated at all. Bercovitch (1997) concurs, arguing that more active and directive mediation strategies like manipulation have a higher success rate because such strategies employ *many* different types of mediator influence. Thus, it appears that facilitation is ineffective at achieving formal agreements only when it is the lone style of mediation used in a crisis.

Actor satisfaction

The second model presented in Table 4.2 relates to crisis actor satisfaction with the outcome of the crisis. This is the weakest of the three models presented. Model 2 is approaching statistical significance but provides little support for the expected relationship between mediation style and crisis actor satisfaction.

This model does reveal that facilitation on its own has a modest effect on crisis actor satisfaction with outcomes ($p \leq 0.10$). Contrary to Hypothesis 2b, though, crises in which facilitation is the highest form of mediation are actually *less* likely than unmediated crises to end with all or most actors being satisfied. The probability of all or most actors in an unmediated crisis being satisfied with a crisis upon its termination is roughly 49 percent. When a crisis is mediated and the third party only uses facilitative tactics, this probability drops by more than half to 20 percent. Although the coefficients corresponding to formulation and manipulation as highest mediation forms are both positive, pointing to increased levels of satisfaction in these mediation contexts, these indicators are not statistically significant.

Since the results regarding formulative and manipulative mediation are inconclusive, we find no strong evidence to confirm Hypotheses 2a and 2c. Hypothesis 2b, on the other hand, appears to be refuted by our results, at least in relation to its conjecture regarding facilitation. Mediator styles and mediation as a whole seem to have little overall effect on the distribution of satisfaction positions among crisis actors. These findings are consistent with those presented in Beardsley *et al.* (2004), which concluded that the level of violence in the international crisis, rather than third-party activity, was the key determinant of actor satisfaction.[12] We provide a more complete discussion of our findings regarding satisfaction and mediation in the corresponding section of the experimental analysis below.

Tension reduction

Turning to the final model presented in Table 4.2, we find traces of evidence that mediation style has an effect on post-crisis tensions between disputants. While the model itself is statistically significant ($p \leq 0.05$), the nature of the overall relationships predicted by this model are generally weaker than the model of formal agreement but stronger than the model of actor satisfaction, as evidenced by the Likelihood Ratio Chi-squared value (8.006). Nevertheless, these data do imply that there is a positive relationship between each style of mediation and the likelihood of tensions between adversaries being reduced after the crisis terminates.

The baseline probability of tensions being reduced between crisis actors is roughly 49 percent in the context provided in Model 3, reflecting the likelihood of unmediated crises being followed by a reduction in tensions between actors. This likelihood increases by roughly 14 percent to an overall likelihood of 63 percent when the crisis is mediated and formulation and/or manipulation are the highest forms of mediation used. When mediators limit their activities to facilitation, this likelihood of tension reduction increases even further to 70 percent.

How do these results compare to our hypotheses regarding mediation's effect on the nature of the post-crisis tensions between disputants? For the most part, the answer is that mediated crises are generally more likely to be followed by a decrease in tensions than unmediated crises, and all three styles of mediation have a positive effect on tension reduction. The results also demonstrate support for our conjecture that less substantively intrusive forms of mediation will be more successful at achieving a reduction in tensions than manipulative tactics. As such, H5b, H5c, and in part, H5a, are confirmed.

However, per Hypothesis 5a, we argued that intervention efforts marked by formulation as the highest form of mediation should have the most pronounced positive effect on tension reduction. This contention is not supported statistically – crises that only exhibit facilitative mediation are the most likely to be followed by a reduction in tensions between crisis actors. Furthermore, formulation as the highest mediation level does not have a notably larger success rate than manipulation.

The potential of facilitation to resolve tensions among disputants is demonstrated by the French Hostages in Mauritania crisis involving Polisario forces and discussed earlier in the chapter. In this crisis, UN Secretary-General Kurt Waldheim simply contacted and transmitted messages among officials from Algeria, Polisario, and France, and agreed to be the conduit through which the hostages would be brought back to France. By bridging a communication gap between the parties, Waldheim secured a quick and smooth release of the hostages despite the high level of hostilities among the crisis actors. He allowed the parties to formulate the solution, and long-term tensions were decreased between France and Algeria.

It appears that manipulative tactics add the least to the tension-reduction process. Even when mediation styles are considered in terms of which one has the largest impact on the crisis, the less substantively involved forms have a stronger effect on tension reduction (Beardsley *et al.* 2004). Hence, it seems that when mediators intervene in crises and use manipulative devices, the formulative, and especially facilitative, tactics that they also use have a more profound effect on reducing long-term tensions between crisis actors.

In crises in which mediators engage in both facilitation and formulation, facilitation has the more profound effect on the nature of long-term relations among disputants. This is illustrated by the events of the 1995 Red Sea Islands crisis between Yemen and Eritrea. This crisis grew out of a dispute over three economically desirable islands in the Red Sea known as the Hanish islands. A small Yemeni fishing community lived on the islands, but Eritrea claimed them on historical grounds – its forces had been there since the beginning of its 30 year war with Ethiopia. (See Figure 3.2 for a map of this region.)

On December 15, 1995, Eritrea attacked the Hanish islands, triggering a crisis for both itself and Yemen.[13] Two days later, the presidents of the two countries conversed and decided to issue a ceasefire. Despite the continuation of a high level of tensions among the crisis actors, the ceasefire took hold on December 18, and both sides agreed to have it monitored by one Yemeni and one Eritrean representative, as well as a member of the U.S. embassy in each country.

The status of the Hanish islands was still under dispute, and the ceasefire had not terminated the crisis. To help facilitate the process, UN Secretary-General Boutros Boutros-Ghali mediated the dispute on December 29. He met with both Eritrean and Yemeni representatives, facilitating discussions between the two. Boutros-Ghali also used formulative tactics, including highlighting commitments and helping to devise a framework for an acceptable outcome. On December 31, Boutros-Ghali announced that Yemen would withdraw its forces from the Hanish islands and that both sides agreed to send the matter to arbitration for final decision. This announcement ended the crisis, and on May 21, 1996, the two parties signed an accord stating that they would accept the arbitration verdict and handle the dispute only by diplomatic means. Boutros-Ghali's facilitation of communication between the two sides was important for the termination of this crisis in the short-term, as well as its legacy. His formulative tactics were not nearly as important as was getting Eritrea and Yemen to bridge the communication gap. Tensions were reduced between the two parties, as the issue was settled once and for all when an international court handed down its decision regarding the status of the islands in 1998. Eritrea and Yemen both received portions of the islands (Yemen received a larger share), and both sides stated that they accepted the decision in full (Ostowani 1998). While facilitation does serve this goal of long-term tension reduction, it is less effective in leading crisis actors to formal agreements or in ensuring actor satisfaction with the outcome of crisis.

Mediation style in simulated crises

The preceding findings were derived from analyses of historical data on mediation style and crisis dynamics, but additional data, generated from crisis simulations, allows an investigation of hypotheses ill-suited to examination through ICB data. We begin with a brief discussion of some methodological issues. We then present and discuss the results of the experimental analyses, comparing them to the ICB-based results where appropriate and building toward an integrated set of conclusions about mediation style and crisis outcome.

Methodology

The analyses conducted in this chapter focus on the effect that mediation and mediator style have on various measures of crisis outcome, and the following analyses reflect findings derived from data generated by the experimental research design presented in Chapter 2. While that earlier chapter contained a thorough description of this "base" design, it only provided a superficial overview of the elements of this design pertaining to the matter of mediation style. We present summary statistics regarding the experimental data collected for the analyses in this chapter, followed by specific details of how mediation style was operationalized in our simulations. We then present a description of the specific variables used in the experimental analyses and how these analyses relate to the set of hypotheses of concern in this chapter.

Two hundred and fourteen subjects participated in the 107 Ecuador-Peru simulated crisis negotiations that serve as the universe of analysis for our investigations of mediation, mediator style, and crisis outcomes in this chapter.[14] These simulations were conducted in Spring and Fall 2001. One-third of the negotiations that we conducted involved no mediator, one-third included a facilitative mediator, and one-third a manipulative mediator.

As noted in Chapter 2, a select group of graduate and undergraduate students at the University of Maryland were trained to serve as mediators in the Ecuador-Peru crisis simulations. The ultimate goal of all mediators in these simulations was to encourage the negotiators to agree to any of the simulation's peaceful outcomes and to attempt to prevent either side from launching a military strike on the other. That is, the mediators were focused on crisis management, rather than conflict resolution. The behavior of each mediator reflected a specific mediation style – either facilitation or manipulation. Facilitators encouraged the negotiators to work toward compromise and to think about the needs of the opposing state but could not recommend any specific outcomes or options to either negotiator. Manipulative mediators, on the other hand, subjected negotiators to a much more aggressive and active intervention. Manipulators proposed and advocated those options and solutions that they thought most likely to lead to a rapid but peaceful termination of the crisis. In addition, manipulative mediators had "carrots and sticks" at their disposal – including the ability to impose trade sanctions, cut off foreign aid, and/or allow arms sales – to entice the disputants to agree to a proposed outcome. If the mediator chose to employ any of these rewards or punishments, the expected-utility payoff for the negotiator would be affected in a positive or negative manner, respectively. In those simulations that contained a manipulative mediator, the participants' decision-support system (DSS) revealed to each negotiator (but not to the mediators) the effect of actions taken by the manipulative mediator in terms of each state's utility points, so that the extent of the mediator's leverage was clear to the negotiators. The complete text of the experimental scenario in Appendix B explains the options available to manipulative mediators in this context.

After receiving lengthy instruction on the concept of mediation, simulation mediators were trained in the two most extreme mediation styles, facilitation and manipulation. Using Bercovitch's (1997) concise conceptual overview of mediation style as a guideline, mediators were instructed regarding the main purposes and philosophies of each mediator style, as well as the repertoire of actions that they were permitted to draw from when "playing" each role.

Mediators were told that the main purpose of facilitative mediators was to serve as a channel of communication between the parties and to assist them in reaching an agreement without adding anything substantive to the process. Consistent with the work on interactive problem-solving and third-party consultation (see especially Burton 1984, 1990; Kelman 1992; and Keashly and Fisher 1996), simulation mediators were informed that facilitators should have a presence in the negotiations only to assist crisis actors in reaching an agreement on their own. The parties themselves, not the mediator, should devise the frameworks for and control the processes of negotiation, and should formulate and conclude their own agreements.

Facilitative mediators were told that they could employ any tactics short of making substantive additions/suggestions, using leverage, or engaging in heavy-handed persuasion and/or threats. Stressing the need for compromise, making sure both parties' concerns and needs/goals are respected, reiterating statements, serving as a conduit for communication, asking questions, and clarifying the situation were part and parcel of the facilitator's tactical repertoire. Facilitators were given a list of ten suggested tactics that they could employ while trying to contribute to a negotiated settlement among negotiators (see Figure 4.2). Even more importantly, facilitative mediators were also provided an explicit list of things that they could *not* do in order to ensure that they did not perform actions that characterize formulative or manipulative mediation styles.

In contrast, manipulators were told that they were expected to push for a peaceful resolution to the crisis (i.e., agreement) by using all means at

Things you can and should do as a facilitator

1. Ask the parties to brainstorm.
2. Assist parties in understanding messages that are passed back and forth and the details of the conflict if necessary.
3. Ask each party what their fears and interests are and promise not to share these with the other party unless such action is requested or approved by the providing party. Point out that these fears and concerns are legitimate.
4. "Feel the pain" of each side. In messages sent to the individual parties in private or both parties in public, point out that each side has legitimate concerns.
5. Ask which issues they want to discuss and let them determine the agenda and order in which issues are discussed.
6. Reiterate how the negotiations have gone and what has been agreed upon, especially when the parties are at an impasse or when discussion has been completed on a specific topic.
7. Praise positive actions.
8. Constantly reiterate that *compromise is the key*, that each side will not be able to get all of what they wanted.
9. Be prepared to act as the sole channel of communication between parties if requested.
10. If one party asks your opinion (i.e., "Should I take this offer?" or "Should I offer this?"), respond with questions once again. E.g., "Does the offer satisfy you? If not, what else do you want or need?"

Things you *cannot* do as a facilitator

1. Add anything substantive to the process.
2. Redefine issues.
3. Set the agenda and/or determine the order of issues to be discussed.
4. Propose new options for agreements.
5. Formulate possible resolutions.
6. Make them aware of the political and economic costs or international repercussions of non-agreement.
7. Use carrot and stick measures, manipulate the world state parameters, or threaten to manipulate global sentiment or other aspects of the international environment.
8. Raise costs of disagreement or rewards for agreement. Do not use leverage.
9. Make reference to the DSS, utility values, or your knowledge of any of this. You are not supposed to know that they have a DSS or anything about the conflict beyond the scenario that we give you and anything further that the parties tell you while the negotiations are occurring.

Figure 4.2 Guidelines for facilitative mediators

their disposal, including threats and punishments if necessary. Using the work of Touval and Zartman (1985) and Bercovitch (1997) as a guideline, mediators were informed that manipulators should stop at nothing to prevent war between disputants and should contribute heavily to the negotiations in substantive terms. The manipulator should always be prepared to offer suggestions and reinforce conciliation. According to this approach, once negotiators begin engaging in positional bargaining and/or reach a stalemate, the manipulator should take primary responsibility for directing the negotiations toward agreement.

Manipulators were trained to be much more aggressive about their mediation approach in general and to use all of the powers at their disposal to push the sides to compromise. They were told to suggest outcomes and compromises and use their leverage to push for an agreement that either they formulated or that the negotiators themselves were debating. The actions in a manipulative mediator's repertoire included those of facilitators and formulators, but also incorporated persuasion, sanctions, threats, and rewards. Manipulators were given a list of eight suggested actions that they should execute when appropriate in their attempt to push parties toward a negotiated settlement (see Figure 4.3). Manipulative mediators were also provided the same list of suggested actions given to facilitators (the first section of Figure 4.2), since they were permitted to use these tactics as well. Mediators who adopted the manipulative style not only had the power to pressure negotiators toward agreement through the use of carrots and sticks, but they also had the ability that formulators have to propose to crisis actors specific agreements that they think should be acceptable to all sides.

Facilitators and manipulators were also provided distinct opening statements that were used at the beginning of every simulation. This was done not only to ensure consistency across cases, but also to give the negotiators at the outset a sense as to the type of mediator they were going to be dealing with. The differences in these opening statements, presented in

Things you can and should do as a manipulator

1. Begin by pushing for preliminary agreement on side issues (borders, river access).
2. Move on to the land division issue, asking each side what their red lines are and telling them you will not share this information with the other side. Find out what the agreement range includes based on the information they provide you.
3. Once you have information on their red lines and you figure out if there is a zone of agreement, push them toward an agreement that falls within that zone. Using private messages between yourself and each party helps.
4. Use flattery.
5. Don't let them escalate the conflict. E.g., If Peru threatens to mobilize its troops if Ecuador doesn't withdraw its troops, write the following to Peru: "Let us try positive actions first before threats. I am confident that we can get Ecuador to withdraw its troops in the context of a framework for general agreement."
6. If a negotiator is regularly belligeront and/or closes its borders, mobilizes its troops, or denies river access (Peru), apply your sanctions.
7. Give them credit when they engage in confidence-building measures.
8. Besides applying sanctions, also stroke their egos. Provide carrots if necessary.

** Manipulators may also carry out any of the actions that facilitators are permitted to carry out.

Figure 4.3 Guidelines for manipulative mediators

Figure 4.4, provide an apt contrast between the two mediation styles under consideration. Finally, all simulations were monitored to ensure reliability within mediation style prior to – and during – the actual experiments. On only one occasion did we have to drop a case from the sample because a mediator "acted out of character" in terms of the style of mediation that they were "playing;" in this case, a facilitative mediator became too assertive. In general, however, mediators' actions reflected the style in which that had been trained to mediate. One can see distinct differences between the transcripts of facilitated and manipulated simulations, and these reflect the different styles.

From *facilitative* mediators to both Ecuador and Peru

"Hello, you have brought us here today to serve as mediators during your negotiations regarding the border dispute you are involved in. We are here to assist you in devising an agreement that is acceptable to both of you and that takes into account both of your interests, fears, and concerns. These negotiations can result in 3 possible situations: continuing the dispute, one of you launching an all out war on the other, or reaching a compromise. While neither of you will be able to reach 100 or maybe even 70 percent of your initial goals, we can work toward a compromise that is satisfactory to both of you and that will be much better than a bloody war that is not advantageous to either of you. The negotiation should begin by each of you putting your fundamental needs, concerns, and fears on the table. We as mediators ask you to be sensitive not only to your concerns, fears, and interests, but to those of your fellow negotiators as well. From there, we will try to move toward a negotiated settlement of the dispute. We as the mediation team look forward to assisting you in reaching a negotiated settlement that is acceptable to both of you by creating a space in which you can discuss the issues at hand."

From *manipulative mediators* to both Ecuador and Peru

Message 1: "Hello, we are here today to resolve this conflict in both your interests. We have three options open to us. We can continue with this dispute, either of you can launch a ruinous war that you will probably lose, or we can settle this conflict. The mediation group believes that we can resolve this peacefully and to both countries' benefit. While neither side will be able to achieve 100 or even 70 percent of its goals, we can certainly reach a conclusion that is more satisfactory then a gamble on war. The mediation group will agree to help you reach your objectives by keeping our trade status with you open, and by giving both of you foreign aid if the negotiation works. We hope that there will be no need for us to impose sanctions. We ask first that you both agree to withdraw and/or demobilize your troops, and send the mediation group the proposal that you desire and that you think the other side could realistically accept."

Message 2: "The mediators suggest that we agree on a non-binding framework that includes open borders, open trade, foreign aid for both states, open access to Amazon navigation, and some type of land division. If this is acceptable, then we then just need to work out what is a good division of the land."

Figure 4.4 Mediator opening messages

Analysis of experimental data: variables and hypothesis testing

Using experimental data, we employ bivariate cross-tab and linear regression analyses to test the relationships between crisis mediation/mediator style and several different crisis outcomes, as outlined in H2a, H2b (satisfaction), and H3a (expected-utility payoffs) through H4b (duration). Specifically, we examine data that were collected on three different outcome measures – negotiator satisfaction with the outcome, expected utility of the outcome, and negotiation duration. Analyzing each of these three measures of crisis outcome provides a more nuanced and comprehensive understanding of the effects of crisis mediation than an analysis of historical data alone.

The ICB data on crisis actor satisfaction analyzed earlier in the chapter were derived from coders' interpretations of states' reactions to the conclusion of a crisis. The ICB satisfaction coding relates to perceptions of whether a state "won" or "lost" the crisis. The simulations, on the other hand, allowed for a more direct measure of an individual negotiator's reaction to the crisis and its outcome than is possible with historical data. Both leaders and the newspapers that report on leaders' remarks have strong motivations to color their own perception of victory, defeat, and satisfaction due to the need to please certain populations, and leaders' ultimate desire to retain power. This is especially true when it comes to the issue of mediation. Mediators are often representatives of powerful countries and international organizations. Publicly voicing displeasure about the contributions of such a mediator could jeopardize the crisis actor's future relations with the third party – a risk many would consider unwise to take. On the other hand, admission that a mediator had strongly influenced the country's position in a negotiation could have possible negative political repercussions. Experimental methods thus allow us to more effectively gauge negotiator satisfaction and perception of the mediator than can be done via use of historical data.

Participants in the Ecuador-Peru simulation completed a post-crisis survey immediately following the conclusion of their simulations. In this survey, participants reported on whether they found the outcome of the crisis to be satisfactory to them as negotiators. The indicator of satisfaction used in the analysis below reflects their answers (yes or no) to this question. As such, the experimental satisfaction measure is a direct measure of how negotiators feel about the outcome of the crisis rather then a coder's interpretation of how a negotiator might feel about the end of a crisis.[15]

The research design also allows us to look beyond the limited question of whether negotiators were satisfied with the outcome of a crisis. We can also explore the objective value of an outcome to each party by determining the utility value of the outcome for both Ecuador and Peru in each simulation. A comparison of utility values across repeated iterations of the Ecuador-Peru crisis simulation provides a measure of crisis outcome that cannot be replicated using historical ICB data. Thus, we test H3a and H3b using only experimental data, in a multivariate linear regression. The dependent variable used in this analysis is a scale indicator of utility value – each outcome is assigned a specific utility value out of a possible 1,000 (higher scores indicate higher utility).

The controlled setting of the experimental environment also allowed us to examine Hypotheses 4a and 4b, relating to the interplay between crisis duration and mediation. Here, we must keep in mind that elapsed time in a simulation can only approximate this phenomenon in an actual crisis setting. What can take weeks or months in the real-world is condensed into minutes and hours in the laboratory. The experimental design specified that the simulation would last no longer than 120 minutes, divided into twelve ten-minute negotiating rounds. At the end of each round, the utility values associated with outcomes change to reflect the effects of the passage of time. In a real-world situation, payoffs would rarely change so quickly. Rather, such changes would occur after a more prolonged negotiating round (a day or a week, for instance). Hence, it is nearly impossible to simulate the passage of real-time and its impact on crisis decision making by using the experimental method.

Nevertheless, data from simulated crises allow an examination of the relationship between mediation efforts and duration in a way that ICB data do not. In historical cases, there is a complex mix of factors that affect crisis duration, making valid comparisons across different crises difficult and creating challenges for isolating the effect that mediation has on duration. Conversely, comparing repeated iterations of the *same* crisis negotiation conducted in a controlled setting, with only mediation conditions changing among iterations, does allow for consideration of the relationship between mediation style and duration. Hence, we only use experimental data to test H4a and H4b. Once again, we utilize a multivariate linear regression analysis to examine these data; the dependent variable is a scale indicator of how many minutes the negotiation lasted prior to crisis termination, either via agreement or military attack.

Despite our ability to examine disputant satisfaction via experimental techniques, not all crisis outcomes for which there exist ICB data and that concern us can be measured and/or analyzed by way of crisis simulations. For instance, we cannot use this method to test arguments regarding tension reduction (Hypotheses 5a through 5c) because the simulated crisis is – by design – a one-shot iteration.

Similarly, we do not use the experimental method to test hypotheses that relate specifically to the likelihood of crises terminating in formal agreements. The rates of agreement in our simulations were high across the board – higher than in the "real-world." This high rate of agreement is likely an artifact of our experimental design. While student-negotiators are never explicitly told that they need to reach agreement and they all have the option of launching a military attack during the course of the simulation, they may feel like they are "supposed to" reach an agreement, that this is what their professors want or expect from them. The tendency toward agreement, however, was not so acute that it prevented us from drawing some general conclusions from a comparison of mediated and unmediated cases (see below). Nonetheless, consideration of the relationship between crisis mediation *styles* and the rates of agreement can be more effectively analyzed using ICB data.

Similar to the ICB-based analyses, the independent variables used in the investigation of experimental data are all indicators of mediation conceived as highest style. Simulations were classified as unmediated, mediated by a facilitator, or mediated by a manipulator. Facilitative mediators were restricted to performing those facilitative functions, sketched out in Figure 4.2, whereas manipulative mediators employed all three styles of mediation (see Figure 4.3). Negotiators were aware that manipulative mediators had the capacity to offer to each participant both carrots (increased foreign aid) and sticks (economic sanctions).

Results

Some common trends emerged from analyses of ICB and simulation data: for instance, as previously reported in Table 4.2, mediated crises were significantly more likely to end in agreements among the crisis actors than were unmediated crises. The same trend holds true in an analysis of experimentally generated data – while 70 percent (21 of 30 simulations) of unmediated crisis simulations ended in agreements (rather than war between Ecuador and Peru), 95 percent (72 of 77 simulations) of mediated simulations ended in agreement, a statistically significant difference ($\chi^2 = 10.691$, $p < 0.0025$). This finding not only serves to bolster our previous finding on the positive relationship between mediation and crisis ending in agreement but also validates our experimental methodology, which replicated real-world trends in crisis mediation. The simulation data do not reveal anything about the relationship between mediation *style* and rates of agreement, however.

Negotiator satisfaction

As reported earlier, ICB data provided no support for the idea that – regardless of mediation style – mediated crises are more likely to conclude in outcomes considered satisfactory to the crisis actors (Hypotheses 2a and 2b). We reexamine this issue using experimental data, as we believe the data on satisfaction generated from the simulations provide a more accurate and direct measure of satisfaction with the outcome of the crisis.

Table 4.3 displays data on the levels of satisfaction with outcomes as reported by participants' responses to a post-simulation survey. Analysis of the experimental measure of the level of negotiator satisfaction reveals

Table 4.3 Levels of negotiator satisfaction

	Satisfied with outcome	*Not satisfied with outcome*	*Total*
Unmediated	25 (58.1%)	18 (41.9%)	43 (23.6%)
Facilitative mediation	50 (75.8%)	16 (24.2%)	66 (36.3%)
Manipulative mediation	56 (76.7%)	17 (23.3%)	73 (40.1%)
Total*	131 (72.0%)	51 (28.0%)	182 (100.0%)

$\chi^2 = 5.361, p < 0.05$.

Note
*Data on negotiator satisfaction was not collected during the earliest simulation iterations. There is no reason to believe that the excluded cases were not randomly distributed.

that mediation does have a significant impact on negotiator satisfaction, which was not the case with the examination of the ICB measure of satisfaction.

Seventy-six percent of negotiators involved in mediated simulations indicated that they were satisfied with the outcome of the crisis, while only 58 percent of unmediated respondents indicated that the outcome was satisfactory to them. If one goal of crisis management is to try to ensure that those who represent crisis actors are content with the outcome of the crisis, then this statistically significant finding indicates that mediated processes are a desirable means of management.

These findings do not, however, support the hypothesis that a more aggressive mediation style would lead to outcomes considered to be more satisfactory. As Table 4.3 indicates, facilitation and manipulation were almost equally likely to generate satisfactory outcomes for the Ecuadorian and Peruvian negotiators. Thus, we find partial support for Hypotheses 2a and 2b.

Expected utility of outcome

In Hypotheses 3a and 3b, we contend that mediated crises will lead to outcomes with greater utility-point payoffs (that is, outcomes that are more beneficial) than will unmediated crises, and that manipulative mediation will generate the greatest average payoffs for the crisis actors. Given our research design, according to which Peru has a power advantage in this situation, we expect significant variation in the expected utility of outcomes achieved by the two states in this negotiation, with Peru more likely to secure outcomes with higher utility values. Therefore, the analysis of the relationship between mediation style and utility payoffs also takes into

Table 4.4 Effects of mediation on expected utility payoffs

	B	*SE*
Facilitation	−0.457	(30.125)
Manipulation	50.900**	(22.580)
Role of negotiator (Ecuador or Peru)	−222.448***	(17.797)
Constant†	623.033***	(19.510)
Adj. R^2	0.445***	
N	201 negotiators	

*$p<0.10$; **$p<0.05$; ***$p<0.00$.

Notes
Standard errors are in parentheses.
†The constant in this model is the expected utility payoff under conditions of no mediation for a participant negotiating on behalf of Peru.

consideration whether an individual negotiator represented Ecuador or Peru, as reflected in the model presented in Table 4.4.

As expected, a significant and sizable difference does exist between the payoffs earned by Ecuadorian and Peruvian negotiators – the average expected utility payoff for the two roles varies by more than 222 (out of a possible 1,000). More specific to our hypotheses, though, this regression model also reveals that there is, in fact, a significant relationship between mediation and expected utility. Overall, the independent variables in this model – mediation style and country of negotiator – explain 45 percent of the overall variation in the dependent variable, expected utility payoff, across iterations ($p<0.000$).

Consistent with Hypothesis 3a, negotiators working with a manipulative mediator were able to secure more beneficial outcomes for their respective countries than were negotiators in unmediated simulations (our baseline case); as the coefficients in Table 4.4 indicate, the mean expected utility of the outcome for negotiators in simulations mediated by a manipulative third party increased by 51 over the average payoff in unmediated crises.

Interestingly, however, the benefits of mediation for crisis negotiators were only apparent in simulations that involved a manipulative mediator. The payoffs to negotiators in facilitated crises do not significantly differ from those simulations that were unmediated.

We cannot conclude, then, that all styles of mediation offer negotiators the best chances for an outcome that will be considered more beneficial to their country. Negotiators were, in fact, no better off with facilitative mediation than they were with no mediation; this evidence provides no support for the assertions made in Hypothesis 3b. It was only with manipulative mediation that expected utility payoffs were bolstered significantly. This finding supports the premise that the impact of mediation should not be assessed without looking more closely at the style of mediation employed and lends support to those who advocate manipulation as the style of mediation best suited for crisis management.

Duration of negotiations

The controlled setting of the experimental environment allowed us to examine Hypotheses 4a and 4b, relating to the interplay between crisis duration and mediation. In general, those simulations that involved a mediator ended sooner than unmediated simulations did, consistent with our expectations. Based upon the coefficients reported in Table 4.5, the average length of an unmediated simulation was 54 minutes (standard deviation = 2.38), with the longest unmediated negotiation going on for 108 minutes. Mediated negotiations ended an average of 7.97 minutes earlier than did unmediated simulations.

Furthermore, manipulated crises ended significantly earlier than did facilitated crises. Simulations involving the more active and aggressive type of mediator (which, on average, lasted only 41 minutes) ended 9.93 minutes sooner than did those in which the mediator could not use leverage to push the parties into agreement. In fact, the average duration of facilitated crises – 51 minutes – was not significantly different from that of unmediated crises. Thus, we find evidence to support Hypothesis 4a, but not H4b. While manipulative mediation does have a significant effect on when crisis actors accept a given outcome, facilitative mediation does not, further supporting the propositions that analyses of mediation and its effectiveness *must* take into consideration the type of mediation employed in a crisis, and that manipulative mediation can bring with it some crisis management benefits that facilitation does not appear to add.

Consideration of how long a crisis persists is an especially crucial question, since crises are volatile situations that, more often than not, lead to outbreaks of violence or war. The less these crises are allowed to linger, the less likely it is that the tensions inherent in crisis situations will escalate to the point of violence or war. In fact, analysis of the experimental data

Table 4.5 Duration of crisis simulation (in minutes)

Highest form of mediation	*B*	*SE*
Facilitation	−2.687	(4.297)
Manipulation	−12.618**	(4.189)
Constant†	53.792***	(2.38)
Adj. R^2	0.085**	
N	101 simulations	

**p* < 0.10; ***p* < 0.05; ****p* < 0.00.

Notes
Standard errors are in parentheses.
†The constant in this model is the expected utility payoff under conditions of no mediation.

reveals a significant and negative relationship between the likelihood of a crisis ending in agreement and the duration of the negotiation. There was a difference of about 11 minutes between negotiations that ended in agreement (46.2 minutes) and those that ended in war (57.0 minutes), significant at $p < 0.05$. Earlier resolution of the crisis is an important achievement for those interested in managing a crisis, and it is one that manipulative mediation makes more likely.

Conclusion

In sum, we observe numerous important trends in both the ICB and experimental data that meet a number of our expectations regarding the effect that mediation in general and mediator styles specifically have on crisis outcomes, and that provide us with a broad understanding of this set of relationships. Corroborating earlier findings of Morgan (1994) and Dixon (1996), we find that mediation is a highly successful form of international crisis management. In comparison to unmediated crises, mediated crises are more likely to terminate earlier, involve the crisis actors signing a formal agreement, and end with negotiators being satisfied with the outcome. In addition, post-crisis tensions between disputants have a higher likelihood of being reduced when third parties have mediated a crisis, indicating that this form of intervention also has some value as a means of resolving the underlying issues of international conflicts.

However, it does not appear that mediation in general offers parties a higher degree of objective benefits at the conclusion of a crisis than they would have achieved on their own. This finding seems to run contrary to the scholarly argument that disputants ask for or accept mediation because they believe it will provide them with more overall benefits than would be otherwise possible (see Touval and Zartman 1985). Even though crisis actors undoubtedly have individual interests that are often opposed to each other when making the decision to accept mediation, it may be that shared interests directed toward ending the crisis override concerns of aggregate gains. Considering the argument that mediation is most likely to occur when parties are entrenched in positional bargaining stances, or when their bilateral management efforts have failed (Touval and Zartman 1985; Bercovitch 1992, 1997; Zartman and Touval 1996), crisis actors may be primarily driven by their desire to bring an end to an increasingly unbearable situation and thus cooperate with each other and the mediator in achieving that goal. On the other hand, as argued in Chapter 1, it could be that perceived *relative* gains play a larger role than aggregate benefits in the calculus of crisis actors' decisions to accept the intercession of a mediator. We do not test such assertions statistically in this book,[16] but we encourage future studies that attempt a more complex analysis of the relationship between disputant or mediator goals and the effectiveness of mediation efforts.

That being said, our findings do indicate that some mediators are more effective crisis managers than others, depending upon the mediation style that they employ. Touval and Zartman (1985) have argued that mediators with leverage and the mandate to use it are more likely to generate an agreement between parties than other types of mediators. Our results demonstrate evidence in support of that assertion – more aggressive and substantively intrusive styles are most successful at generating formal agreements between actors.[17] They are also most effective at shortening the lengths of crises. There is a reciprocal relationship between these two outcomes as well – shorter crises, in general, are much more likely to end in agreement. Crises in which mediators adopt a manipulative style also conclude with disputants achieving higher average benefits than crises that are either unmediated or marked only by facilitation.

The evidence regarding the impact of a less substantively intrusive mediation style – facilitation – is more mixed. On the one hand, this mode of mediator involvement is most effective at achieving post-crisis reduction in tensions between adversaries. By contrast, crises marked only by mediation as facilitation conclude with negotiators receiving lower benefits than those that are unmediated or characterized by manipulative mediation and conclude no more rapidly than unmediated crises.

Consistent with the earlier findings of Morgan (1994) and Wilkenfeld *et al.* (2003), mediators adopting "higher" levels of mediation are consistently more successful at bringing about crisis endings that prevent war (e.g., shorter crises, more agreements) than those assuming lower levels of involvement. If a mediator's primary goal is crisis management (see Young 1967; Milburn 1972; Touval 1982; Wehr and Lederach 1996; Kleiboer 1998), then it seems that manipulation is the most effective means of achieving this goal.

How do different mediation styles go beyond crisis management to affect the resolution of the issues underlying the conflict from which a crisis erupts? Those styles that bring about a post-crisis reduction in tensions go the furthest toward resolving conflicts. It should be noted that reducing post-crisis tensions is not a perfect indicator of a resolved conflict: many protracted international conflicts have lasted decades and many ethnic-based conflicts have lasted centuries, with only intermittent crisis episodes (e.g., the "real-life" Ecuador and Peru border conflict). However, there are scores of stand-alone crises that are not part of protracted conflicts; for these cases, if tensions are reduced following a crisis, this is a good sign that the issues underlying the dispute have been resolved to a high degree. With this in mind, while manipulation and formulation are both successful means of resolving conflicts, our evidence points to facilitation as having the largest positive effect on reducing tension between actors after the crisis concludes (see Beardsley *et al.* 2004 for a presentation of even stronger evidence of the effectiveness of facilitation in reducing tensions). Hence, these results also provide some support for those scholars who contend that facilitation is a successful mediation strategy for resolving conflicts (see Burton 1972, 1987, 1990; Fisher 1972; Carnevale and Pegnetter 1985; Bercovitch 1992; Kelman 1992; Princen 1992; Rothman 1992; Jabri 1996; Keashly and Fisher 1996; Kleiboer 1998).

Finally, the absence of significant differences between facilitative and manipulative styles in generating greater satisfaction with outcomes sheds some further light on the findings in the existing literature on mediation style, in general, and on crisis mediation more specifically. As noted earlier, those scholars who promote facilitation over formulation and manipulation argue that it serves to ensure that the outcome to the crisis is generated by the crisis actors themselves, and it prevents situations in which crisis actors might feel that they were forced to accept an undesirable outcome as a result of pressure employed by a third party (i.e., a manipulative mediator). Our findings reveal no support for the notion that negotiators will resent outcomes resulting from formulation and manipulation. In light of the above-noted results regarding tension reduction, while both facilitation and manipulation are likely to produce outcomes that are highly satisfactory to negotiators at the conclusion of the crisis, it seems that facilitation is more likely than manipulation to ensure that these parties remain satisfied with the crisis outcome in the future. Thus, it may be the case that actors are highly satisfied at the point of crisis termination when any sort of mediation is involved because mediation will usually produce the signing of agreements more efficiently than if the parties were left to their own devices. Thus, crisis actors are likely to be pleased that the tense situation and/or stalemate is over. However, once enough time passes that they are able to re-assess the status quo that results from the crisis termination, this satisfaction is more likely to persist if they feel that they have played a primary role in the resolution of the crisis.

Notes

1 Skjelsbaek (1986), Mitchell (1993), Hopmann (1996), and Keashly and Fisher (1996) offer alternative categorizations of mediation style.

2 Polisario is a movement with both conventional and militant wings, mainly consisting of members of the Sahrawi ethnic group. It formed in the early 1970s with the expressed intent of liberating the Western Sahara region from (at different times) Spanish, Moroccan, and Mauritanian rule. In 1976, it formally declared the existence of the Sahrawi Arab Democratic Republic. This entity, which had a government in exile, was recognized by the OAU and several Latin American states, but not by the UN.

3 Before World War I, Poland was under the control of czarist Russia. It was captured by Germany during the war but gained independence from Germany and Russia when the Allies agreed to the provisions of Woodrow Wilson's Fourteen Points declaration regarding Poland's sovereignty status. After the Russian Revolution, Bolshevik forces attempted to regain control over Poland.

4 Manipulation is also sometimes referred to as "power" mediation (see especially Keashly and Fisher 1996 and Bloomfield, Nupen, and Harris 1998). These same scholars label formulative mediation as "pure" mediation.

5 Hypotheses 3a, 3b, 4a, and 4b are only tested using experimental data. Hence,

they do not include reference to the formulative style of mediation, since the experiments did not evaluate this style.

6 The measure of tension reduction reported here refers to the non-recurrence of crisis between these adversaries within five years of the termination of the crisis. The measure reported in Appendix A refers to a reduction in tension during the course of the crisis.

7 The other six forms of outcome identified by ICB are semi-formal agreement, tacit understanding, unilateral act, imposed agreement, faded crisis, and, for those outcomes that don't fit neatly into any other category, the catch-all grouping of "other."

8 In our general discussion and analysis of the form of outcome variable in Chapter 3, we grouped together formal, semi-formal, and tacit agreements into a single agreement category. In the present analysis, we included only those cases ending in formal agreements as a sharper indicator of this phenomenon.

9 Since the coding of the most recent case additions to the ICB dataset was completed in the Fall 2003, those crises that terminated later than 1996 are not coded for the tension reduction variable, as the five-year threshold for determining whether or not tensions have been reduced had not yet passed.

10 South Yemen did not exist as a separate country until 1967. Prior to that, the Yemen Arab Republic had consisted of what eventually became North and South Yemen. In 1965, two rival nationalist groups – the Front for the Liberation of Occupied South Yemen (FLOSY) and the National Liberation Front (NLF) – instigated a campaign to control South Yemen. The NLF seized power after defeating its FLOSY rivals, and it declared the People's Republic of South Yemen as a separate entity in 1967. A Marxist faction of the NLF eventually gained power and changed the name of the country to the People's Democratic Republic of Yemen (PDRY) in 1970 and established close ties with the Soviet Union. Oman was a British protectorate until 1971. Since 1963, Dhofarian rebels had been engaging in military confrontations with the country's ruling sultan. Originally, these rebels had separatist goals; the movement eventually focused energies on overthrowing the sultan. In 1967, the movement changed its name to the Popular Front for the Liberation of the Occupied Gulf (PFLOG), and its goal was to instigate revolutionary movements against conservative regimes throughout the Arab Peninsula.

11 The analyses of mediation style and crisis outcomes in Beardsley *et al.* (2004) differ from those carried out in this book in two important ways: 1) Beardsley *et al.* utilized a more extensive model in their investigation of the effects of mediation style conceived in terms of "highest form"; and 2) they also examined the effects of mediation style conceived in terms of "most crucial form" – which style of mediation had the greatest *impact* on crisis processes and outcomes.

12 An additional factor that likely contributes to the overall weakness of the model of actor satisfaction is the large amount of missing data regarding this crisis outcome measure in the ICB dataset, due in large part to the difficulty that coders experienced in making post-hoc judgments about actors' views of the crisis outcome. Single actor cases or cases in which there are no adversarial actors are also coded as missing data for the ICB actor satisfaction variable.

13 In November 1995, Eritrea claimed that Yemen instigated tensions by putting troops on the Hanish islands. Yemen countered with the argument that tensions between the two countries were raised after Eritrea ordered all Yemenis off the islands on November 11; it argued that the increasing Yemeni military presence was a response to Eritrea's attempt to land naval vessels on the islands. Eritrean and Yemeni delegations held talks on December 7 and agreed to handle the dispute diplomatically, which caused the Eritrean offensive that

occurred a week later to be even more of a shock to Yemen. Yemen claimed that these attacks were an Eritrean act of aggression.

14 The minor discrepancies in the number of cases analyzed for each model are accounted for by computer glitches and failure of some subjects to answer surveys fully.

15 We are unable to use our experimental method to fully analyze all of the hypotheses related to actor satisfaction, since we do not explore the effects of formulation via the simulations. Thus, while we are able to test Hypotheses 2a and 2b by using experimental data and compare these results to those acquired from the ICB-based analyses, we cannot do the same in regards to Hypothesis 2c.

16 In relation to our experiments, at no point before, during, or directly after the simulation are negotiators given access to their opponent's utility scores. Thus, they are unaware of each other's relative gains.

17 It is important to note that positive and negative leverage are likely to have differential effects on the negotiation process and/or outcome. Greenberg, Barton, and McGuiness (2000) argue that carrots seem to be more advantageous than sticks at attaining long-term dispute resolution, though sticks can help to bring about short-term crisis resolutions (e.g., ceasefires). We do not analyze the potential differential effects of carrots and sticks in this study, but we encourage further systematic research on this topic.

5 Crisis mediation and relative power

As we have seen, an evaluation of the style of mediation invoked by a third party helps to enhance our understanding of the dynamics of mediation in international crisis. In this and the following chapter, we explore in more detail two specific characteristics of the relationship among crisis actors and how these factors interact with the efforts of a third party to bring a crisis to a peaceful conclusion. In this chapter, we focus on the power relationship among states involved in crises, while Chapter 6 considers how the degree to which a crisis is ripe for resolution affects the impact that mediation has on crises. Specifically, our main concern when analyzing crisis actor power and zones of agreement is how each of these contextual factors modifies the expected effectiveness of different mediation styles – facilitation, formulation, and manipulation – on the outcomes of crises.

Power in international conflicts and crises

Defining state power

Power is traditionally conceived as the ability of one actor to affect the behavior of another actor, and similarly, in international relations, states are considered to be powerful when they can influence the decisions and policies of other states. Brecher and Wilkenfeld (2000) contend that the power of a given state in the international system is a product of several characteristics of that state's capabilities – the size of the state's population and territory, its gross domestic product (GDP), the nature of its relationships with major powers (that is, the nature of its alliances), and its military and nuclear capabilities at the time the crisis emerged. State power thought of in these terms is most often referred to as "aggregate" power.

Others, like Kriesberg (1996), argue that consideration of power as a function of state capabilities is insufficient, and that a more complete measure of power considers the situation facing a state, otherwise known as the state's context- or issue-specific power. A state with lesser capabilities – or lower levels of aggregate power – can have an advantage over others in particular situations, including conflicts and crises, as well as during conflict resolution and crisis management endeavors. Building on the work of others (see especially Keohane and Nye 1977; Lockhart 1979), Habeeb argues that "the power balance of an issue-specific relationship is determined by three variables: alternatives, commitment, and control" (1988: 21). In other words, a state's issue-specific power depends on how reliant it is on others to achieve its desired outcome, the degree to which it wants or needs this outcome, and its ability to achieve its goal(s) by acting unilaterally (and, thus, to control its own fate). Habeeb points to the negotiations between the United States and Panama over control of the Panama Canal as a situation in which the state with greater capabilities – the United States – had to contend with a state that had greater issue-specific power – Panama – which controlled the canal. In the analyses below, we attempt to account for the relevance of both state capabilities and situational factors as components of a state's overall power.

Relative power in international relations

International relations scholars have long focused on the power relations among states as explanatory factors for a wide variety of behavioral patterns, including alliance formation, strategic interactions, and negotiation strategies. Singer (1963) argues that a state's aggregate power determines its influence and the degree to which it can translate promises into rewards and threats into punishments in its relations with other states. Hopmann (1996) notes, though, that a true understanding of a state's power in the international system relies upon its *relative* capabilities and influence in a situation: "Influence is *symmetrical*," he writes, "when [state] B can use counter-threats or counter-promises to cancel or to in some other way substantially negate A's attempt to influence B. Conversely, influence is *asymmetrical* when B has little or no such ability to exert influence in reply to A" (1996: 108, emphasis added).

It is this relative nature of state power that we will consider when examining the interplay of crisis actor power and mediation. Analyses in this chapter explore whether mediator behavior has a different effect in symmetrical situations – or crises characterized by *power parity* among crisis actors – than it does in asymmetrical situations, characterized by power discrepancies or *disparity* among crisis actors. Truly asymmetrical situations are those in which one state possesses an advantage in regard to both aggregate and contextual/issue-specific elements of power.

Analysts and researchers maintain that the relative power of states is a relevant factor related to the outbreak of hostilities between and among states, but there is no consensus about *how* relative power affects the outbreak of hostilities. Power-transition theorists, including Organski (1960), Kugler and Organski (1989), and Kugler and Lemke (1996), argue that war is most likely under conditions of power parity among states. According to this argument, when there is a preponderant power in the international system, that power will seek to maintain the status quo and hence guard against conflicts, wars, and crises that can disturb this status quo. Balance of power theorists, like Claude (1962) and Wright (1965) argue that power parity *diminishes* the chances of war: according to this theory, as the power of states comes into balance (i.e., as states approach parity), uncertainty over the likely outcome of a conflict involving the states in the system increases, as no state can be assured that it can overwhelm and defeat those with which they are equals. Under these conditions, balance of power advocates argue, states will be less likely to take an aggressive stance in the international system.

This debate about relative power and the likelihood of the eruption of conflicts reflects more significant scholarly disagreements about the workings of the international system and will likely continue. Nevertheless, a review of data can provide us with insights about how the relative power of crisis actors affects the dynamics of the unique class of events known as international crises. In this chapter, we attempt to arrive at a deeper understanding of this relationship by exploring both historical and experimental data on power relations and crises.

Relative power and crisis management

The relative capabilities of states in crisis situations are relevant to how crises will likely evolve and be resolved. For instance, Morgan (1994) provides empirical evidence that the probability of a crisis escalating to war is highest when there is a large disparity in military capabilities between parties and the weaker party exhibits high resolve. Similarly, the relative power of crisis actors is purported to affect decisions about efforts to de-escalate and resolve international crises, including which type of approach may be implemented and how likely it is to be effective.

Relative power and negotiation

Many scholars argue that negotiation is unlikely to occur in conflicts in general when the relative power relationship between or among disputants is characterized by power disparity (see especially Pruitt and Carnevale 1993; Bercovitch and Houston 1996; Kleiboer 1996). The expectation is that power disparity will cause the stronger party to view negotiation as an obstacle to complete conquest – if this party negotiates, it will have to compromise for the conflict to terminate, so why not just try to achieve victory unilaterally? As Modelski explains, "It goes against the grain of human nature to seek a negotiated solution when one can be imposed by demanding it" (1964: 149). Pruitt and Carnevale argue that this is true regarding both aggregate and issue-specific power: "One's power may seem greater than that of the other party, encouraging an effort to exploit the other. One's case may seem stronger than that of the other party, encouraging an appeal to an arbitrator or judge" (1993: 6).

Hypotheses offered by Terris and Maoz (2001) are consistent with the expectation that asymmetric conflicts and crises are ill suited to negotiation. They posit that conflicts characterized by greater power disparities between disputants will be more resistant to negotiation as a method of conflict resolution than those conflicts where the parties' power relationship is more symmetrical in nature. However, Terris and Maoz's analyses demonstrate that there is no statistically significant relationship between the relative power among conflicting parties and whether they agree to meet at the negotiating table. These non-findings are consistent with those presented by Dixon (1993), who discovered that, for conflicts involving only democratic countries, the probability that negotiation would be used was also unaffected by the relative power of the states involved in a conflict.

These empirical findings support the idea that conflicts characterized by power disparity are, in fact, receptive to negotiation efforts. Deutsch (1973) argues that negotiation will not only *occur* among disputants of unequal power, but that it is more likely to be successful in asymmetric conflicts, so long as disputants are in agreement about the nature of the relative power relationship among them. According to Deutsch, a "mutual recognition of differential power" (1973: 46) among parties to a conflict is conducive to conflict resolution through negotiation, as it makes more evident to the adversaries which party will be expected to make more concessions (usually the weaker party). Such shared expectations will facilitate the bargaining and negotiation process. A series of case studies of negotiation in international conflicts conducted by Rubin and Zartman (1995) provides empirical support for Deutsch's hypothesis. They conclude that, in general, negotiations characterized by a power imbalance among parties are more likely to result in more satisfactory outcomes for all parties than are negotiations among equal parties.

Despite the expectation that stronger countries will be reluctant to engage in negotiations with less powerful actors or vice versa, history is replete with examples of asymmetric negotiations in the international system. In such circumstances, negotiation may be the only thing that prevents the more powerful state from overrunning – figuratively or literally – a weaker state. And while the stronger power in an asymmetric negotiation clearly holds an advantage, the weaker power can secure a satisfactory outcome through negotiation.

This is true even during times of international crisis, as demonstrated by the 1987 India Intervention in Sri Lanka crisis. In June 1987, Indian officials attempted to deliver humanitarian aid to Indian Tamils living in Sri Lanka. After Sri Lanka denied the Indian delegation entry into Sri Lanka's territorial waters, India responded by airlifting humanitarian aid to the Indian population living in Sri Lanka – an act Sri Lanka perceived to be a blatant violation of its sovereignty, thus triggering an asymmetrical international crisis between Sri Lanka and the more powerful India. Despite the power imbalance, India agreed to rely on negotiation efforts with Sri Lanka to resolve the crisis, and the negotiations generated an outcome satisfactory to both sides: India was given permission to deliver humanitarian assistance in return for working with Sri Lanka to establish a peace plan between the two states. The peace plan was put into action one month after the conclusion of the 1987 crisis, leading to a significant reduction in tensions between the two countries.

Watkins (2002) points out that when faced with a power disparity in a negotiation, actors can adopt specific tactics to help ensure beneficial outcomes. Weaker actors can succeed in negotiations, he argues, if they guard against advocating "all-or-nothing" proposals, if they sequence discussions of issues in a way that will help them, and if they maximize their own power by gaining as much information as possible about the situation and the other actors involved. While Watkins' lessons are drawn from analyses of business negotiations, his principles are relevant, as well, in the international system.

Relative power and mediation

Just as there is disagreement as to whether power disparity is an obstacle or an advantage to negotiation efforts, disagreements exist about whether mediation will occur in asymmetrical situations. Hopmann (1996), for instance, argues that mediators will be unwelcome in conflicts characterized by disparity among disputants. By definition, the involvement of a mediator must be acceptable to all parties to a dispute, conflict, or crisis. As such, any party that views a mediator as a threat or simply as unneeded or unwanted essentially has the power to veto the inclusion of a willing third party.

Just as the stronger parties in asymmetrical conflicts are expected to be the most resistant to negotiation, they are also expected to be more highly opposed to third-party intervention than weaker parties. As Kleiboer notes, "a marked power disparity will strengthen the stronger party's view of the mediator as a stumbling block toward the achievement of total victory ... [and] will enhance [the stronger party's] reluctance to make any concession or compromises during mediation essential for attaining successful results" (1996: 368). A more powerful party to the conflict may expect that the third party will try to push for a solution or outcome that is perceived to be fair to all sides but which, in practice, may "be less than the powerful side's reservation value" (Princen 1992: 63). In addition, powerful states will likely be concerned that a third party may improve the power and bargaining position of the weaker party (Wehr 1979; Groom and Webb 1987; Greig 2001). Since mediators may "empower weaker parties in the interest of an equitable settlement" (Kleiboer 1996: 370; see also Pruitt and Carnevale 1993), such reluctance on the part of the stronger party is not surprising.

Despite this generally negative forecast of the likelihood of mediation in asymmetric disputes, mediation does occur in actuality in conflicts marked by power disparity. In an empirical analysis of international disputes between 1945 and 1995, Bercovitch and Jackson (2001) discover that mediation is preferred over bilateral negotiation as a form of conflict management when the power disparity between parties is most extreme.

However, our review of ICB data on international crises revealed that, while mediation transpires in both symmetric and asymmetric crises, it is significantly more likely to occur under conditions of symmetry, consistent with expectations that states with a preponderance of power in a specific crisis episode may be unwilling to accept the involvement of a mediator. As shown in Chapter 3, mediators have been involved in almost half of all symmetric crises (45 of 97 cases, or 46.4 percent) but in only about one-quarter of asymmetric crises (74 of 270 cases, or 26.8 percent). That is, while the vast majority of crises in the international system are likely to involve states of unequal power, those that include states of equal power are significantly more likely to involve a mediator ($\chi^2 = 11.74, p < 0.000$).[1]

Relative power and mediation success

Scholars contend not only that the relative power of disputants will influence *whether* a conflict or crisis is mediated but also what the effect of that third party will be (see Wall and Lynn 1993; Dixon 1996; Wall, Stark, and Standifer 2001). Based upon theoretical (see Young 1967; Kriesberg 1996), qualitative (see Ott 1972; Zartman 1981; Touval 1982), quantitative (see Bercovitch 1985, 1996; Raymond and Kegley 1985; Bercovitch and Houston 1996), and prescriptive (see Nickles and Hedgespeth 1991) analyses, many scholars find that conflicts characterized by power parity among negotiators are better suited for the achievement of successful mediated outcomes than are situations characterized by power discrepancies.[2] In support of this view, Bercovitch, Anagnoson, and Wille (1991) find that mediation was successful in only 6 percent of the negotiations of international disputes characterized by power asymmetry, and that disputes marked by the highest degree of mediation success were those in which all parties were relatively weak and equal in power capabilities.

Some analysts do not support the argument on the merits of power parity in mediated conflicts and crises. Organski (1960) and Wright (1965) warn that the work of a mediator could be undermined in the presence of power symmetry because the situational power balance may, in fact, spark competition among parties as each tries to gain the upper hand in the dispute. In support of this argument, Greig (2001) provides evidence that mediation efforts are less likely to be followed by the use of force by disputants (an important measure of success) in power-asymmetric interstate rivalries than in symmetric rivalries. He notes that conditions of power parity may "suggest to rivals that ... they may have sufficient power to impose through force their preferred settlement" (Greig 2001: 710). Thus, they *both* may be more willing to accept risks of using force, rather than working with a third party to find a more peaceful outcome.

Mediation may be effective under conditions of power disparity for reasons that have nothing to do with competition. Deutsch (1973) argues that the key to successful mediation of asymmetric conflicts lies in the weaker party recognizing its position in the conflict and being prepared to make more concessions than the stronger party during the mediated negotiations. On the other hand, Pruitt and Carnevale (1993) point out that even though stronger parties are less likely to concede and more likely to use threats than weaker parties, when the more powerful parties do make concessions, such actions are especially effective because they are seen as "genuine efforts at conciliation (rather) than concessions from weakness" (1993: 147). It seems, then, that mediators can be successful in asymmetric conflicts if they can convince the stronger party of the need for some concessions while making sure the weaker party understands that it will have to compromise to an even greater degree.

Several empirical analyses have yielded results that indicate no significant relationship between disputant power and conflict settlement at all (Miall 1992; Dixon 1994). Greig (2001) examined the effect of power distribution on the likelihood of both short-term mediation success and the reduction of long-term dispute severity following mediation. He found no statistically significant relationship between the distribution of power between disputing rivals and either measure of outcome. To date, then, the debate continues as to whether and to what degree power impacts the potential of third-party mediation efforts in international conflicts and crises.

Relative power and mediation style

While there exists a general dearth of theoretical and/or empirical analyses of the relationship between mediation style, mediation success, and the power relations of disputants, a few studies have tackled this question. Bercovitch and Houston (2000) indicate that parties' internal and external sources of power are likely to influence "the type of mediator behavior sought and accepted by the parties as well as its ultimate effectiveness" (2000: 198). They find that the degree of control that the parties can exert over the process and structure of negotiation – a function of power, in part – is important in the use of facilitative strategies and less important in the use of more directive strategies, when the mediator can direct the process and substance of the negotiation to a higher degree.

In addition, several empirical studies conducted by Bercovitch and his associates (see Bercovitch 1985; Bercovitch, Anagnoson, and Wille 1991;

Bercovitch and Houston 1996) have yielded results that show a statistically significant relationship between mediation effectiveness and both mediation style and the power relations between parties. Specifically, these studies find that more active and directive mediation strategies – formulation, and especially, manipulation – have higher rates of success in bringing about abatement and settlement of disputes than do communication-facilitation strategies.[3] They also demonstrate that mediation is most effective at managing or resolving disputes when the power differentials between parties are small rather than large. What is lacking in these studies is that they do not look at the *combined* effect of relative power relations and mediation style. We attempt to remedy this omission by conducting such an analysis, using both historical and experimental data.

Rates of incidence: relative power and mediation style

Before delving deeper into an analysis of the separate and interactive effects of mediation style and relative power on crisis outcomes, we present some summary statistics on two items of interest to this study: 1. Incidence rates of asymmetric vs. symmetrical power relations in crises, and 2. Incidence rates of each of the three styles of mediation discussed in Chapter 4 under these different types of relative power conditions. The latter is especially important because we want to know if there are high degrees of variation in approaches to crisis mediation across both types of power conditions, or if mediators attempt to match mediation style with specific relative power situations.

As mentioned in Chapter 3, the International Crisis Behavior (ICB) dataset includes data on the power capabilities of individual states involved in international crises, and the system-level ICB data include a measure of power discrepancy among crisis actors for each case. This indicator is continuous in nature and is based upon a comparison of the power scores of relevant actors, with calculated values ranging from 0 (including the 1969 Football War between El Salvador and Honduras and the 1990–91 Rwanda-Uganda crisis) to 179 for the 1999 crisis in Kosovo, involving 10 member states of NATO and the Federal Republic of Yugoslavia. Those crises with lower power-discrepancy values involve actors that are relatively equivalent powers.

We have classified all crises for which the power discrepancy score is equal to 0 or 1 as *symmetric crises*, characterized by power parity among the crisis actors. Similarly, *asymmetric crises* are those in which disparities exist among the crisis actors, as demonstrated by ICB power discrepancy scores of greater than 1. Based on this measure, the majority of crises – 270, or 74 percent – are asymmetric crises, while 97 crises (26 percent) are symmetric crises.[4] These findings support the power-transition argument that power discrepancies foster hostile relations among states and the

Table 5.1 Mediation style and relative power of crisis actors

	Asymmetric crises	*Symmetric crises*	*Total*
Facilitation	13 (81.3%)	3 (18.7%)	16 (15.2%)
Formulation	28 (54.9%)	23 (45.1%)	51 (48.6%)
Manipulation	24 (63.2%)	14 (36.8%)	38 (36.2%)
Total	65 (61.9%)	40 (38.1%)	105 (100.0%)

$\chi^2 = 3.625, p = 0.0815.$

potential emergence of conflict and crisis, but it is the case that crises can and do emerge as well when there is equality among states.

As noted in Chapter 2, a major re-coding effort has resulted in the addition of a range of mediation-related variables to the existing ICB dataset. Using these new data, we find that each of the three major mediation styles – facilitation, formulation, and manipulation – has been used in crises characterized by power parity as well as those characterized by power disparity. As revealed in Table 5.1, though, ICB data indicate that facilitation is much more likely to be used under conditions of power disparity than it is under conditions of power parity among crisis actors.

While facilitation of symmetric crises has proven to be rare, history demonstrates that crises which involve a third party that adopts this role can be successfully managed. In December 1985, a crisis emerged between Burkina Faso and Mali – two states of essentially equal power – regarding disputed territory along the border between these two states (a region known as the Agacher Strip). Years earlier, both states had agreed that they would work with the other to determine an acceptable border between the two states in a peaceful manner, but a crisis (known as the "Christmas War") was triggered when Burkina Faso attempted to conduct a census in the Agacher Strip, a move seen by Mali as a step to assert control over the territory. This move by Burkina Faso triggered public uprisings in the disputed region and the eventual movement of Mali troops into towns in the Agacher Strip. This crisis was resolved less than a month after its outbreak with the help of mediation efforts by Nigeria and Libya. In this situation, the mediators restricted their role to facilitating discussions among the two states, encouraging them to work with one another to find a resolution, and accepting an invitation from the disputants to help enforce the agreed upon settlement. Thus, the mediators adopted a facilitative style that proved to be successful in moving the parties toward a peaceful resolution to the crisis. This approach in crises marked by power parity is atypical, however.

More common in symmetric crises was the approach adopted by the United States, and then-Assistant Secretary of State Richard Holbrooke, who served as a mediator in the 1996 Aegean Sea crisis involving Greece and Turkey. This crisis, characterized by power parity between the crisis actors, was triggered following the running aground of a Turkish ship on the uninhabited island of Imia, located in Greek territorial waters. Greece and Turkey had a long-standing disagreement regarding sovereignty over Imia and whether this island was a part of Turkey or Greece. The presence of the Turkish ship on the island prompted a local Greek official to raise a Greek flag on the island of Imia, a move that triggered a crisis for Turkey, which responded by sending military forces to Imia. This act triggered a crisis for Greece, which promptly sent its military forces to the island as well. Four days after the crisis was triggered, Holbrooke led an American effort to end this crisis. Noting that "the two sides [in this crisis] cannot talk to each other," Holbrooke and other U.S. officials served as a conduit for communication between Greece and Turkey (CNN 1996). In this way, the United States acted as a facilitative mediator.

However, in this crisis, the United States took another step in its mediation efforts as Holbrooke and other officials from the State Department, Pentagon, and White House advocated a specific solution to this problem. The Holbrooke-led team encouraged both Greek and Turkish leaders to remove their military forces from Imia and to allow the status of Imia to return to what it was prior to the crisis, according to which neither a Turkish nor a Greek flag would be flown over the island and the status of its sovereignty would remain ambiguous. Indeed, officials from both of the disputing states accepted this U.S.-backed position, and the crisis was resolved before military hostilities broke out between the long-time rival states. By advocating a specific resolution to the crisis, the U.S. clearly acted in a manner consistent with the formulative style of mediation – the style most often seen in the course of symmetric crises.

While mediation was associated with successful crisis management efforts in both the Burkina Faso-Mali crisis and the Aegean Sea crisis, it remains to be seen how effective mediation is as a crisis management or conflict resolution tool in symmetric versus asymmetric crises, in general. The analyses that follow provide some insights into this question.

Effectiveness of crisis mediation: relative power and mediation style

Building upon our findings in the previous chapter regarding the differential effects of mediation given the style employed by the mediator, here we seek to examine whether and how the relative power of disputants influences the impact of mediation during crisis conditions. We agree with those scholars who propose that the relative power of crisis actors is a relevant factor to consider in examining crisis mediation dynamics. Furthermore, we adopt the perspective that a mediator will have a more profound effect on crises under conditions of power disparity, when there is essentially an "uneven playing field" among the crisis actors. It is under these conditions that we expect mediators to be able to assert their influence.

As ICB data in Table 3.6 indicate a smaller percentage of asymmetric crises involve mediation than do symmetric crises. While mediation is relatively rare in asymmetric crises, it has been argued that mediation can be especially effective during such situations of power disparity. The more powerful disputant's acceptance of the involvement of a mediator will likely be perceived by the weaker party as a concession, as a gesture that the stronger party does not seek to wholly exploit the weaker party. As such, the very inclusion of a mediator in an asymmetric crisis can change the dynamics of the relationship between or among the crisis actors, such that weaker parties will be more likely to believe that the crisis management process is a fair one and more likely to accept the suggestions of a mediator about potential solutions to the crisis. When the weaker party consents to the mediator's proposals, this can also signal to the stronger party that the weaker party understands its position in the conflict and is willing to act accordingly by compromising.

In symmetric crises, on the other hand, it is likely that each of the parties will believe that the mediator will heighten its marginal power in a situation – that is, that each crisis actor will expect that the mediator will help them, at the expense of other actors. From this mindset, it is much more likely that disputants will soon become disappointed in the contributions of a mediator – who, in practice, is more likely to request concessions from all sides than it is to make each side feel stronger. As disappointment sets in, crisis actors will be less likely to look to the mediator for guidance or to heed the mediator's advice or warnings.

Based on this logic, we argue that the impact of the mediator under conditions of power parity is more likely to be negligible, whereas in conditions of power disparity, the effect of a mediator on crisis dynamics and its outcome is more likely to be significant. Based on the arguments we made in Chapter 4 regarding mediation style and the findings of several studies conducted by Bercovitch and his associates noted above, we also assert that manipulative mediation will have the greatest impact on nearly all crisis outcomes. We have noted the relevance of mediation style in Chapter 4, and here we expand our framework of crisis mediation by considering how the relationship between mediation style and crisis outcome changes when its effects are combined with those of the relative power relations of the crisis actors.

In sum, although mediation is more likely to occur during symmetric crises, it will have a larger positive impact on crisis management and conflict resolution during asymmetric crises, and asymmetric crises that involve manipulative mediation are more likely to be successfully managed than all other crises. As explained in Chapter 4, an exception to this expectation is that we anticipate that formulative and facilitative mediation styles will be more effective than manipulation at resolving long-term conflicts, hence these modes of mediation will be more likely than manipulation to aid in the reduction in tensions between actors following the termination of the crisis. With this reasoning in mind, we test the following hypotheses in this chapter:

Hypothesis 6a: Asymmetric crises in which manipulative mediation is used will be more likely to terminate in formal agreement than all other crises.

Hypothesis 6b: Asymmetric crises in which formulative or facilitative mediation is used will be more likely to terminate in formal agreement than unmediated crises or mediated symmetric crises.

Hypothesis 6c: Asymmetric crises in which formulative mediation is used will be more likely to terminate in formal agreement than asymmetric crises exhibiting only facilitative mediation.

Hypothesis 7a: Asymmetric crises in which manipulative mediation is used will be more likely to result in negotiators being satisfied with the crisis outcomes than all other crises.

Hypothesis 7b: Asymmetric crises in which formulative or facilitative mediation is used will be more likely to result in negotiators being satisfied with the crisis outcomes than unmediated crises or mediated symmetric crises.

Hypothesis 7c: Asymmetric crises in which formulative mediation is used will be more likely to result in negotiators being satisfied with the crisis outcomes than asymmetric crises exhibiting only facilitative mediation.

Hypothesis 8a: Asymmetric crises in which manipulative mediation is used will be more likely to result in negotiators perceiving the mediator as having a positive effect on crisis management than all other crises.

Hypothesis 8b: Asymmetric crises in which facilitative mediation is used will be more likely to result in negotiators perceiving the mediator as having a positive effect on crisis management than mediated symmetric crises.

Hypothesis 9a: Crisis actors in asymmetric crises exhibiting manipulative mediation will achieve more beneficial outcomes than actors in all other crises.

Hypothesis 9b: Crisis actors in asymmetric crises exhibiting facilitative mediation will achieve more beneficial outcomes than actors in unmediated crises or mediated symmetric crises.

Hypothesis 10a: Asymmetric crises in which manipulative mediation is used will end more rapidly than all other crises.

Hypothesis 10b: Asymmetric crises in which facilitative mediation is used will end more rapidly than unmediated crises or mediated symmetric crises.

Hypothesis 11a: Asymmetric crises in which formulative mediation is used but manipulation is not will be more likely to be followed by a reduction in tensions between crisis actors than all other crises.

Hypothesis 11b: Asymmetric crises in which facilitative or manipulative mediation is used will be more likely to be followed by a reduction in tensions between crisis actors than unmediated crises or mediated symmetric crises.

Hypothesis 11c: Asymmetric crises in which facilitation is the only mediation style used will be more likely to be followed by a reduction in tensions between crisis actors than asymmetric crises exhibiting manipulative mediation.

In order to examine this collection of hypotheses, we once more present analyses based on the multi-method approach outlined in Chapter 2. Hypotheses 6a though 7c (agreements and satisfaction, respectively) and 11a through 11c (tension reduction) will be tested using ICB data on mediation style, relative power, and crisis outcomes. H7a, H7b (on satisfaction), and H8a through H10b will be tested using data derived from the experimental simulation based on the 1981 Ecuador-Peru border crisis.

Relative power and mediation style in ICB cases

We begin our examination of the inter-relationships among mediation style, power relations of the crisis actors, and crisis outcomes by turning to the ICB dataset. We first address some methodological issues, and then discuss the results of these analyses.

Methodology

Once again, our initial focus is on three ICB measures of crisis outcomes: the achievement of a formal agreement, satisfaction among crisis actors with the outcome, and post-crisis tensions between actors. To evaluate the combined effects that mediation style and the relative power relations of crisis actors have on crisis outcomes, we employ multivariate logistic regression. Power relations are evaluated both for their own individual impact on crisis outcomes, and for the combined, or interactive effects of relative power and mediation style.

All models reported on in this chapter include four independent variables to examine the separate effects of mediation style and the relative power relations of the crisis actors. For mediation style, we employ individual indicators of facilitation, formulation, and manipulation, conceived in terms of "highest form of mediation." We also include a dichotomous measure of the relative power relations of the crisis actors, with "0" indicating symmetric crises and "1" indicating asymmetric crises.

Several models also explore the interaction effects of relative power and mediation style on outcome. These models utilize three interaction terms that were derived by multiplying the indicator of the relative power relations of the crisis actors for a given crisis by the indicator of the "highest form of mediation" used in that crisis. Interaction terms were used since the combined effects of these two factors – relative power and mediation style – are what ultimately concern us in this chapter. The same independent variables were also utilized in each of these models: the individual indicators of each style of mediation conceived in terms of highest form, the dichotomous indicator of the relative power relations of the crisis actors, and the interactions of the latter and each indicator of mediation style, with one exception. Due to the very small number of asymmetric crises in which facilitation was the highest form of mediation used (only three times since 1918), however, this variable was dropped from each model.

For each dichotomous interaction term, crises coded "0" are either symmetric, marked by the absence of the mediation style of concern regarded as the "highest" mediation form, or a combination of these two conditions. Crises coded "1" are both asymmetric *and* marked by the presence of the mediation style of concern regarded as "highest form." The indicator of no mediation is used as the reference category when interpreting the results of each analysis.

Results

Formal agreement

Table 5.2 displays the results of two models relating relative power and mediation style to the achievement of a formal agreement at the termination of a crisis. Mediation style by itself and the interactive effects of mediation style and relative crisis actor power each have a significant impact on the likelihood of a crisis ending with a formal agreement. The Likelihood Ratio Chi-squared values associated with both models are high, and both of these overall models are highly significant ($p < 0.000$).

Table 5.2 shows that when we control for relative power, manipulation and formulation remain strongly associated with the achievement of agreement. As we see in Model 1, when crisis actor power relations are held constant, manipulation has the strongest positive impact on the probability of a crisis terminating with a formal agreement. The baseline probability of crises terminating in a formal agreement in the context dictated by Model 1 is 12 percent. (This baseline is calculated by holding all independent variables, each of which are dichotomous, at their modal

Table 5.2 Relative power, mediation style, and formal agreement in ICB

	MODEL 1 *Main effects only*		*MODEL 2* *Main effects + Interaction terms*	
Facilitation	0.191	(0.788)	0.194	(0.789)
Formulation	1.633***	(0.353)	2.496***	(0.637)
Manipulation	2.504***	(0.391)	2.902***	(0.731)
Relative power relations	−0.122	(0.317)	0.406	(0.512)
Formulation × relative power relations	—	—	−1.335*	(0.781)
Manipulation × relative power relations	—	—	−0.483	(0.867)
Constant	−1.888***	(0.313)	−2.314***	(0.472)
N	350	—	350	—
$LR\chi^2$	56.50***	—	59.59***	—
df	4	—	6	—

*$p \leq 0.10$; **$p \leq 0.05$; ***$p \leq 0.005$.

Notes

Standard errors are in parentheses. The dependent variable was operationalized as follows: 0 = no formal agreement, 1 = formal agreement.

values.) In comparison, crises in which a third party adopts the most substantively intrusive style of mediation have a 62 percent overall likelihood of terminating in a formal agreement. Crises in which formulation is the highest form of mediation used do not fare as well as those involving manipulation, but the results still indicate that formulative mediation is more effective at producing formal agreements than if the crisis actors were left to their own devices to do so. When formulation is the highest style of mediation adopted in a given crisis in this context, the crisis is over three times more likely – a 41 percent overall probability – to end in a formal agreement than if it was unmediated. The findings regarding facilitation as the highest form of mediation are inconclusive. Each of these findings is consistent with those presented in Chapter 4. However, as Model 1 demonstrates, the relative power of crisis actors, on its own, has no independent influence on the likelihood of a crisis ending in a formal agreement.

Model 2 incorporates the interactive effects of individual mediation styles and relative power relations. While the main-effect indicators of both formulation and manipulation are again statistically significant, the crucial finding here is that when formulation is the highest form of mediation in a crisis, the relative power of crisis actors does significantly affect the probability of an agreement being achieved.

The baseline probability of crises terminating in a formal agreement in the context presented in Model 2, when holding all independent variables at their minimum values (i.e., "0"), is roughly 10 percent. When a third-party adopts formulation as the highest style of mediation in *symmetric* crises, the chance of those crises ending in formal agreements is about

55 percent. In asymmetric crises, however, the probability of a formulator leading parties to formal agreement drops to 32 percent. Despite the fact that the vast majority of historical cases of mediation (74 percent) have been among parties with unequal levels of power, the data indicate that the effectiveness of formulation as a crisis management tool is much more profound when the crisis actors are relatively equal powers. This finding runs counter to the assertion made in Hypothesis 6b regarding the effect of formulation on formal agreements. The interaction of relative power and the more extreme mediation styles of manipulation and facilitation are insignificant, and as such, we have no evidence to support Hypotheses 6a and 6c.

Comparing the results of the two models, manipulative mediation retains the strongest positive relationship with the likelihood of a formal agreement between disputing parties, regardless of the nature of the relative power relations between these parties. However, crises are also highly likely to terminate in this manner when interveners limit their activities to those associated with a formulative style of mediation. Interestingly, the positive effect of formulation is significantly stronger during symmetric crises than when the relative power relations of the crisis actors are marked by disparity.

Contrary to the assertions of many power transition theorists, mediation – at least when it takes the shape of formulation – seems to be especially effective at assisting in the achievement of formal agreements during situations of power parity. These results support the arguments made by scholars that conflicts characterized by power parity among the negotiators are better suited for the achievement of successful mediated outcomes than are situations characterized by power discrepancies among disputants (see especially Young 1967; Nickles and Hedgespeth 1991; Kriesberg 1996). Our findings also corroborate past empirical evidence of the positive relationship between mediation success and power parity (see especially Ott 1972; Zartman 1981; Touval 1982; Bercovitch 1985; Raymond and Kegley 1985; Bercovitch, Anagnoson, and Wille 1991; Bercovitch and Houston 1996). Hence, if a mediator can intervene in a symmetric crisis, convince each side of the need for making concessions, and help draw up formal agreements that involve such concessions, it has a reasonable likelihood of being successful, as a closer look at several ICB cases demonstrates.

In 1986, Bahrain experienced a crisis with Qatar in the al-Dibal incident. These two Persian Gulf states, both of which had formerly been part of the British Empire until they were granted independence in 1971, were essentially equal in terms of their overall power standing. The crisis arose out of a long-standing territorial dispute involving the Hawar Islands, located adjacent to the Qatar Peninsula. Beginning in the 1930s, intermittent incidents of rising tensions over this issue had transpired between the two countries, but none had reached crisis level until Bahrain began constructing a coast guard station on one of the disputed Hawar islands – al-Dibal. On April 26, 1986, Qatari soldiers landed on al-Dibal, declared that the island was a "restricted zone," and proceeded to arrest Bahraini officials stationed there. This triggered a crisis for Bahrain, whose perceived threat level rose further when Qatar placed its flag on the island two days later. Qatar responded by denouncing the occupation.

A group of Middle Eastern states – Oman, Saudi Arabia, the United Arab Emirates, and Kuwait – mediated the crisis in early May 1986. These mediators helped to devise a framework for agreement between Bahrain and Qatar, in line with their adoption of a formulative mediation style. This agreement included the removal of Qatari troops, as well as construction workers, from al-Dibal. Both tasks were completed by June 15, 1986, when the Qatari troop withdrawal terminated the crisis. The agreement that the mediators helped to devise was the most important factor in easing tensions between the relatively equal powers of Bahrain and Qatar.

Mediation limited to formulation was not as successful in the 1978–79 "Fall of Amin" crisis that occurred, among Uganda, Libya, and Tanzania after Ugandan troops invaded Tanzania and occupied the Kagera Salient, a piece of territory north of the Kagera River. Tanzania, in turn, sent troops into Uganda to challenge its leader, General Idi Amin.[5] Libya, allied with Amin's Uganda, perceived this situation as a crisis for its country, as well. Mediation efforts in this situation, in which Uganda and Libya combined held a preponderance of power in comparison to Tanzania, were troubled from the onset. The weaker Tanzania was initially reluctant to accept the OAU as a mediator in the crisis. Tanzania's leaders eventually conceded and invited OAU crisis mediation efforts but proceeded to boycott meetings organized by the OAU. Tanzania further rejected a comprehensive peace plan formulated by the OAU mediation team as it failed to include a condemnation of Uganda's actions during the crisis. Following these failed mediation attempts, with Tanzanian forces encroaching further into Uganda, Amin eventually fled Uganda. Thus, despite its attempt to formulate a solution to the crisis, the OAU's efforts failed in the face of the continued belief of the weaker Tanzania that the mediator was not representing the interests of Tanzania in its mediation efforts.

Actor satisfaction

While the interactive effect of mediation style and the relative power relations of crisis actors has some influence on the likelihood of crises terminating in formal agreements, the same cannot be said in relation to actor satisfaction with the outcomes of crises. However, mediation style and relative power by themselves do have an effect on satisfaction levels. Table 5.3 displays the results of the two models of actor satisfaction that we

Table 5.3 Relative power, mediation style, and actor satisfaction with outcome in ICB

	MODEL 1 Main effects only		*MODEL 2 Main effects + Interaction terms*	
Facilitation	−1.314*	(0.818)	−1.312*	(0.817)
Formulation	0.437	(0.390)	0.233	(0.719)
Manipulation	0.696*	(0.412)	0.685	(0.754)
Relative power relations	1.193***	(0.360)	1.113**	(0.508)
Formulation × relative power relations	—	—	0.304	(0.860)
Manipulation × relative power relations	—	—	−0.015	(0.900)
Constant	−1.091	(0.360)	−1.022**	(0.475)
N	222	—	222	—
$LR\chi^2$	16.96***	—	17.11**	—
df	4	—	6	—

$*p \leq 0.10$; $**p \leq 0.05$; $***p \leq 0.005$.

Notes

Standard errors are in parentheses. The dependent variable was operationalized as follows: 0 = less than all or most crisis actors satisfied with outcome, 1 = all or most crisis actors satisfied with outcome. Single actor cases or cases where there are no adversarial state actors have missing values coded for the actor satisfaction variable.

tested. The Likelihood Ratio Chi-squared values associated with these models are not as high as those related to the formal agreement models, but both of these overall models are statistically significant ($p \leqslant 0.01$). The baseline probability of crises terminating in a manner satisfactory to the parties in the context provided by both models is 52 percent.

Reinforcing the results reported in Chapter 4, Table 5.3 shows that when controlling for the effects of the relative power relations of the crisis actors, the relationship between facilitation and actor satisfaction is significant and negative; crises in which facilitation is the highest form of mediation used have only a 25 percent chance of ending with all or most actors being satisfied with the crisis outcome. Thus, when mediators limit their activities to the least substantively intrusive form of mediation, crisis actors are less than half as likely to be content with the outcome than if the crisis was not mediated at all.

The coefficients related to the other styles of mediation – formulation and manipulation – are both positive, consistent with the analysis of actor satisfaction in Chapter 4 and indicate that manipulation as the highest mediation form has the strongest positive effect of all mediation styles. In Model 1, the relationship between manipulation and satisfaction is significant, unlike our findings in Chapter 4, which did not examine power considerations. That is, manipulated crises are more likely than all other crises to end with all or most actors being satisfied with the outcome when controlling for the relative power relations of crisis actors. Controlling for the relative power of the adversaries reveals a clearer relationship between manipulative mediation and actor satisfaction than did the models utilized in Chapter 4 and by Beardsley *et al.* (2004), neither of which accounted for relative power relations. In fact, the results regarding manipulation that are summarized here lend support to Hypothesis 2a, which was presented in Chapter 4.

The relative power relations of the crisis actors also have a significant effect on the probability of a crisis terminating with all or most actors being satisfied. Specifically, we find that crisis actors are more likely to be satisfied with the results of asymmetric crises than symmetric crises. Considering only Model 1, when a crisis involves actors whose power relationship is asymmetric in nature, there is a 52 percent likelihood of all or most of them being satisfied with the outcome (equal to the baseline probability), compared to only 25 percent for situations in which the actors are roughly equal in power.

Contrary to our earlier findings regarding power and the likelihood of formal agreement, the effect of relative power relations on satisfaction levels are consistent with the empirical evidence uncovered by Rubin and Zartman (1995) that negotiations involving power disparity among parties are more likely to result in satisfactory outcomes for all parties. In addition, our findings also support Deutsch's (1973) theory that when disputing parties mutually recognize that a power differential exists between them, they will be more likely to successfully resolve their disputes, as such power disparity makes it more clear who will be expected to make a larger degree of concessions.

ICB data do not reveal any significant relationship between mediator styles and actor satisfaction with outcomes during *specific* relative power scenarios, as neither of the interaction terms that test the combined effect of mediation style and relative power are significant. Thus, we are unable to find any support for Hypotheses 7a through 7c by using historical data. To try to understand the interactive effect of mediator style and relative power, then, we explore this relationship in more depth by using data from the Ecuador-Peru border crisis simulation; the results of this experimental examination are discussed later in this chapter.

Tension reduction

Table 5.4 displays the results of the two models of post-crisis tension reduction, our last ICB measure of crisis outcome. The Likelihood Ratio Chi-squared values associated with these models are quite low, and neither overall model is statistically significant. In general, it appears that both overall models are weak at best in terms of explaining tension reduction.

Nevertheless, we do find evidence that, when controlling for both the relative power relations of the crisis actors and the interactive effect of

Table 5.4 Relative power, mediation style, and tension reduction in ICB

	MODEL 1 *Main effects only*		*MODEL 2* *Main effects + Interaction terms*	
Facilitation	0.884	(0.606)	0.884	(0.606)
Formulation	0.451	(0.330)	1.063**	(0.551)
Manipulation	0.518	(0.373)	0.999	(0.651)
Relative power relations	−0.112	(0.255)	0.147	(0.306)
Formulation × relative power relations	—	—	−0.974	(0.691)
Manipulation × relative power relations	—	—	−0.696	(0.795)
Constant	0.121	(0.238)	−0.082	(0.272)
N	340	—	340	—
LRχ^2	5.75	—	8.20	—
df	4	—	6	—

*$p \leq 0.10$; **$p \leq 0.05$; ***$p \leq 0.005$.

Notes

Standard errors are in parentheses. The dependent variable was operationalized as follows: 0 = post-crisis tension escalation, 1 = post-crisis tension reduction. Crises that terminated toward the end of 1996 and later contain missing data for the tension reduction variable, as the five-year threshold for determining whether or not tensions have been reduced had not yet passed when coding of these cases was completed in fall 2003.

these relations and mediation style (Model 2), formulation has a statistically significant and positive relationship with a post-crisis reduction in tensions. The baseline probability of a crisis being followed by a reduction in tensions in the context of Model 2 in Table 5.4 is 52 percent. This likelihood increases to 74 percent when formulation is the highest form of mediation used in a crisis. This finding lends support to Hypothesis 5a, which was presented and discussed in Chapter 4.

Thus, we discover new insights about the potential utility of formulation over other styles of mediation for contributing to tension reduction: Mediators seem to be especially effective when they have suggestive powers that assist parties in focusing on a specific outcome. Beardsley *et al.* (2004) note that these outcomes should be as closely aligned with the perceived distribution of capabilities between actors as possible. Such an outcome, which formulators can help to uncover, is less likely to leave disputants unsatisfied or feeling like the victims of an unfair set of circumstances in the future; in turn, they will be less likely to seek a modification of the status quo in the future (Beardsley *et al.* 2004).

Despite formulation's *independent* effect on tension reduction, we found no evidence to support any of our hypotheses (H11a through H11c) regarding the *interactive* effect of mediation style and relative power on the nature of post-crisis tensions between actors. The indicators of facilitation and manipulation as highest mediation form also no longer have independent influences on the likelihood of tension reduction when controlling for the relative power relations of the crisis actors. Future tests are needed to see how these interaction terms and the independent effects of mediation style perform in the context of a more robust model of tension reduction that includes a control for relative power relations as well as additional explanatory factors.

Relative power and mediation style in simulated crises

While ICB data allow for some insights into the effect of mediation style and disputants' power relations on crisis outcomes, there are important aspects regarding these relationships that remain elusive when using the historical record. Less can be discerned from ICB about the crisis actors' perceptions of the mediator, and analysis of ICB data is also less useful in pinpointing the potential effect of crisis mediation on measures of crisis dynamics that vary greatly from crisis to crisis, such as the value to crisis actors of agreements reached and the duration of the crisis.

To go beyond what we can investigate using real-world data, we modified our "base" experimental research design centered on a land-dispute crisis between Ecuador and Peru, which we described in detail in Chapter 2. These alterations to our research design allowed us to compare the outcomes of mediated and unmediated crisis negotiations under conditions of power parity and disparity and under varying conditions of mediation style. As in the analyses of ICB data above, we begin with a brief discussion of some methodological issues. We then present the results of experimental analyses, comparing them to the ICB analyses where appropriate.

Methodology

While Chapter 2 contained a thorough description of our basic experimental design, it contained little information about how we altered this design in order to compare outcomes of symmetric versus asymmetric crises. We discuss here the specific details of the simulation modifications. Following this, we present a description of the specific variables used in the experimental analyses and some summary statistics regarding the experimental data collected for the analyses in this chapter. We end this section by presenting how these analyses relate to the set of hypotheses of concern in this chapter.

Relative power and the experimental scenario

As described earlier, the experiments reported on in this book utilize a scenario based on the Ecuador-Peru Border Dispute of 1981. This crisis involved an historical instance of successful mediation after military clashes along the borders of these two states triggered an international crisis. The actual Ecuador-Peru dispute is a classic example of an *asymmetric* crisis. In the 1981 crisis, Peru had an advantage over Ecuador both in terms of capabilities (i.e., aggregate power) and the situation at the core of the dispute (i.e., issue-specific power). Changes to the experimental design were necessary, therefore, to explore the relationship between mediation and power symmetry.

In order to evaluate the impact of mediation styles in conditions of power asymmetry versus power symmetry, the simulation scenario and the accompanying decision-support system were altered to create a situation in which there was no objective power disparity between Ecuador and Peru. Doing so required distorting some of the historical facts of the 1981 crisis. Specifically, Ecuador and Peru were made equals in terms of aggregate power, and the status of the disputed territory was changed so that neither country had sovereignty over this stretch of land. See Appendix B for a discussion of the specific changes that were made to the original power-disparity scenario. In this appendix, both versions of the scenario (power asymmetry and power symmetry) are presented in their entirety.

In Fall 2003, 138 students enrolled in an Introduction to International Relations course at the University of Maryland participated as experimental subjects in the power parity version of the Ecuador-Peru simulated crisis negotiations. Participation was required for this course. As noted in Chapter 4, another 214 participated in the previous asymmetric version of the simulation. Among symmetric crises, 38 percent were unmediated, 32 percent were facilitated, and the remaining 30 percent involved a manipulative mediator, while among asymmetric simulated crises, 28 percent were unmediated, 34 percent involved a facilitator, and 38 percent included a manipulative mediator.

Analyses of experimental data: variables and hypothesis testing

Using experimental data, we employ bivariate cross-tab and difference of means statistical analyses to test the relationships between crisis mediator style, the relative power relationship of crisis actors, and several different measures of crisis outcome, as outlined in H7a, H7b, and H8a through H10b. Specifically, we examine data that were collected on four different outcome measures – expected utility of the outcome, negotiator satisfaction with the outcome, negotiator perception of the mediator's effect on the negotiations, and negotiation duration. Hence, these analyses provide us with a more nuanced and comprehensive understanding of the effects of crisis mediation and relative power relations than an analysis of historical data alone.

Three of the four crisis outcome measures noted in the above paragraph – expected utility of the outcome, negotiator satisfaction with the outcome,[6] and negotiation duration – were analyzed via experimental means in Chapter 4. For an in-depth discussion of these outcomes, their values, and their operationalizations, see the simulation methodology section in Chapter 4.

In order to measure negotiator perception of the mediator's effect on the negotiation process, we required participants in the Ecuador-Peru simulation to complete a post-crisis survey immediately following the conclusion of their simulations. In this survey, participants reported not only on whether they found the outcome of the crisis to be satisfactory to them as negotiators, but if they had a mediator, they were also asked to report whether or not they believed that the mediator effectively helped them to manage their crises. The indicator of perception of the effect of mediation style used in the cross-tab analysis below reflects participants' responses to this question.

It is important to note here that we attempted to collect data for ICB cases on negotiator perception of the mediator's effect on the negotiations during the coding effort described in Chapter 2. We instructed researchers to code the indicator of negotiator perception (MEDVIEW) only if they found statements by relevant public officials indicating their view of the effect of mediation, or if the source they were using specifically indicated the actor's stance on this issue. Reliable information from which to code this variable was sparse, which prevented an accurate coding of the two system-level variables that relied on this actor-level perceptual information – MEDPREF and MEDEDNEG (see Chapter 2). Inability to code these actor-level variables (the missing data rate was roughly 61 percent) means that our analysis of negotiator perception of mediation has had to rely exclusively on experimental data.

Similar to the ICB-based analyses discussed above, the independent variables used in our investigation of experimental data in this chapter are indicators of mediation style, conceived as highest form, and the crisis actors' relative power relations. Simulations were classified as unmediated, mediated by a facilitator, or mediated by a manipulator. They were also classified according to the version of the scenario used for each simulation – power symmetry or power asymmetry.

Results

A comparison of data derived from the two types of relative power scenarios does not provide us with more definitive results regarding the relationship between mediation style and rates of agreement than does an examination of this relationship under conditions of power disparity alone. In addition, while unmediated simulations were less likely to end in agreement than mediated simulations under conditions of power disparity alone (see Chapter 4), a comparison of the rates of agreement among mediated cases in the two power contexts did not differ significantly: 95.3 percent of mediated symmetric crises resulted in an agreement between the Ecuadorian and Peruvian negotiators, while 93.5 percent of mediated asymmetric crises ended in an agreement. Regardless of mediation, we do discover one significant finding regarding the likelihood of agreement vs. war based on an experimental comparison of the two types of power scenarios: participants in the power parity context were significantly more likely to reach an agreement than were those participants working in a context of power disparity among Ecuador and Peru ($\chi^2 = 3.673, p < 0.05$).

Expected utility payoffs

The expected utility payoffs associated with the outcomes achieved by the negotiators demonstrate the degree to which each negotiator was able to serve the needs of the country he or she represented. Analysis of the utility points earned by negotiators under different mediation contexts and in conditions of both asymmetry and symmetry provides an additional measure of the effect of these factors on crisis dynamics and outcome. Table 5.5 displays the results of a pairwise comparison of mean differences in payoffs for negotiators among unmediated, facilitated, and manipulated simulations. (Note that scores for Ecuadorian and Peruvian negotiators have been analyzed separately as each country had unique relative payoff possibilities.)

These data indicate that mediation only had a significant impact on crisis actor payoffs under conditions of asymmetry, and that – when the negotiators represented unequal countries – only manipulative mediation served to improve significantly the payoff earned by the weaker of the two countries, Ecuador. In symmetric crises, the mean payoffs for both Ecuador and Peru increased when a third-party mediator was involved in the negotiations, but the difference between payoffs in mediated and unmediated symmetric crises was not significant. Thus, we find some support for Hypothesis 9a: whereas manipulative mediation affected the outcomes of asymmetric crises – as measured by Ecuador's payoff – it had no significant effect on the outcome of symmetric crises. However, the results do not fully support H9a, as the data reveal no significant difference in payoffs for Peru under different mediation contexts in an asymmetric relationship. In addition, we find no evidence to confirm Hypothesis 9b: facilitative mediation appears to have no greater influence on negotiator payoffs in symmetric crises than it does in asymmetric crises.

Negotiator satisfaction

In general, data collected in post-simulation surveys reveal that negotiators in symmetric crises were only slightly more likely than those in asymmetric crises to be very satisfied with the outcome of the negotiations: 22 percent versus 16 percent. However, these data also reveal that the effects of mediation, and mediation style, on negotiator satisfaction vary under conditions of crisis actor power disparity and parity, as illustrated in Table

Table 5.5 Relative power, crisis mediation, and utility payoffs

Ecuador

		Difference in mean payoffs	
		Asymmetric Crises	*Symmetric crises*
Unmediated	compared to facilitation	+28.0	−53.9
	compared to manipulation	−34.9	−43.2
		n = *31*	*n* = *26*
Facilitation	compared to unmediated	−28	+53.9
	compared to manipulation	−62.8*	+10.7
		n = *36*	*n* = *22*
Manipulation	compared to unmediated	+34.9	+43.2
	compared to facilitation	+62.8*	−10.7
		n = *40*	*n* = *21*

Peru

		Difference in mean payoffs	
		Asymmetric crises	*Symmetric crises*
Unmediated	compared to facilitation	−29.3	−1.8
	compared to manipulation	−68.9	−16.3
		n = *31*	*n* = *26*
Facilitation	compared to unmediated	+29.3	+1.8
	compared to manipulation	−39.6	−14.5
		n = *36*	*n* = *22*
Manipulation	compared to unmediated	+68.9	+16.4
	compared to facilitation	+39.6	+14.5
		n = *40*	*n* = *21*

*$p < 0.05$.

Notes

Significance scores were generated through a Scheffe test, which allows for simultaneous joint pairwise comparisons for all possible combinations of means.

5.6. Under conditions of power asymmetry, negotiators who did not have a mediator involved in their simulation were significantly less likely than others to be very satisfied with the outcome of the negotiation. Only 6.8 percent of negotiators in unmediated, asymmetric crises reported that they were very satisfied following the negotiations, compared to 20.3 percent of those who worked with a facilitative mediator in an asymmetric crisis and 18.3 percent of those whose asymmetric crisis involved a manipulative mediator.

In the symmetric version of the experimental design, however, no significant trends emerge in relation to mediation style and satisfaction. In these symmetric crisis negotiations, then, different mediation styles had no

Table 5.6 Relative power, crisis mediation, and negotiator satisfaction

Asymmetric crises

	Very satisfactory outcome	*Not very satisfactory outcome*	*Totals*
No mediation	3 (6.8%)	41 (93.2%)	44 (24.6%)
Facilitation	13 (20.3%)	51 (79.7%)	64 (35.7%)
Manipulation	13 (18.3%)	58 (81.7%)	71 (39.7%)
Totals	29 (16.2%)	150 (83.8%)	179 (100.0%)

$\chi^2 = 3.883, p = 0.072.$

Symmetric crises

	Very satisfactory outcome	*Not very satisfactory outcome*	*Totals*
No mediation	11 (22.0%)	39 (78.0%)	50 (42.4%)
Facilitation	8 (25.0%)	24 (75.0%)	32 (27.1%)
Manipulation	7 (19.4%)	29 (80.6%)	36 (30.5%)
Totals	26 (22.0%)	92 (78.0%)	118 (100.0%)

$\chi^2 = 0.304, p = 0.430.$

discernible differential effects on negotiators' levels of satisfaction with the outcome.

The trends revealed in the analyses in Table 5.6 support the notion that the power relations between crisis actors are a key determinant in the nature of the relationship between mediation and crisis dynamics. Both facilitative and manipulative mediation have an impact on the likelihood of negotiator satisfaction when there is disparity among disputants, and this mediator effect is muted under conditions of power parity among crisis actors. Hence, there is some evidence to support the arguments made in H7a and H7b. These hypotheses are not confirmed in total, however, because the differences in effect between manipulative and facilitative mediation are minimal.

How do the results of the ICB analysis of negotiator satisfaction compare to those generated from an examination of experimental data? Both sets of data reveal that mediation and the relative power relations of the actors each have some effect on the likelihood of crisis actor satisfaction. However, divergent trends are also apparent from the two different sets of results. In relation to mediation style, we found that facilitation negatively affects actor satisfaction by using ICB data, but that both facilitation and manipulation have a positive impact on satisfaction based on experimental data. We also observe conflicting trends related to the independent effect of relative power relations on actor satisfaction – while symmetric crisis simulations were more likely than asymmetric ones to end with actor satisfaction with the outcome, asymmetric real-world crises are nearly two times more likely than ones characterized by power parity to conclude with all or most actors being satisfied. These divergences between the historical and experimental findings will need to be addressed with more sophisticated designs to be incorporated in future research.

Reaction to mediator

In addition to collecting information from simulation participants about their reaction to the outcome of the simulation, in general, the post-simulation survey also included a question asking those negotiators who had a mediator involved in their simulation if they believed that the mediator effectively helped to manage their crisis. In all, slightly more than half of respondents – 53.3 percent (or 104 out of 195) of participants – reported that the mediator helped crisis management efforts. A closer look at these data, though, demonstrates that a participant's perception of the impact of the mediator was influenced by both the style that the mediator used and whether the participant was involved in a symmetric or asymmetric crisis.

In general, Table 5.7 reports that participants in asymmetric crises were considerably more likely than participants in symmetric crises to find the efforts of the mediator to be helpful, regardless of which mediation style was employed. This evidence supports Hypotheses 8a and 8b, in part. Almost 60 percent of negotiators in crises characterized by disparity between Ecuador and Peru perceived the mediator to be a useful actor in crisis management efforts, whereas less than 45 percent of respondents from crises in which Ecuador was presented to be an equal power to Peru believed that the mediator helped the progress of the crisis towards resolution.

The data presented in Table 5.7, however, demonstrate that the relative power relations of the crisis actors also influence how different styles of mediation are perceived. In asymmetric crises, wherein Peru had a clear power advantage, the style employed by a mediator had no significant effect on participants' responses to the question of the impact of the mediator: 57 percent of those who worked with a facilitative mediator under conditions of power disparity indicated that the mediator helped the crisis negotiation process, while 60 percent of those who worked with a more aggressive, manipulative mediator found the mediator to be a relevant force in bringing the asymmetric crisis to an end.

Table 5.7 Relative power and perceptions of mediator effect on crisis negotiations

Asymmetric crises

	Mediator helped the process	*Mediator didn't help the process*	*Totals*
Facilitation	34 (56.7%)	26 (43.3%)	60 (47.2%)
Manipulation	40 (59.7%)	27 (40.3%)	67 (52.8%)
Totals	74 (58.3%)	53 (41.7%)	127 (100.0%)

$\chi^2 = 0.120, p = 0.365$

Symmetric crises

	Mediator helped the process	*Mediator didn't help the process*	*Totals*
Facilitation	11 (34.4%)	21 (65.6%)	32 (47.1%)
Manipulation	19 (52.8%)	17 (47.2%)	36 (52.9%)
Totals	30 (44.1%)	38 (55.9%)	68 (100.0%)

$\chi^2 = 2.327, p = 0.064.$

However, in symmetric crises, participant perception of the mediator's effectiveness is significantly related to mediation style: 53 percent of negotiators in manipulated symmetric crises felt that the mediator had a positive effect on the negotiations, while only 34 percent of negotiators in facilitated symmetric crises felt this way. Thus, while these results do confirm our expectation that negotiators will be more likely to perceive manipulators, rather than facilitators, as effective, this holds true only under conditions of *power symmetry* among actors. Accordingly, we found evidence that both supports and disconfirms H8a and H8b.

Under conditions of power disparity, then, crisis mediators are seen as influential and relevant by negotiators regardless of which style they employ. This finding, coupled with ICB data which indicate that there is a wider variety of mediation styles employed in asymmetric crises than in symmetric crises (see Table 5.1), supports a position that any involvement of a mediator – ranging from facilitation (such as the providing of "good offices" to disputing states) to manipulation (such as Libyan leader Colonel Qaddhaffi threatening to imprison leaders of North and South Yemen if they didn't agree to resolve their 1972 crisis by unifying into one country) – is likely to have an effect on the evolution and outcome of a crisis.

Findings regarding the perceived lack of mediator impact in symmetric simulated crises involving a facilitative mediator may also help to explain why there have been so few historical facilitated crises involving states of equal power. (As we saw in Table 5.1, a facilitative style of mediation was the highest level of mediation employed in only three of the recorded 40 mediated symmetric crises.) As discussed in Chapter 4, manipulative mediators in the crisis simulations included in their very first messages to the crisis actors recommendations for how to resolve the crisis, and offers of possible rewards and sanctions could be implemented at any time. On the other hand, facilitators began by encouraging parties to work together to find a resolution. Such was the general message of facilitators throughout the simulation, and even if negotiators found themselves in a stalemate or in a situation where hostilities were increasing, the facilitator could not "switch styles" and begin suggesting proposed resolutions.

In the real-world, if a facilitator sensed that it was having little influence in resolving a crisis, it would likely change styles – albeit subtly – and adopt the more substantively intrusive roles of formulator or manipulator, if it had the ability to do so. Thus, in symmetric crises, where parties may be less willing to make concessions and stalemates are more likely, crisis mediators are more likely to move beyond the role of facilitator in order to have an impact on the negotiations and/or outcome.

Duration of crisis negotiations

Experimental research on asymmetric crises revealed that crisis negotiations came to an end significantly more rapidly when a *manipulative* mediator was involved in those negotiations, whereas the average duration of unmediated negotiations did not differ significantly from the average length of those involving a *facilitative* mediator, as noted in Table 4.5. This ability of manipulative mediation to bring a more rapid end to violent and potentially violent crises distinguishes it as a valuable tool for crisis management. As the data in Table 5.8 demonstrate, analyses of experiments involving crisis actors of equal power reveal that neither type of mediation has a significant effect on the duration of a symmetric crisis negotiation.

Since asymmetric crises with manipulative mediation terminated more rapidly than all other crises, we find evidence to support the conjecture put forth in Hypothesis 10a. However, it is apparent that asymmetric crises where facilitation is the highest form of mediation used do not end more quickly than unmediated asymmetric crises. Thus, these results do not confirm Hypothesis 10b.

The data in Table 5.8 also illustrate that the mean duration of negotiations between crisis actors of equal power and involving a manipulative mediator does not differ significantly from those symmetric negotiations involving either a facilitative mediator or no third-party mediator at all.

Table 5.8 Relative power, crisis mediation, and negotiation duration

		Difference in mean duration (measured in minutes)	
		Asymmetric crises	*Symmetric crises*
Unmediated	compared to facilitation	+3.35	+2.92
	compared to manipulation	+13.35*	+3.69
		n=*31*	*n*=*26*
Facilitation	compared to unmediated	−3.35	−2.92
	compared to manipulation	+9.93*	+0.77
		n=*36*	*n*=*22*
Manipulation	compared to unmediated	−13.35*	−3.692
	compared to facilitation	−9.93*	−0.77
		n=*40*	*n*=*21*

*$p<0.05$.

Notes

Significance scores were generated through a Scheffe test, which allows for simultaneous joint pairwise comparisons for all possible combinations of means.

Conclusion

The findings presented in this chapter provide a new cluster of insights into our understanding of the dynamics of crisis mediation. These explorations also demonstrate the value of employing multiple methodologies, including an experimental research design. Analysis of ICB data provided us with a general understanding of how mediation style and the relative power of crisis actors work separately to affect actor satisfaction with outcomes of international crises. These data also demonstrate that different mediation styles are used under different conditions of power symmetry versus asymmetry, and that the likelihood of a formal agreement being reached between parties of a mediated crisis is related to the interaction of the style of mediation adopted and the nature of the power-relations context. The experimental approach allowed us to explore a distinct set of considerations related to crisis mediation. The controlled nature of the experiments facilitated analysis of issues related to how mediation, mediation style, and crisis actor power relations impact the specific utility of crisis outcomes and the duration of crisis negotiations. In addition, the experimental methodology allowed us to collect immediate feedback from subjects, providing us with insights into negotiator satisfaction with outcomes and perception of mediation and mediation style in different power contexts. By combining the findings from analyses of cross-national and experimental data, we are able to develop a much fuller picture of the nature of crisis mediation.

Theorists have long argued that asymmetric crises will be most resistant to the inclusion of a mediator, as a more powerful state might view such a third party as a threat to its power advantage. ICB data on the relative infrequency of mediation in asymmetric crises supports this theory. The importance of this finding is compounded by evidence from both the historical record and simulated crisis negotiations that mediation may have a more significant impact on asymmetric crises than it does on the symmetric crises in which they are actually more often involved.

Crisis actors tend to be more satisfied with the outcomes of asymmetric crises in general, and this is likely due to the fact that these actors can more easily perceive whether the distribution of benefits from the outcomes is aligned with their relative capabilities (Beardsley *et al.* 2004). However, the experimental data also demonstrate that under conditions of power disparity among crisis actors (as it was in about 60 percent of the simulated crisis negotiations we conducted), negotiators who worked with a mediator were significantly more likely to express satisfaction with the outcomes they achieved than were those who did not work with a mediator. No such difference exists among symmetric crises. Similarly, those negotiators involved in asymmetric mediated crises were significantly more likely than those in mediated symmetric crises to believe that the mediator was helpful in getting parties to achieve a satisfactory outcome. An issue remaining for further exploration concerns our inability to find strong relationships in the historical data between actor satisfaction and the interaction terms for power and mediation style.

It is likely that the very inclusion of a mediator in an asymmetric crisis helps change the dynamics of the relationship among the crisis actors even further – the mediator assists parties in understanding the nature of their relations with each other and how that relates to what is expected of them during the negotiation process. As such, it seems that the mediator is tasked with getting the stronger party to put aside its ability to dominate the weaker party and concede to the latter's interests to some degree, while also making sure that the weaker party understands that it will have to compromise its interests to a larger degree than the stronger party.

Distinct results regarding the combined effect of *mediator styles* and relative power relations also exist, and these results demonstrate that mediation style plays an important role in both conditions of power parity and disparity between crisis actors, depending on the specific outcome of concern. For instance, while manipulative mediation seems to have a greater positive effect on crisis processes and outcomes than all other styles of mediation in both symmetric and asymmetric contexts, its distinct effects on different crisis outcomes are dependent on the relative power relations of the disputants. In asymmetric crises, the involvement of a manipulative mediator significantly and positively affects the utility of outcomes achieved by the weaker negotiators more so than when mediators were limited to using facilitative tactics. Simulations involving a manipulative mediator also ended significantly more quickly than did other asymmetric negotiations. Thus, facilitators seem less equipped to accomplish the aforementioned tasks faced by mediators in asymmetric crises. By using their leverage to get each side to concede in ways beneficial to both of them, manipulators are more successful at preventing stronger party domination and removing weaker party intransigence, and hence, ensuring that hostilities don't increase between the parties.

However, these measures of manipulator success do not necessarily translate into negotiators' thinking that the manipulator was more helpful than the facilitator where the parties are unequal in power. While unequal parties are usually more satisfied with crisis outcomes than equal parties, they are not necessarily more satisfied with the activities of manipulative mediators compared to facilitators – manipulators do not always push for agreements that make the unequal parties happy or are truly aligned with the distribution of capabilities between parties. However, it appears that manipulators are viewed as generally more helpful than facilitators during conditions of power symmetry. This is likely due to the fact that when parties are equal in power, it is less clear who is "winning" and who is "losing" a conflict, and who is entitled to more in regard to the issue(s) under dispute. In this atmosphere, it is commonly believed that negotiators will adopt and retain hard-line bargaining positions because neither can overpower the other. As a result, manipulators will be more effective than facilitators at pushing the parties away from these stances because they can employ threats, carrots, and/or sticks to alter the disputants' decision calculi and agree to *any* outcome that overcomes their tit-for-tat strategies. In such instances, Schelling's notion that mediator's proposals are less often accepted "by reason of their inherent fairness or reasonableness than by a kind of resignation of both participants" (1960: 68) may hold true, as both parties are more likely to be engaged in a conflict or attrition when neither side has a clear advantage.

It is not surprising that manipulative mediators in general are more successful at getting crisis disputants to sign a formal agreement to end the crisis that they are embroiled in. However, we also found evidence that when mediators restrict their roles to formulation, they are also highly successful at producing formal agreements when the parties are equal in power. This trend did not exist in relation to manipulative (or purely facilitative) mediation, and additional analyses using more robust models are needed to find out whether manipulators are truly less effective at achieving formal agreements between disputants than formulators.

Finally, we also investigated the interactive effects of mediation and relative power on the likelihood of tensions being reduced between actors. However, the results of this examination are by and large inconclusive. Nevertheless, the general trends in the data on tension reduction are consistent with the results presented in Chapter 4 on this crisis outcome (i.e., facilitative mediation has the strongest positive effect of all mediator styles on tension reduction), with one exception. We did discover a new and interesting finding that formulation is the only style of mediation to have a strong and significant positive effect on tension reduction when one controls for the separate *and* interactive effects of power relations on this crisis outcome. Additional and more complex examinations of the relationship between mediation style, relative power, and post-crisis tension reduction are needed to draw any further concrete conclusions on this matter.

We turn now to an examination of the impact of ripeness on the relationship between mediation and crisis outcomes, by assessing the existence of, and changes to, possible zones of agreement identified by negotiators.

Notes

1 The analysis presented in Chapter 3 looked at the effect that the power relations of disputants has on mediation incidence. However, it has been argued that there is also a relationship between the *power status of the mediator* and the likelihood of mediation, an issue that we do not examine in-depth in this book. Kriesberg (1996) contends that a mediator's position in the power structure of the international system is important in determining whether or not a potential intermediary possesses the proper "status" to mediate. More specifically, he argues that prospective mediators who have greater issue-specific power and influence relative to the conflict of concern will possess greater status to mediate.

2 Successful outcomes are defined differently by each author, ranging from the implementation of ceasefires to the achievement of long-term conflict reduction or resolution.

3 Morgan (1994) also finds evidence that, in general, mediators with greater political and economic capabilities are more likely to prevent war than mediators that lack such capabilities. The key factor here is that manipulative mediators can bring their resources to bear on the outcomes of crises. Since mediators that can adopt a manipulative style typically have greater degrees of such resources than other mediators, one can infer that manipulators will have higher success rates than all other types of mediators.

4 There are 57 cases within ICB for which the power discrepancy score cannot be determined, the vast majority of which are from the pre-World War II and World War II time periods.

5 In 1971, General Amin led a successful military coup against the regime of then-Ugandan President Milton Obote. Obote took refuge in Tanzania immediately after the coup, causing hostile relations between Uganda and Tanzania as Amin accused Tanzanian President Nyerere of supporting a military overthrow of his regime. One month into the 1978–79 crisis, Nyerere stated that Tanzania would be unsatisfied with the outcome of the present hostilities until General Amin was overthrown.

6 Whereas in Chapter 4, we examined whether negotiators were satisfied with the outcome of the crisis, here we consider whether negotiators were *very satisfied* with the outcome. Almost 60 percent of respondents in the symmetric simulation indicated that they were satisfied, while another 22 percent were very satisfied, for a total of 82 percent of respondents indicating some level of satisfaction. Given this overwhelming rate, here we separate out those cases where negotiators were "very satisfied," thereby providing us with a measure of actor satisfaction that contains greater variation.

6 Crisis mediation, ripeness, and zones of agreement

In November 1991, an international crisis involving Armenia and Azerbaijan erupted over the status of the region of Nagornyy-Karabakh, an enclave within Muslim Azerbaijan, but populated overwhelmingly by Armenian Christians. The crisis was triggered by the Azeri government's decision to revoke Nagornyy-Karabakh's standing as an Autonomous Oblast (or region) of Azerbaijan, a designation it had held since 1923. Within weeks, residents within the enclave had organized a referendum, in which an overwhelming majority of the population cast its vote in favor of independence for Nagornyy-Karabakh.

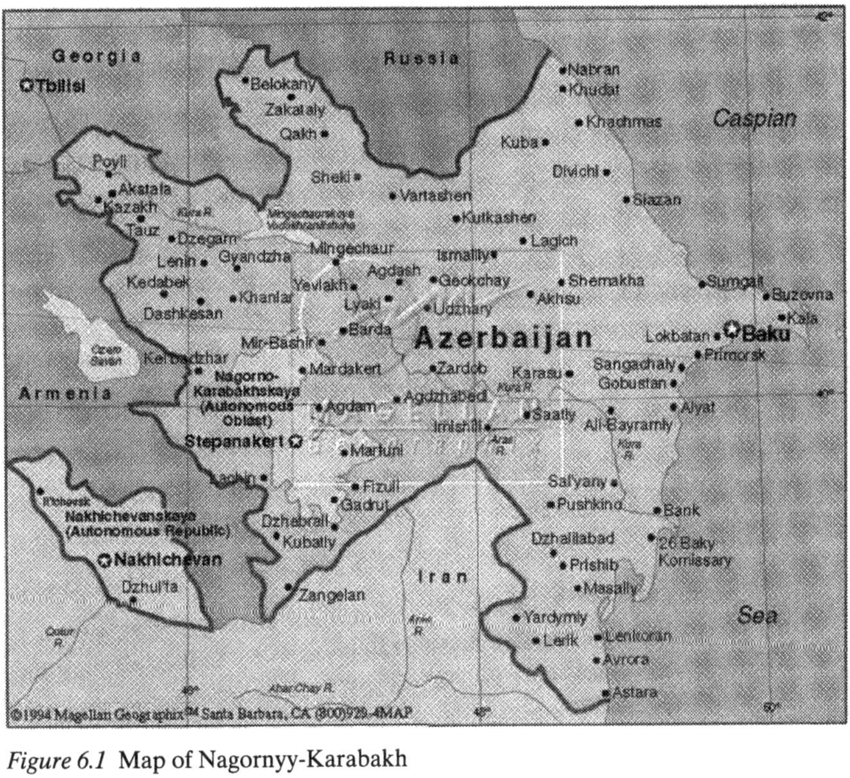

Figure 6.1 Map of Nagornyy-Karabakh

The crisis escalated rapidly, with Azeri and Armenian military forces mobilizing and eventually clashing in and around the disputed territory. The crisis between the two states endured for more than nine months and ended in an unsatisfactory stalemate between the crisis actors. While the crisis eventually faded, military hostilities continued between Armenia and Azerbaijan, and it was not until 1994 that the two countries agreed to a ceasefire.

Mediators, including Russia, Iran, and the Conference for Security and Cooperation in Europe (CSCE, the forerunner of the Organization for Security and Cooperation in Europe (OCSE)), attempted to intervene throughout the 1991–92 crisis, but to no avail. Each mediation effort failed to lead to an end to the crisis or even to an improvement in relations between the disputants. In contrast, mediation efforts by the OSCE in 1994 were the driving force behind the securing of a much-anticipated ceasefire between Armenia and Azerbaijan.

Why was mediation successful in 1994 when it had been so ineffective in 1991–92? Mooradian and Druckman (1999) argue that the differing impact of mediation during these two episodes can best be explained by using the concept of conflict (or crisis) *ripeness*. Whereas in 1992, the conflict was not yet ready to be resolved, by 1994 it was in fact ripe and, as a result, mediators were able to successfully achieve conflict resolution. What had changed? Mooradian and Druckman conclude that, by 1994, both the Armenian and Azeri leaders felt that "both sides had suffered harm that may not be rectified for years" (1999: 723). Between April 1993 and February 1994, approximately 15,000 people were killed as a result of the Armenian-Azerbaijani conflict. In contrast, only 2,000 died in the context of the conflict in 1991 and 1992. This intensification of combat and the dispute in general beginning in the spring of 1993 changed the context of the conflict and the disputants' perceptions of it. The mass casualties prompted both societies and their leaders to come to believe that they would each be better off by resolving the conflict rather than allowing it to continue. By 1994, the leaders of Armenia and Azerbaijan were ready to see the conflict between them end, and, as such, the situation was prime for the intervention by a third party – the OSCE – to capitalize on the situation which, by this time, was ripe for resolution. Had leaders' perceptions of the conflict and of one another *not* changed by 1994, Mooradian and Druckman conclude that this mediation effort would have proven to be unsuccessful as well.

Understanding ripeness

According to Haass (1990), "ripeness is the existence of the prerequisites for diplomatic progress, that is, circumstances conducive for negotiated progress or even solution" (1990: 6). Subsequently, "the absence of ripeness explains why diplomats fail" (Haass 1990: 138–9). (For similar arguments, see also Zartman 1989, 2001; Hancock 2001.)[1] Given this view on the primacy of ripeness as an ingredient for success in the management of international conflicts and crises, one might argue that an essential consideration for a mediator preparing for intervention is *timing*. That is, the timing must be right if a mediator is to have a chance to succeed.

Researchers disagree, though, over whether it is better for mediators to intervene at the beginning or near the end of the conflict process. While some maintain that early intervention is best (see Zartman and Touval 1996), others argue that mediation is most effective when a conflict has already passed through several phases (see Northedge and Donelan 1971; Ott 1972; Pruitt 1981). Still others argue that neither early nor late intervention is particularly effective (see Regan and Stam 2000; Wall, Stark, and Standifer 2001).[2] Bercovitch (1986, 1997), for instance, contends that mediation is most effective when done halfway through the lifecycle of the conflict, after parties' own unmediated efforts have failed. Of course, trying to figure out the halfway point of a conflict while the conflict persists is no small task, as it is impossible to know the endpoint of a conflict or crisis. As Kleiboer (1994) notes, such an appraisal can only be done post-hoc, which is not a useful enterprise for scholars interested in prediction or policy makers faced with time-sensitive decisions regarding whether or not to intervene.

Given the limited value of conceiving ripeness merely as a function of timing, efforts have been made to further specify that "moment" at which a conflict or crisis will become ripe for resolution. Most conceptions of ripeness reflect the essential components identified by Zartman (2001) – changes in the structural nature of the conflict and the disputants' perceptions of the conflict and/or negotiation processes.

Specifically, for a conflict to become ripe, disputants need to be ready and willing to move away from approaches characterized by Fisher and Ury (1981) as *positional bargaining*, whereby adversaries adopt hard-line, diametrically opposed negotiation stances. Fisher and Ury contend that positional bargaining is a severe impediment to concession-making and agreement because it also involves parties attempting to "save face" by insuring that their future actions coincide with their past positions. When parties are "committed to their positions and confrontational policies" (Zartman and Touval 1996: 452), stalemates often follow.

While it is often the case that stalemates also act as severe roadblocks to compromise, agreement, and perceptual change, they can deteriorate to a point at which the parties can no longer tolerate the situation in which they are mired. This set of circumstances is described by scholars as a *mutually hurting stalemate* and is seen as a change in the structural nature of a conflict that acts as the first necessary condition for conflict "ripeness." A mutually hurting stalemate occurs "when the parties find themselves locked in a conflict from which they cannot escalate to (unilateral) victory and this deadlock is painful to both of them" (Zartman 2000:

228; see also Kleiboer 1996). In the Nagornyy-Karabakh conflict described above, Mooradian and Druckman (1999) maintain that Armenia and Azerbaijan each recognized that they were enmeshed in a mutually hurting stalemate when numbers of conflict-related fatalities skyrocketed throughout 1993 and into 1994.

It was at this point during the Nagornyy-Karabakh conflict that Azeri and Armenian leaders both began to recalculate their situations. This reconsideration of the conflict facilitates the second necessary element of a ripe situation: the ability of the disputants to begin to see a "way out" of a conflict. As Coleman (1997) argues, conflict is ripe for resolution only after disputants decide to change their perceptions of the conflict and of their adversaries and to modify their approaches to conflict or crisis resolution, i.e., only after they perceive and decide to pursue a "way out."

The concepts of mutually hurting stalemate and perception of a "way out" are closely linked (Zartman 2000). Zartman and Touval (1996) maintain that, while positional bargaining can and often does stymie conflict resolution efforts, the stalemates that follow from positional bargaining can prompt a needed reconsideration of the conflict situation by disputants. When stalemates regress to a situation in which one or more of the adversaries is no longer able to unilaterally impose a solution to the conflict, "bilateral solutions become conceivable, leading antagonists to believe that there is a workable alternative to combat" (Kleiboer 1996: 363). Explained in game theoretic terms, then, a hurting stalemate appears when the parties' perceptions of their cost/benefit calculi change "from a prisoner's dilemma into a chicken dilemma game" (Zartman 2001: 8–9). Stalemates can lead to disputants' perceptual shifts and reevaluations of hard-line bargaining stances, reevaluations needed to transform a seemingly hopeless situation to one that is ripe for resolution.[3] By undergoing a perceptual shift, Azeri and Armenian leaders in the Nagornyy-Karabakh conflict were eventually able to recognize ways out of the conflict. As a result, mediation efforts following this perceptual shift were successful.[4]

Mediation and ripeness

There is a belief among many theorists and observers that, as noted above, mediation will prove to be fruitless in any situation that has not yet reached ripeness (see, for instance, Rubin 1991; Wall and Lynn 1993; Kleiboer 1996; Greig 2001; Hancock 2001). Haass (1990) maintains that attempts to mediate in conflicts or crises that are not yet ripe can even worsen the conflict at hand. Zartman and Touval (1996) view the issue with a bit more complexity, arguing that there is a paradoxical relationship between ripeness and mediation: the benefits of mediation are only likely to be realized when a conflict escalates to the point that parties are committed to positional bargaining (i.e., are involved in a mutually hurting stalemate), yet mediation is only likely to succeed if the parties can overcome their positional stances and begin to reevaluate their policies (i.e., see a "way out"). Of special importance to the study at hand, Zartman and Touval also add that such reevaluation is highly likely to occur under crisis conditions. Whatever the case may be, it is clear that any analysis of mediation and its effectiveness requires consideration of the question of whether a situation is ripe for resolution.

Others argue, though, that a mediator can play the role of "ripener" – helping to create and/or enhance conditions whereby disputants will be more inclined to make concessions and move towards agreement. Touval and Zartman (1985) contend that, when needed, a mediator must produce the hurting stalemate that leads the parties' "decision toward de-escalation, concession, and compromise" (1985: 16), thus creating an opening for effective mediation. In addition, Young (1967) notes that a mediator can foster ripeness by injecting flexibility into the bargaining situation and thus pushing disputants to reconsider the issues at hand and potential solutions. Likewise, Stevens (1963) argues that a mediator can and should create a domain in which agreement is possible – what he refers to as a contact zone – if one doesn't exist and assist the parties to weigh and rank existing alternative agreements within that domain.

This conception of mediators as catalysts for ripeness runs counter to the idea that ripeness is a prerequisite for mediation, and the analyses in this chapter set out to evaluate how ripeness and mediation interact in crisis situations. The exact nature of this interaction and its precise relationship with crisis outcomes is still in question – while several analysts have noted that ripeness is important, if not necessary, for successful mediation, few have explored this dynamic in a systematic manner. In this chapter, then, we hope to begin to identify the specific mechanisms linking these three factors – mediation, ripeness, and outcome. Consistent with other hypotheses explored in this book, we also pay special attention to the question of how mediator style relates to both the ripeness of a situation and crisis outcome.

Mediation style and ripeness

Much of the literature on mediation and ripeness ignores the fact that mediators can adopt several different styles when intervening. For those studies that do acknowledge the distinctions in mediation style, there is disagreement as to how these different styles might interact with the ripeness of a given situation. Formulation may be particularly helpful once two negotiating parties are in a stalemate because it becomes more and more difficult for each side to see the validity of the other's suggested solutions, and concession is often misconstrued as capitulation. The entrance of a third party with suggestive power can break the stalemate by causing parties to consider, and perhaps even accept, new possible resolutions of the dispute that aren't necessarily part of their former cognitive structure

(Schelling 1960). Besides promoting solutions to the conflict that have already been identified, however, a formulative mediator may also invent solutions (Touval and Zartman 1985), thereby proactively "creating" ripeness where it did not formerly exist.

However, most researchers who advocate creating ripeness or taking advantage of pre-existing ripeness to achieve a settlement point to the use of manipulation. Rubin (1991) and Zartman and Touval (1996) conclude that creating ripeness may involve a much more active engagement of the mediator, moving that role from communication and formulation to manipulation. The manipulator may use carrots and sticks to "cause the minimum point of acceptable agreement ... to change in ways that favor reaching agreement ... to create overlapping bargaining space and the possibility of agreement" (Hopmann 1996: 241). Zartman (2001) suggests that a manipulator is at an advantage versus a facilitative mediator because the manipulative mediator can increase the size of the stakes for the disputants, attracting the parties to share in a "pot" that otherwise would have been too small, or limit the actions of the parties in conflict, providing objective elements to break the stalemate. Edmead (1977) notes that during a hurting stalemate, even a small offer or withholding of mediator resources can induce parties to change their policies. Thus, coercion, sanctions, rewards, and promises can manipulate stalemates so that they begin to "hurt" (Rubin 1991) and create a willingness to concede that was not there previously.

Interestingly, for situations in which hostilities are high (a condition often present in crisis situations), Hiltrop (1985, 1989) argues that the use of pressure tactics by mediators is positively associated with settlement when the parties' bottom line positions are far apart – in other words, when the zone of agreement is small or non-existent. In addition, increasing time pressure (another condition often associated with crises) pushes the mediator to assume a more intrusive role in attempting to expand zones of agreement. Combining this trend with the fact that disputants are also more likely to make concessions under time pressure, and the likelihood of agreement under such conditions is enlarged.

Despite expectations that manipulative mediators will be best equipped to foster and maintain ripeness, Zartman (2001) cautions that the use of manipulative tactics to create ripeness, though often necessary, is nevertheless a delicate and potentially dangerous activity. Hence, manipulation should be used with extreme caution so as not to cause a breakdown in negotiations or move a conflict further away from being ripe for resolution. The analyses that follow explore whether these potential negative effects of manipulation outweigh the predicted positive impact of this style of mediation on the degree to which a conflict is ripe for resolution.

Operationalizing ripeness

Just as disagreement exists over whether a conflict must be ripe before mediation begins, or whether mediation can itself foster ripeness, there is disagreement about how to operationalize this concept. Several authors operationalize ripeness as a function of timing – such as early, midway, or late in the crisis. As discussed earlier, though, this method is post-hoc in nature and has little theoretical connection to the characteristics and mechanisms that affect ripeness.

Mooradian and Druckman (1999) argue that the Nagornyy-Karabakh conflict became ripe after a substantial number of Armenians and Azerbaijanis had been killed. According to this conception, fatalities can serve as an indicator of ripeness. This model, similar to the one adopted by Bercovitch and Langley (1993), provides no guidance, however, for conflicts or crises that have not yet escalated to the point at which hostilities have broken out. Even a cursory review of history reveals that mediation can be effective in conflicts that have not yet reached the point of bloodshed. As such, body counts are only one indicator that a situation *might* be ripe. Finding a more generalizable indicator has proven to be a significant challenge for conflict resolution analysts and policy makers alike.

Berridge notes, "diagnosing 'ripe moments' is not exactly a scientific exercise and it is not always possible to tell if these circumstances exist until they are put to the test, that is, by negotiation" (2002: 200–1). This latter observation – that one won't know whether a conflict is ripe until conflict resolution efforts have begun – gives rise to the concern expressed by Kleiboer (1994) and others that ripeness is a tautological concept. A conflict will be considered ripe if conflict resolution efforts – be it negotiation or mediation – are successful and unripe if these efforts are unsuccessful. Haass (1990), for instance, aims to demonstrate the essential role that ripeness plays in ending a conflict by exploring disputes in the Middle East, over Cyprus, and between India and Pakistan. He concludes that mediation efforts in these conflicts – persisting at the time of his writing in 1990 and as of the writing of this book – failed because these conflicts were not ripe; on the contrary, he argues that mediation efforts in the disputes over the Beagle Channel islands, between Rhodesia and Zimbabwe, and at Camp David between Egypt and Israel succeeded because those conflicts were, in fact, ripe. Case studies like those presented by Haass help enhance our understanding of the challenges that all mediators face in trying to resolve a conflict or crisis, but they do little to reveal how one might recognize ripeness in an on-going conflict.

As noted earlier, few studies have *systematically* analyzed the role that ripeness plays in conflict resolution. Those scholars who have attempted such analyses generally focus their efforts on the hurting stalemate component of ripeness (see, for example, Bercovitch and Langley 1993 and Moordian and Druckman 1999), operationalizing this component of ripeness in terms of conflict cycles or levels of violence, for example. They focus less on the actual processes of reevaluation and perceptual changes (i.e., viewing a "way out") – the second component of ripeness, thought by many researchers to be the most important factor for understanding the impact of ripeness.

In an effort to move beyond the problems associated with both post-hoc conceptualizations of ripeness and a focus on hurting stalemates, we attempted to identify indicators of the "way out" component of ripeness in the cases comprising the International Crisis Behavior (ICB) dataset. We instructed researchers involved in the ICB coding update described in Chapter 2 to seek out information on the actor-level MEDWILCOM variable, using the following question as a guideline: Was the actor willing to compromise before mediation occurred? We planned to use the coding of this variable to appraise the "ripeness" of crises as mediation was initiated by evaluating whether or not the crisis actors had begun to overcome their positional bargaining stances and reevaluate their policies (that is, see a "way out"), indicated by concessionary moves.

As was the case with the actor-level variable measuring the disputant's view of the effects of mediation (described in Chapter 5), coders were to record values for this variable only if they found actual statements by relevant public officials indicating a willingness to compromise, or if the source they were using specifically indicated the actor's stance related to compromise as mediation began. However, it was quickly apparent that, along with the actor's view of the effect of mediation, this would be among the most difficult variables to code. Reliable actor-level information was sparse, and as a result, we also had problems coding the corresponding system-level variable that relied on this information – the proportion of all crisis actors that expressed a willingness to compromise before mediation occurred (MEDCOMP). After concerted efforts by researchers, data remained missing for these variables for roughly 53 percent of mediated crises. Furthermore, we concluded that the conceptualization of a "way out" as indicated by these variables was insufficient: just because two disputants are willing to compromise independent of each other does not mean that they *mutually share* a vision of a "way out" or that such a "way out" exists from an objective standpoint. This additional reflection on our conceptualization of crisis ripeness combined with the frustrations faced in trying to collect systematic data on this phenomenon encouraged a rethinking of how we might operationalize the mutually acceptable "way out" and its relationship to mediation.

Using an experimental approach, we decided to borrow a page from the negotiation literature and focus on the bargaining space between disputants in seeking to operationalize the concept of a mutually acceptable "way out." Specifically, we measure this component of ripeness by looking at the *zone of agreement* (ZOA) created by the respective reservation prices (i.e., the "bottom" or "red" lines – see Fisher and Ury 1981) of the disputants in a conflict or crisis.[5] The lower an actor sets its reservation price, the more concessions it should be willing to make during a negotiation, and the more conducive to resolution the conflict will be. If *all* actors in a conflict have relatively low reservation prices, there is likely to exist a substantial zone of agreement, or range of outcomes acceptable to all parties. Figure 6.2, from Raiffa (2002), presents a classic depiction of the zone of agreement in terms of the reservation levels of a buyer and a seller.

The existence of a zone of agreement (ZOA) indicates that there exist outcomes conducive to a peaceful resolution of a conflict or crisis. In principle, any agreement that lies within this space should be acceptable to both sides (Hopmann 2001). The objective existence of a zone of agreement does not mean, however, that parties will be able to identify those solutions. Morgan (1994), for instance, points out that even if a ZOA exists, the parties may still reject an agreement within this zone if that agreement does not rise to the most beneficial outcome from their perspective (i.e., their "green" lines). Disputants may decide that the risk of continuing the conflict or crisis is worthwhile because unilateral victory would produce an outcome that is more beneficial to them, or they may determine that rejection of an agreement that lies within the ZOA may lead to a better offer from their adversary.

Thus, the existence of a ZOA does not ensure agreement, and conflicts for which a ZOA exists can elude resolution. This is where mediation plays a key role: the involvement of a mediator can help to increase the chances that disputants will find the outcomes that are within that ZOA. Furthermore, as Hopmann (2001) notes, disputants will be more likely to identify acceptable outcomes when there is a *larger* ZOA, indicating more possibilities for such agreement.

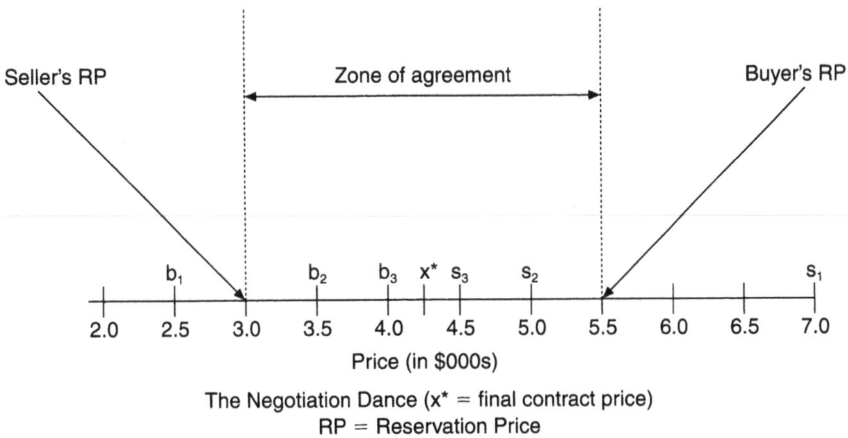

Figure 6.2 Zone of agreement

Source: Reprinted by permission of the publisher from *Negotiation Analysis: The Science and Art of Collaborative Decision Making* by Howard Raiffa, p. 113, Cambridge, Mass.: The Belknap Press of Harvard University Press, Copyright © 2002 by the President and Fellows of Harvard College.

We see a direct relationship between the existence of a ZOA, the breadth of that ZOA, and whether a conflict is ripe for resolution. The more expansive the ZOA, the more acceptable possibilities for agreement (or "ways out") are available, the more likely that those "ways out" will be evident to disputants, and the more likely that the conflict will be ripe for resolution. Similarly, the smaller the ZOA in a specific situation, the less likely the conflict is ripe; and the absence of a ZOA altogether indicates that a conflict is unripe and that conflict resolution or management efforts will likely be futile under current conditions.

Using ZOAs as an indicator of ripeness allows us to look at ripeness not just as a dichotomous variable – a crisis is or is not ripe – but also to look at *degrees* of ripeness. Little research has been done on the impact that different degrees of ripeness might have on the outcomes of mediated negotiations. Many game theoretic approaches to ripeness indicate that there may be such a phenomena as too much ripeness – too large a "way out." Morrow (1992) indirectly suggests that an expansion of the ZOA might not assist in crisis resolution because it may complicate the bargaining situation such that negotiations may fail, while Krasner (1991) argues that increasing the number of possible Pareto optimal outcomes, associated with expanding ZOAs, may exacerbate competition over the distribution of gains in those outcomes.

This chapter will focus on the absence or presence and nature of a "way out" in crisis negotiations, how many different "ways out" exist in any particular dyadic negotiation, whether mediation in general or a specific style of mediation expands the number of "ways out" available to negotiators and/or leads them to a specific way out by inducing them to reassess their reservation price, and the relationship between the perception of an acceptable agreement and the outcome of a crisis.

Zones of agreement, mediation style, and outcome

Most scholars are in agreement that ripeness is an important factor in determining whether or not a conflict or crisis will be resolved. We concur with this assessment and argue that a crisis is much less likely to follow a path to war if it is "ripe" for resolution. Furthermore, we contend that the *degree* of ripeness will also affect how successfully a crisis is managed and/or resolved. Our conjectures regarding this effect run contrary to the warnings of many game theorists, as noted above. We contend that a larger ZOA (i.e., a higher degree of ripeness), in fact, should facilitate successful resolution to a particular crisis more so than lesser degrees of ripeness. Returning to several of the crisis outcome measures that we have utilized throughout the experimental analyses, we argue:

Hypothesis 12: The larger the initial zone of agreement between negotiators, the more likely the crisis will be to end in agreement, rather than war.

Hypothesis 13: The larger the initial zone of agreement between negotiators, the more likely are these actors to be satisfied, rather than dissatisfied, with the outcome of the crisis.

Hypothesis 14: The larger the initial zone of agreement between negotiators, the greater the benefit these actors will achieve at the conclusion of the crisis.

We also concur with those who argue that ripeness is an important factor in determining the effectiveness of a mediator, but we do not believe that a situation must be ripe before a mediator should intervene. Rather, we are in agreement with those who contend that mediators can help to make a situation ripe – that is, act as a "ripening agent" – by encouraging or pushing the parties to compromise and shift their initial reservation prices. While we feel that all mediators can act as "ripening agents," we believe that manipulative mediators have a greater capacity to affect the ripeness of a situation, and that this is one of the reasons that manipulation has proven to be a successful approach to crisis management. More specifically, we propose:

Hypothesis 15a: Crises in which manipulative mediation is used will exhibit greater expansion of the zones of agreement between negotiators than all other crises.

Hypothesis 15b: Crises in which facilitative mediation is used will exhibit greater expansion of the zones of agreement between negotiators than unmediated crises.

Hypothesis 16: Crises in which manipulative mediation is used will be more likely to result in negotiators perceiving the mediator as having a modifying impact on their individual bargaining zones than crises in which facilitative mediation is the highest form of mediation.

Following from this, and acting essentially as a set of corollary hypotheses to H12 through H14, we also offer a series of propositions related to the dynamic nature of zones of agreement and its effect on crisis outcomes. If mediators, and especially manipulators, can expand zones of agreement, then in line with our conjectures regarding the breadth of zone of agreement and crisis outcomes, we also suggest that the likelihood of crises being successfully resolved is linearly and directly related to the degree of expansion that zones of agreement undergo. Mediators, then, can act through the mechanism of expanding zones of agreement to more effectively manage crises. Thus, we contend:

Hypothesis 17: The greater the expansion of the zone of agreement between negotiators during the course of crisis negotiations, the more likely the crisis will be to end in agreement, rather than war.

Hypothesis 18: The greater the expansion of the zone of agreement between negotiators during the course of crisis negotiations, the more likely are these actors to be satisfied, rather than dissatisfied, with the outcome of the crisis.

Hypothesis 19: The greater the expansion of the zone of agreement between negotiators during the course of crisis negotiations, the greater the benefit these actors will receive at the conclusion of the crisis.

In their review of U.S. involvement in Israeli-Egyptian relations, Mandell and Tomlin (1991) note that National Security Adviser Henry Kissinger used mediation to change the cost/benefit views of Israel and Egypt in the process of helping them find "a new zone of agreement between the parties by redefining key issues" (1991: 52). Our analysis is designed to see whether mediators can, in fact, succeed in expanding zones of agreement and how static and dynamic aspects of the ZOA in a particular situation affect the outcome of a crisis.

ZOA and mediation style in an experimental setting

In order to gain a better understanding of the interactions among the central factors of ripeness, mediation, and crisis outcomes, we conducted a series of experiments that allow us to track the breadth of the ZOA and its changes during mediated and unmediated crisis negotiations, as well as during different types of mediated negotiations – those where the mediator adopted a facilitative style versus those involving a manipulative mediator. Our research design also provides us with direct feedback about negotiators' perceptions of mediation and with a range of data on the nature of the outcomes of crisis negotiations, as indicated by the aforementioned hypotheses. After discussing several aspects of the experimental design as it relates to ZOAs from a methodological standpoint, we present the results of analyses that we conducted using experimental data. The data from these experiments allow us to evaluate the degree to which ripeness is a prerequisite for successful mediation and whether different mediation styles have different effects on the ripeness of a conflict.

ZOA and the experimental scenario

In real-world cases, there are an infinite number of possible crisis outcomes. Furthermore, it is rarely the case that one can get reliable or accurate information from disputants about their respective reservation prices, a point clearly demonstrated by the difficulties we faced when attempting to collect ICB data on zones of agreement. Some information on goals might be available from officials following the conclusion of a conflict, but this information is likely to be skewed not only by the passage of time but reaction to the actual outcome of the conflict. Consciously or not, in recollecting a conflict, officials may tend to align their *original* goals with the ultimate outcomes of the conflict or crisis.

Given the challenges of examining zones of agreement in historical cases, we have opted for an experiment-based analysis. Like other analyses in this book, the experiments reported on here are based on simulated negotiations between Ecuador and Peru at the time of the 1981 border crisis.[6] A modification to the general experimental methodology was needed, however, in order to measure ZOAs in the simulation context.

For the purposes of measuring ZOAs among crisis negotiators, we did not change the scenario or materials presented to student participants but, rather, collected additional information from them throughout the course of the simulated crisis negotiations. Participants during the ripeness-focused simulations were asked to complete additional survey questions before, during, and after the simulation. These questions asked participants to record their respective reservation prices in terms of the number of utility points that they were trying to earn for their state.

After training but before the experiments began, each negotiator was asked to examine the decision-support system (DSS) for his/her country in order to assess the desirability of different conditions and outcomes and to determine his/her individual bargaining zone in terms of utility points. Negotiators then recorded (but did not share with either their adversary or mediators) the amount of utility points they hoped to earn for their country (their ultimate goal, i.e., their "green line") and their reservation price (or "red line") – the lowest amount they would be willing to accept before choosing to opt out. Participants were asked to record their goals and reservation prices again at the beginning of each ten-minute negotiating round.

Unlike real-world situations, the controlled setting of our experiments provides a finite (although large) number of possible outcomes to the simulated Ecuador-Peru crisis. A total of 416 possible outcomes existed for negotiations that were either unmediated or involved facilitative mediation, while, for negotiations with a manipulative mediator, a total of 13,312 possible outcomes existed. (The manipulative simulations have a far greater number of possible payoff outcomes due to the manipulative mediators' "carrots and sticks," which affect the outcomes for each of the states involved.) Each of these possible outcomes would deliver a distinct utility-point payoff to both Ecuador and Peru.

In order to determine whether a ZOA existed and, if so, the extent of the ZOA at the outset of each simulation, we examined the initial reservation prices reported by the negotiators in a dyad and determined the set of possible outcomes that would allow each negotiator in the dyad to achieve its minimum-acceptable outcome or better. That is, we determined the breadth of the ZOA between the negotiators, defined as the ratio of all possible outcomes that provided both Peru and Ecuador with utility points equal to or greater than the reservation price of each to the total number of possible outcomes. The higher the ratio, the larger the ZOA. Thus, we can measure whether each crisis dyad was ripe (an absence of a ZOA indicated no ripeness) and the degree to which each was ripe. Data reported by negotiators during each round of the simulation also allowed us to track whether ZOAs in each simulation dyad contracted, expanded, or remained the same throughout the course of the negotiation.

In order to examine the issues of ripeness, as measured by zones of agreement, and mediation style, a total of 52 crisis simulations were conducted using students at the University of Maryland enrolled in an undergraduate International Negotiation course in Fall 2001 and Fall 2002. Of these 52 simulations, 37 percent were unmediated, 33 percent involved a facilitative mediator, and the remaining 30 percent of simulations involved a manipulative mediator.

Analyses of experimental data: variables and hypothesis testing

As established in previous chapters, we use a combination of statistical techniques to analyze each of the relationships related to ZOA and mediation that are described in Hypotheses 12 through 19. Specifically, we utilize logistic regression analyses to examine the effect that mediation, ZOAs, and changes in ZOAs have on the likelihood of a formal agreement being reached and negotiator satisfaction with the crisis outcome, both of which are dichotomous indicators. On the other hand, we use linear regression analysis to examine the two relevant continuous indicators – the number of utility points earned by the actors in the dyad at the conclusion of a crisis and the change in zone of agreement that each dyad underwent throughout the course of the crisis. Finally, we use bivariate cross-tab analysis to investigate negotiators' perceptions of the effect that mediators had on individual bargaining zones.

Two of the dependent variables analyzed in this chapter are exclusive to our examination of mediation and ZOA. The change in ZOA variable is an indicator of the total *change* in the ratio used to measure ZOA (described above) from the beginning until the end of the crisis. The negotiator perception variable is a dichotomous indicator of the answer that participants gave to the survey question asking them whether they thought the mediator affected their own bargaining zones (0 = no, 1 = yes). For an in-depth discussion of all other crisis outcome variables used in these analyses, their values, and their operationalizations, see Chapter 4.

In our analyses of the effect of initial ZOA on several crisis outcomes, our main explanatory variable is the initial ZOA itself, which is operationalized as the ratio described earlier. We also consider mediation style conceived as "highest form" in these analyses.[7] These mediation style indicators are used as independent variables in the analysis of negotiators' perceptions of the mediator's effect on their individual bargaining zones.

In all relevant examinations, "no mediation" is used as the reference category when interpreting the corresponding results. Finally, to control for the differential effects that each negotiator's utility value may have on the total dyadic utility score used as a measure of crisis outcome, we also include a dichotomous indicator of the country of the negotiator in these specific regression equations, with 0 indicating Ecuador and 1 indicating Peru.

Results

Unripe crises

Within our pool of simulations (52 total), only four can be categorized as wholly unripe – that is, no initial zone of agreement existed in these cases. Negotiators in these simulations set their reservation prices in such a way that none of the possible 416 outcomes would have satisfied both negotiators as the simulation began. Interestingly, while only 26.7 percent of all simulations resulted in war versus agreement among the parties, *all four* unripe crises resulted in one of the parties launching a military attack against the other.

While it is impossible to draw statistically significant conclusions from such a small sample, these findings are notable nonetheless for lending modest support to the notion that some degree of ripeness is needed for effective conflict or crisis resolution efforts (see especially Zartman 1989, 2001; Haass 1990; Mooradian and Druckman 1999; Hancock 2001). More specific to the question of mediation, two of the four unripe simulations were unmediated, while the remaining two occurred under conditions of facilitative mediation. There were no cases in which a manipulative mediator worked in an unripe crisis. It may be the case that manipulators would have sufficient power and leverage to help foster ripeness even in situations that lacked an initial ZOA, but investigation of this question will be left to future research.

Impact of initial zones of agreement

The mean zone of agreement at the outset of these simulations was 0.263 (SD = 0.223). The breadth of initial zones of agreement ranged from 0 (as noted above) to 0.80. That is, in the ripest case, 80 percent of the possible agreements in the simulation would have satisfied the initial reservation prices of both Ecuador and Peru, while in the most typical case, 26 percent of all possible agreements would have satisfied these initial parameters.

While it was noted that all unripe crises ended with the use of force, we expand our analysis to examine to what degree the breadth of this initial ZOA affects the outcome of the crisis for all cases, controlling for the impact that different styles of mediation and country type have on the relationship between initial ZOA and crisis outcomes. Findings on this question are presented in Table 6.1.

Model 1 reveals an overall weak relationship between the initial breadth of the ZOA, mediation and mediator style, and the likelihood of agreement in a given crisis. The Likelihood Ratio Chi-squared value associated with Model 1 is low, and the overall model is not statistically significant. As with other simulation data, a disproportionately high percentage of all dyads resulted in agreement (rather than war), perhaps because students thought they were supposed to avoid war. These experimental results regarding mediation and agreement are consistent with those presented in Chapter 4, which are used for comparative purposes since all simulations conducted for the analyses in both that chapter and the current one were conducted using the "base" scenario characterized by power disparity between Ecuador and Peru.

Regardless of the insubstantial explanatory power of Model 1 taken as a whole, we do find that the breadth of the initial ZOA between negotiators does significantly and positively affect whether disputants achieve an agreement versus one of the disputants declaring war. The baseline probability of crises terminating in agreement rather than war when all dichotomous variables are held at their modal values and all interval variables are held at their mean values is roughly 67 percent in the context provided by Model 1. This means that a case in which 26 percent of all possible agreements would have satisfied the initial minimum goals of both Ecuador and Peru still has a 67 percent chance of terminating in agreement. A completely unripe crisis, on the other hand, has a 54 percent chance of concluding with an agreement. In contrast, negotiators in the most ripe crisis in our universe of analysis (wherein the initial ZOA included 80 percent of all possible outcomes) would have an 83 percent chance of avoiding war. While these percentages are high, they are not absolute, giving us an indication that something else besides mediation and the initial ZOA is contributing to the generally high number of cases ending in agreement.

Model 2 reveals the absence of a significant relationship between each independent variable and whether an individual negotiator is satisfied with the outcome of a crisis. Thus, while our analyses in Chapter 4 indicated that whether or not a crisis is mediated affects negotiator satisfaction on its own, this is no longer the case when we hold constant the initial ZOA between these negotiators.

On the other hand, Model 3, which measures the effect of initial ZOA on negotiators' utility point payoff, is statistically significant (adj. $R^2 = 0.385$, $p < 0.000$). According to this model, the mean payoff for an Ecuadorian negotiator working without a mediator was 376 out of 1,000. Peruvian negotiators, on the other hand, collected an average payoff of 508. This significant difference is not surprising, given the power discrepancy between Ecuador and Peru in the structure of these simulations, and

Table 6.1 Initial ZOA, mediation style, and crisis outcome

	MODEL 1 *Agreement reached*		*MODEL 2* *Negotiator satisfaction*		*MODEL 3* *Utility points earned*	
Initial ZOA	2.174*	(1.672)	1.213	(1.010)	41.208	(59.705)
Facilitation	0.600	(0.807)	−0.502	(0.504)	30.097	(30.865)
Manipulation	0.874	(0.825)	−0.044	(0.523)	63.372**	(31.564)
Country of negotiator[†]	—	—	—	—	204.5***	(25.531)
Constant[‡]	0.179	(0.626)	0.535	(0.426)	376.240***	(29.041)
N	52 dyads	—	104 negotiators	—	103 negotiators	—
$LR\chi^2$	2.784	—	2.354	—	—	—
Adj. R^2	—		—		0.385***	
df	3	—	3	—	4	—

*$p \leq 0.10$; **$p \leq 0.05$; ***$p \leq 0.005$.

Notes
Standard errors are in parentheses.
[†]Baseline case in this model is negotiator as Ecuador.
[‡]Baseline case in this model is an unmediated simulation.

is consistent with the findings in Chapter 4. This model also reveals that utility-point payoffs increase significantly under the condition of manipulative mediation (versus no mediation). Consistent with findings in Chapter 4, facilitative mediation has no significant effect on payoffs in an asymmetric crisis situation – the payoffs associated with facilitation are not significantly different than those associated with unmediated crises. Most relevant to the hypotheses presented in this chapter, though, Model 3 indicates that the extent of the zone of agreement at the outset of a crisis negotiation has no significant impact on the utility-point values achieved, regardless of the style of mediation that is used in this crisis.

In sum, the breadth of the initial ZOA between crisis actors only seems to be a determinant of whether or not a crisis terminates in war. Consistent with Hypothesis 12, we find that the larger the initial ZOA between crisis actors, the more likely the crisis is to end with the actors signing an agreement, rather than one of them launching a military attack. Despite the significant effect that the static degree of ripeness has on this outcome measure, we find no evidence supporting H13 or H14 – "riper" crises are not more or less likely than other crises to conclude with actors being satisfied with the outcome, and they do not provide crisis actors with significantly different payoffs than other crises.

Mediation and zone of agreement changes

As noted, many practitioners and observers alike believe that mediators can serve to ripen a conflict, to transform it into a situation better positioned for resolution. We hypothesize that manipulative mediators will be better equipped to affect negotiators' individual reservation prices and, subsequently, their collectively constructed zones of agreement, due to their ability to offer inducements and threaten sanctions against the parties involved in a crisis. Unlike facilitators, manipulators can also propose new, alternative solutions that – left to their own devices – the negotiators may not have explored.

Our experimental research design allows us to explore the effect of mediation on the evolution of zones of agreement and to examine in detail the degree to which mediation style is relevant in this relationship. As the results displayed in Table 6.2 demonstrate, mediation style is, in fact, a significant consideration when looking at the ability of a mediator to impact ZOAs.

Both facilitation and manipulation have a significant impact on the degree to which a ZOA changes in a simulation, but the effects of these two styles of mediation are radically different. ZOAs in unmediated simulations, on average, contracted by 6 percent; these situations actually became less ripe over time. Facilitators are associated with an even more dramatic contraction of the ZOA than crises that involve no mediator. The ZOA between crisis actors shrank by more than 14 percent during the

Table 6.2 Mediator style and zone of agreement changes

	Change in ZOA	
Facilitation	−0.0791**	(0.046)
Manipulation	0.09102**	(0.046)
Constant†	−0.0634**	(0.030)
N	52 dyads	—
Adj. R^2	0.088***	
df	3	—

*$p \leq 0.10$; **$p \leq 0.05$; ***$p \leq 0.005$.

Notes
Standard errors are in parentheses.
†Baseline case in this model is an unmediated simulation.

course of an average facilitated crisis. Manipulative mediation, on the other hand reverses the trend toward ZOA contraction and actually leads to about a 3 percent expansion of the ZOA during the course of the negotiation.

Thus, while we find support for Hypothesis 15a regarding the effect of manipulation on ZOAs, we find evidence that counters our claim in Hypothesis 15b concerning the effect of facilitation. These results do give further credence, however, to one of the main arguments of this book: it is important to account for the distinct effects of mediation style when analyzing how mediation affects crisis processes and outcomes. If we had not conceptually disaggregated the phenomenon of mediation into distinct categories of activity, we would not have discovered a statistically significant relationship between mediation and changes in ZOAs. However, we find evidence to support those scholars who point to manipulation in particular as the strongest possible "ripening" mediation activity (see especially Rubin 1991; Hopmann 1991; Zartman and Touval 1996; Zartman 2001). Given the independent influence that time has on ZOA change in our simulations, the observed effect of manipulation is even more impressive since crises with a manipulative mediator end more rapidly than all other crises. Thus, manipulation has a larger effect on ZOA expansion in a smaller amount of time.

As noted, participants in these mediated simulations also completed post-crisis surveys, in which they reported whether they believed that the mediator affected their respective bargaining zones throughout the course of the negotiation. Interestingly, the survey results indicate that participants were aware of the effect that manipulative mediators had on encouraging negotiators to redefine their goals, as the data in Table 6.3 reveals.

Of the 59 participants whose simulations involved a mediator and who reported a change in their reservation price, 59 percent (or 35 respondents) indicated that the mediator was at least somewhat responsible for the change in their reservation price. Those participants who worked with

Table 6.3 Participants' perception of mediator effect on zone of agreement

	Mediator had an effect on ZOA	*Mediator had* no *effect on ZOA*	*Totals*
Facilitation	12 (42.9%)	16 (57.1%)	28 (47.5%)
Manipulation	23 (74.2%)	8 (25.8%)	31 (52.5%)
Totals	35 (59.3%)	24 (40.7%)	59 (100.0%)

$\chi^2 = 5.897, p < 0.007$.

a manipulative mediator, though, were significantly more likely than those who worked with a facilitator to credit the mediator with affecting individual bargaining zones and, subsequently, collective zones of agreement. Almost three-fourths of those who worked with a manipulative mediator reported that the mediator had an impact on their willingness to modify reservation levels and goals, while less than half of those participants who worked with a facilitative mediator indicated that changes were a result of the efforts of the third party. Thus, we find evidence to support our contention in Hypothesis 16.

Zone of agreement changes and crisis outcome

We have argued that manipulative mediation's ability to expand zones of agreement may be one of the reasons why we find manipulative mediation to be a highly successful means of crisis management. Since success in these terms is defined as a manipulator's ability to produce specific crisis outcomes, this argument assumes that there is also a significant relationship between the expansion of the zone of agreement in a crisis and its outcome. Table 6.4 displays results from analyses intended to explore this assumption.

The findings presented in this table demonstrate that ZOA change does have a significant impact on whether or not a crisis ends in agreement, but that no significant relationship exists between this independent variable and negotiator satisfaction or utility points earned. The absence of a significant impact of ZOA change on these latter two measures of crisis outcome raises questions about whether and to what degree it is the ability of manipulators to change ZOAs that leads to favorable crisis outcomes. As it is, then, we find no evidence that confirms the arguments we put forward in H18 and H19.

Even more questions are raised, however, by the nature of the relationship between ZOA change and the likelihood of agreements, represented by Model 1 in Table 6.4. The Likelihood Ratio Chi-squared value associ-

Table 6.4 Zone of agreement changes and crisis outcome

	MODEL 1 *Agreement reached*		*MODEL 2* *Negotiator satisfaction*		*MODEL 3* *Utility points earned*	
Change in ZOA	−2.846*	(2.099)	−0.595	(1.077)	−47.75	(65.33)
Country of negotiator†	—	—	—	—	205.80***	(26.20)
Constant‡	0.978***	(0.329)	0.616***	(0.216)	409.72***	(18.94)
N	51 dyads	—	102 negotiators	—	102 negotiators	—
$LR\chi^2$	2.242*	—	0.314	—	—	—
Adj. R^2	—		—		0.374***	
df	1	—	1	—	2	—

*$p \leq 0.10$; **$p \leq 0.05$; ***$p \leq 0.005$.

Notes

Standard errors are in parentheses.

†Baseline case in this model is negotiator as Ecuador.

‡Baseline case in this model is an unmediated simulation.

ated with Model 1 is low, indicating that its overall explanatory power is also minimal, but the overall model is statistically significant ($p \leq 0.10$). There is a statistically significant relationship between ZOA change and the likelihood of agreements, but it is in the opposite direction as that proposed in Hypothesis 17. We find that this relationship is *negative*, indicating that an *increase* in the breadth of a zone of agreement actually *reduces* the chances that a crisis will end in agreement.

The baseline probability of crises terminating in agreement rather than war when the indicator of ZOA change is held at its mean value is roughly 75 percent in the context provided by Model 1. Since the mean change in ZOA from the outset to the conclusion of a simulation was −0.060 (SD = 0.202), this means that a case in which the ZOA between negotiators decreased by 6 percent from the beginning to the end of the negotiation has a 75 percent chance of terminating in agreement. If there was no change in ZOA between actors, this likelihood equals 72 percent. The changes in ZOA in our experiments ranged from −0.796 (a decrease of 80 percent) to 0.260 (an increase of 26 percent). At the low end of this spectrum, a crisis has a 90 percent chance of terminating in agreement; at the high end, a crisis only has a 56 percent chance of concluding in this manner.

Model 3, which considers the effect of a change in ZOA on the expected utility payoff for a negotiator while controlling for which country the negotiator represented, is statistically significant overall (adjusted $R^2 = 0.374$). However, the variation in expected utility payoff explained by this model results from changes in the control variable – the country role of the negotiator – rather than from changes in ZOA, whose indicator is not statistically significant. Not surprisingly, given the context of power asymmetry in this model, Peru received higher average payoffs at the conclusion of a crisis than did Ecuador.

Bearing in mind that the simulations analyzed in this chapter have a 73.3 percent agreement rate, it is not shocking that crises are still more than half as likely to end in agreement with any degree of change in ZOA under consideration. However, it remains a matter of fact that expansion of the ZOA between actors lessens their likelihood of reaching an agreement. Even though ZOA change is not significantly related to negotiator satisfaction or expected utility payoff, the coefficients associated with this indicator of ZOA change are negative in the models of both of these crisis outcomes. These results raise questions about whether and to what degree it is the ability of manipulators to change ZOAs that leads to favorable crisis outcomes. Thus, it seems that there is another mechanism at work behind the success of mediation in general, and especially manipulation.

Conclusion

In this portion of the study, we provided an overview and analysis of the effect that crisis ripeness has on the ability of mediators to influence the outcome of a crisis. Using an experimental method allowed us to move beyond the limited conception of ripeness-as-hurting-stalemate to concentrate on the perceptual change that many scholars and practitioners feel is the crux of the phenomenon of ripeness: for a conflict or crisis to de-escalate, exhibit compromise on the part of one or more parties, and/or conclude with an agreement, the disputants need to see a "way out" of the crisis. Concentrating on this "way out" aspect, we utilized an innovative operationalization of ripeness for empirical studies of negotiation and mediation. Borrowing the concept of zone of agreement from the negotiation literature, we offered one of the first applications of this principle via the medium of quantitative analysis of international negotiation and mediation. In addition, we presented one of the first applications of ripeness conceived of and measured as a continuous variable. The results of this endeavor were both informative and puzzling, and future work is encouraged and needed in order to hone our understanding of the concept of ripeness-as-zone-of-agreement.

The main findings of the analyses contained in this chapter are summarized as follows. The breadth of the zone of agreement between crisis actors, whether envisaged in either static or dynamic terms, has a significant effect on the likelihood of a crisis terminating in agreement versus war. However, the static and dynamic conceptions of ZOA are found to have divergent effects on this likelihood. While a larger ZOA at the outset of a negotiation increases the chances that a crisis will end in agreement rather than war, expansion of this ZOA during the course of the negotiations seems to decrease the probability of agreement. Perhaps, then, the warnings provided by Morrow (1992), Krasner (1991), and the empirical evidence of several game-theoretic studies of crisis bargaining are to be heeded: it may in fact be the case that there is a phenomenon of "too large a ZOA," that expansion of the original ZOA provides negotiators with too many options for agreement and therefore an inability to coordinate on one specific outcome. In this sense, then, it may be the case that the initial ZOA formed by the distance between the disputants' reservation points has a very profound effect on the course of negotiations, that the substance of negotiators' initial reservation prices looms over the entire negotiation process.

Keeping this in mind, we also discovered evidence that manipulative mediation expands the zones of agreement between crisis actors, which was to be expected given the ability of these mediators to apply sanctions and rewards to prod negotiators to shift their reservation points and compromise. Not all forms of mediation are more likely to expand ZOAs between actors, however, as ZOAs in facilitated crises actually *contracted* more than those in unmediated crises. Fittingly, negotiators who worked with manipulators were much more likely to perceive the mediator as having an effect on their individual reservation prices than those who worked with facilitators. These results support the theory that mediators with leverage will more profoundly affect bargaining zones than those lacking such power (see especially Rubin 1991; Hopmann 1991; Zartman and Touval 1996; Zartman 2001).

In addition, we found that while the breadth of the ZOA (conceived in both static and dynamic terms) has an effect on the likelihood of agreements being achieved, it has no discernible influence on the payoffs received by negotiators or their satisfaction with the outcome of a crisis. Corroborating the findings we presented in Chapter 4, manipulative mediation has the largest positive effect on negotiator utility scores of any style of mediation.

Comparing these results to those reported in the previous chapters, it seems that mediation and the degree of ripeness associated with a given crisis both have independent effects on rates of agreement, and that more forceful mediation and higher degrees of ripeness increase the likelihood that a crisis will end in agreement. However, it appears that the effectiveness of mediation, and especially manipulative mediation, as a crisis management tool does not stem from mediators' effects on the ripeness of a crisis. Thus, there seems to be something else at work that is causing mediation in general, and especially manipulative mediation, to appear to be an effective means of crisis resolution. It may be the case that mediation – especially manipulation – can stimulate crisis actors to reach an agreement, regardless of the ZOA that exists between them.

Furthermore, while we do find evidence that supports the argument that the degree of crisis ripeness does affect the likelihood of a successfully negotiated outcome (see Zartman 1989, 2001; Haass 1990; Mooradian and Druckman 1999; Hancock 2001), ripeness does not seem to matter in providing individual negotiators with more beneficial outcomes or leaving them more satisfied with these outcomes. Thus, depending on the measure of outcome of interest, ripeness may not be a relevant factor. In addition, even though a higher degree of crisis ripeness is an important factor for avoiding war, the relationship between these two factors is not absolute.

While our small sample of unripe crises likely contributes to the somewhat blunted explanatory power exhibited by ripeness in this study, once again, it seems that there are also other important factors besides crisis ripeness at work behind successful crisis management. Mediation is obviously important, but we also found that the relative power relations between crisis actors affect the likelihood of a crisis being managed in an effective manner.

In addition, since our analysis of ZOA was only conducted under conditions of power disparity between the crisis actors, it may be the case that the effects of ZOAs on crisis outcomes and the effects of mediation on the breadth of the ZOA are different under conditions of power parity between the actors. As discussed in Chapter 5, under conditions of power parity it is often the case that it is less clear who is "winning" and who is "losing" a conflict, and who is entitled to more in regard to the issue(s) under dispute. Under these conditions, manipulators in particular will be more effective at pushing the parties away from hard-line bargaining stances because they can employ threats, carrots, and/or sticks to alter the disputants' decision calculi and agree to *any* outcome. And we find evidence that parties are more satisfied with manipulative mediation than facilitative mediation when the parties are relatively equal in power. Hence, it may be the case that expansion of the ZOA by means of manipulative mediation will actually increase the likelihood of agreement and satisfaction levels in symmetric crises.

Finally, the fact that our investigation of the effect of mediation on ZOA and outcome included a small sample of unripe crises (a total of four) hinders our ability to say anything about how mediation may affect a crisis that is not yet ripe. Accordingly, we were unable to investigate whether or not manipulation's tendency to lower negotiator reservation points could actually favorably affect crisis outcomes when no ZOA exists between actors at the beginning of the crisis. Hiltrop (1985, 1989) finds that, under crisis-like conditions, the use of pressure tactics by mediators is positively associated with settlement only when the ZOA between disputants is small or non-existent. Thus, it may be the case that mediator-induced expansions of the zone of agreement will increase the likelihood of agreement between actors in those cases that are completely unripe or minimally ripe, but that after some point ZOA expansion has diminishing returns. Unfortunately, due to the very low number of unripe cases in our analysis and the fact that each of these cases was either unmediated or mediated by a facilitator, we were unable to accurately assess the effect that ZOA expansion and manipulation have on such cases.

Notes

1 For a comprehensive review of the literature on ripeness, see Wall and Lynn (1993) and Wall, Stark, and Standifer (2001).

2 Princen (1992) offers the most complex view of the dilemma regarding early vs. late intervention: timing is an "optimization problem between, on the one hand, entering early, in which case the high likelihood of acceptance and low likelihood of uncontrollable escalation are countered by the low level of process influence; and, on the other, entering late, in which case the high likelihood of escalation is countered by the high expected process influence" (1992: 54). As alternatives to mediation worsen, a mediator will possess more potential influence and bargaining power, and hence more procedural control; however, the chance of "uncontrollable escalation" will be higher.

3 In a study that employs a game theoretic approach to ripeness and mediation, Terris and Maoz (2001) utilize the terminology of "growing versatility" as an operational synonym for the change in disputant perceptions of the conflict.

4 As of this writing, OSCE-led negotiations between Armenia and Azerbaijan continue, and Nagornyy-Karabakh remains *de facto* autonomous region within Azerbaijan. Attempts at resolving the conflict have progressed very little. An armistice has yet to be signed between Armenia and Azerbaijan, which means they are still officially "at war" even though they have agreed to a ceasefire.

The situation between Armenia and Azerbaijan remains tense, and though no further crises have erupted since 1994, the threat of violence still looms large as the underlying conflict remains unresolved.

5 See Hopmann (2001) for a brief overview of the concept of zone of agreement as it is used in the literature on negotiation.

6 All simulations measuring ZOA were based on the Ecuador-Peru scenario characterized by power disparity between the two states. In other words, these simulations were conducted using the "base" experimental design as laid out in Chapters 2 and 4.

7 See Chapter 4 for a discussion of how mediation style was operationalized as "highest form" for use in the experimental scenario.

7 Conclusion

As this study has made clear, international crises are infrequent, but nevertheless extremely disruptive events for the international system, capable of escalation to serious levels of violence and often presaging fundamental reorientations of relations among states, both regionally and globally. Our goal has been to shed light on mediation as one approach to resolving or controlling these potentially dangerous situations that has been employed by various actors in the international system – international and regional organizations, individual and groups of states, prominent individuals, and non-governmental organizations. While mediation can be used in conjunction with other conflict management measures, such as military interventions and peacekeeping forces, sanctions and embargoes, and censure, we have found that isolating the impact of mediation and identifying the circumstances under which it is effective can contribute to a greater understanding of the dynamics of this powerful tool of crisis management and conflict resolution.

We have also attempted to make a distinct contribution to the analysis of crisis and mediation by utilizing a research strategy that employs both historically based and experimental data. By doing so, we hope to provide a more comprehensive understanding of the manner in which international actors practice mediation and the conditions under which it is most likely to be effective. As Mintz (2004) notes, while multi-method research is rare in international relations, such approaches allow for greater generalizability of findings and enhanced specificity of theories which "lead to robust and standardized results, thus contributing to scientific advancement in international relations" (2004: 11). This multi-method approach has required great care, both in the collection of appropriate historical data on mediated international crises and in the construction of an experimental environment to replicate the conditions under which crisis decision makers and mediators operate in the real-world. Thus, it is our hope that this study will be read and used not only by those seeking a greater understanding of the dynamics of crisis mediation, but also by scholars and analysts whose research questions cannot easily be addressed by a single methodology.

In the pages below, we briefly review the major substantive findings of this study, and then make some concluding comments about our methods, how they might be replicated, and for whom they might be useful. We first present Table 7.1, which provides a summary of the findings for the hypotheses tested in this study.

Perhaps the most fundamental of our findings has been that a general decline in the frequency of international crises since the end of the cold war has been accompanied by a fairly dramatic increase in the proportion of crises in which mediation has been attempted. The sharp 47 percent decline in the number of crises from the 1963–89 polycentric period to the post-cold war unipolar system can be explained in part by the decline in power of the Soviet Union culminating in its disintegration into 15 independent states, coupled with the emergence of the United States as the dominant military power in the system. While the global system remains dangerous, crises involving nation states in adversarial situations are now outnumbered by conflicts based on ethnicity, nationality, and religion, most of which do not directly threaten the fundamental structure of the international system or regional subsystems. Nevertheless, those *crises* that have occurred in recent years – including Afghanistan, Iraq, North Korea, Kashmir, Kosovo, Eritrea-Ethiopia – continue to constitute serious threats to the stability of the system. Additionally a number of long-term protracted conflicts that remain – India-Pakistan, Arab-Israel, the Korean Peninsula, Taiwan Strait – are each capable of spawning dangerous confrontations.

It is in this environment that we find a dramatic increase in the use of mediation – from 27 percent in the immediate post-World War II bipolar era, to 35 percent for polycentrism, and finally to 46 percent for the post-cold war era through 2001. Our findings show that mediation is particularly prevalent when ethnicity is involved, when crisis actors are geographically contiguous, and when crises occur at the subsystem rather than the dominant system level. Mediation is also used more often in crises occurring in the Americas than all other geographic regions. In the course of our study, we look beyond the issue of identifying the conditions under which crises are likely to be mediated. In addition, we consider what actors and organizations are most likely to become involved as mediators. What are the goals of the mediators? And, what effect does mediation have on crisis outcomes? It is this final question that we explore in greatest detail.

In this concluding section, we focus on the effect of mediation on crisis outcomes. It is in this context that we have introduced three key factors that we postulate will intervene in the mediation process, and impact both the dynamic of the mediation process and the probability of its success in crisis management. These factors are the particular style that mediators adopt (facilitation, formulation, and manipulation), the nature of power relations among the adversaries, and the extent to which the crisis is ripe

Table 7.1 Summary results for hypotheses tested

Independent variable (methodology)	*Hypothesis*	*Findings*
Chapter 4		
H1a: Style of mediation (ICB)	Crises in which manipulative mediation is used will be more likely to terminate in *formal agreement* than all other crises	Supported
H1b: Style of mediation (ICB)	Crises in which formulative or facilitative mediation are used will be more likely to terminate in *formal agreement* than unmediated crises	Partially supported (formulation only)
H1c: Style of mediation (ICB)	Crises in which formulative mediation is used will be more likely to terminate in *formal agreement* than crises exhibiting only facilitative mediation	Supported
H2a: Style of mediation (ICB and experimental)	Crises in which manipulative mediation is used will be more likely to result in negotiators being *satisfied with the crisis outcomes* than all other crises	Partially supported by ICB (manipulation more likely than all others only when controlling for relative power relations) and by experiments (mediated more likely than unmediated in general)
H2b: Style of mediation (ICB and experimental)	Crises in which formulative or facilitative mediation are used will be more likely to result in negotiators being *satisfied with the crisis outcomes* than unmediated crises	Partially supported in hypothesized direction by experiments (facilitation more likely than unmediated, but formulation was not tested) and partially supported in opposite direction by ICB (facilitation only)

Table 7.1 continued

Independent variable (methodology)	*Hypothesis*	*Findings*
H2c: Style of mediation (ICB)	Crises in which formulative mediation is used will be more likely to result in negotiators being *satisfied with the crisis outcomes* than crises exhibiting only facilitative mediation	Not supported
H3a: Style of mediation (experimental)	Actors in crises exhibiting manipulative mediation will achieve outcomes with *higher utility value* than actors in all other crises	Supported
H3b: Style of mediation (experimental)	Actors in crises exhibiting facilitative mediation will achieve outcomes with *higher utility value* than actors in unmediated crises	Not supported
H4a: Style of mediation (experimental)	Crises in which manipulative mediation is used will *end more rapidly* than all other crises	Supported
H4b: Style of mediation (experimental)	Crises in which facilitative mediation is used will *end more rapidly* than unmediated crises	Not supported
H5a: Style of mediation (ICB)	Crises in which formulative mediation is used but manipulation is not will be more likely to be followed by a *reduction in tensions* between crisis actors than all other crises	Partially supported (only when controlling for relative power relations)

H5b: Style of mediation (ICB)	Crises in which facilitative or manipulative mediation are used will be more likely to be followed by a *reduction in tensions* between crisis actors than unmediated crises	Supported
H5c: Style of mediation (ICB)	Crises in which facilitation is the only mediation style used will be more likely to be followed by a *reduction in tensions* between crisis actors than crises exhibiting manipulative mediation	Supported
Chapter 5		
H6a: Power relations (ICB)	Asymmetric crises in which manipulative mediation is used will be more likely to terminate in *formal agreement* than all other crises	Not supported
H6b: Power relations (ICB)	Asymmetric crises in which formulative or facilitative mediation are used will be more likely to terminate in *formal agreement* than unmediated crises or mediated symmetric crises	Partially supported in opposite direction (formulation more likely under symmetry)
H6c: Power relations (ICB)	Asymmetric crises in which formulative mediation is used will be more likely to terminate in *formal agreement* than asymmetric crises exhibiting only facilitative mediation	Insufficient data available
H7a: Power relations (ICB and experimental)	Asymmetric crises in which manipulative mediation is used will be more likely to result in negotiators being *satisfied with the crisis outcomes* than all other crises	Partially supported by experiments (mediated more likely than unmediated under asymmetry in general, but difference between effects of manipulation and facilitation are minimal)

Table 7.1 continued

Independent variable (methodology)	*Hypothesis*	*Findings*
H7b: Power relations (ICB and experimental)	Asymmetric crises in which formulative or facilitative mediation are used will be more likely to result in negotiators being *satisfied with the crisis outcomes* than unmediated crises or mediated symmetric crises	Partially supported by experiments (mediated more likely than unmediated under asymmetry in general, but difference between effects of manipulation and facilitation are minimal)
H7c: Power relations (ICB)	Asymmetric crises in which formulative mediation is used will be more likely to result in negotiators being *satisfied with the crisis outcomes* than asymmetric crises exhibiting only facilitative mediation	Not supported
H8a: Power relations (experimental)	Asymmetric crises in which manipulative mediation is used will be more likely to result in negotiators perceiving the mediator as having a positive *effect on crisis management* than all other crises	Partially supported in hypothesized direction (mediated under asymmetry more likely than mediated under symmetry) and partially supported in opposite direction (manipulation more likely than facilitation under symmetry)
H8b: Power relations (experimental)	Asymmetric crises in which facilitative mediation is used will be more likely to result in negotiators perceiving the mediator as having a positive *effect on crisis management* than mediated symmetric crises	Partially supported in hypothesized direction (mediated under asymmetry more likely than mediated under asymmetry) and partially supported in opposite direction (manipulation under symmetry more likely than facilitation under asymmetry)
H9a: Power relations (experimental)	Crisis actors in asymmetric crises exhibiting manipulative mediation will achieve more *beneficial outcomes* than actors in all other crises	Partially supported (weaker party only)

H9b: Power relations (experimental)	Crisis actors in asymmetric crises exhibiting facilitative mediation will achieve more *beneficial outcomes* than actors in unmediated crises or mediated symmetric crises	Not supported
H10a: Power relations (experimental)	Asymmetric crises in which manipulative mediation is used will *end more rapidly* than all other crises	Supported
H10b: Power relations (experimental)	Asymmetric crises in which facilitative mediation is used will *end more rapidly* than unmediated crises or mediated symmetric crises	Not supported
H11a: Power relations (ICB)	Asymmetric crises in which formulative mediation is used but manipulation is not will be more likely to be followed by a *reduction in tensions* between crisis actors than all other crises	Not supported
H11b: Power relations (ICB)	Asymmetric crises in which facilitative or manipulative mediation are used will be more likely to be followed by a *reduction in tensions* between crisis actors than unmediated crises or mediated symmetric crises	Not supported
H11c: Power relations (ICB)	Asymmetric crises in which facilitation is the only mediation style used will be more likely to be followed by a *reduction in tensions* between crisis actors than asymmetric crises exhibiting manipulative mediation	Not supported

Table 7.1 continued

Independent variable (methodology)	*Hypothesis*	*Findings*
Chapter 6		
H12: Zone of agreement (experimental)	The larger the initial zone of agreement between negotiators, the more likely the crisis will be to end in *agreement*, rather than war	Supported
H13: Zone of agreement (experimental)	The larger the initial zone of agreement between negotiators, the more likely are these actors to be *satisfied*, rather than dissatisfied, with the outcome of the crisis	Not supported
H14: Zone of agreement (experimental)	The larger the initial zone of agreement between negotiators, the greater the *benefit* these actors will achieve at the conclusion of the crisis	Not supported
H15a: Zone of agreement (experimental)	Crises in which manipulative mediation is used will exhibit greater *expansion of the zones of agreement* between negotiators than all other crises	Supported
H15b: Zone of agreement (experimental)	Crises in which facilitative mediation is used will exhibit greater *expansion of the zones of agreement* between negotiators than unmediated crises	Supported in opposite direction
H16: Zone of agreement (experimental)	Crises in which manipulative mediation is used will be more likely to result in negotiators *perceiving the mediator as having a modifying impact on their individual bargaining zones* than crises in which facilitative mediation is the highest form of mediation	Supported

H17: Zone of agreement (experimental)	The larger the expansion of the zone of agreement between negotiators during the course of crisis negotiations, the more likely the crisis will be to end in *agreement*, rather than war	Supported in opposite direction
H18: Zone of agreement (experimental)	The larger the expansion of the zone of agreement between negotiators during the course of crisis negotiations, the more likely are these actors to be *satisfied*, rather than dissatisfied, with the outcome of the crisis	Not supported
H19: Zone of agreement (experimental)	The larger the expansion of the zone of agreement between negotiators during the course of crisis negotiations, the greater the *benefit* these actors will receive at the conclusion of the crisis	Not supported

for resolution. We use combinations of aggregate and experimental data to examine several aspects of crisis outcome: whether agreements have been reached, the extent to which the parties are satisfied with the outcome, whether the outcome to the crisis has led to a sustained reduction in tensions among the adversaries, the extent to which mediation has impacted the duration of the crisis and associated negotiation, the impact of mediation on the expected utility derived by the parties, and negotiators' perceptions of the mediator.

Our findings show that mediated crises are more likely than others to terminate with the conclusion of a formal agreement, to terminate earlier, to lead to higher levels of satisfaction among the parties, and to lead to a sustained reduction in tensions among the adversaries. Our results also suggest that more aggressive and substantively intrusive styles of mediation are most successful in generating formal agreements between actors. These manipulative forms of mediation are also most effective in shortening the duration of crises. In this regard, we observe a reciprocal relationship between these two outcomes – shorter crises, in general, are much more likely to end in agreement. And manipulation also results in a greater average benefit for both parties, as measured by the expected utility payoff received by simulation participants. Facilitative mediation, on the other hand, is better suited than manipulation for generating a post-crisis reduction in tensions between parties. Facilitation, however, usually provides the parties with lower benefits than manipulation, and facilitated crises do not end more quickly than those with no mediation at all.

Many international relations theorists have argued that crises characterized by asymmetric power relations among adversaries are most resistant to mediation, on the grounds that the more powerful state will perceive a threat to its power advantage. Our findings on crises in the twentieth century tend to confirm this argument. However, both aggregate and experimental findings show that it is actually among these relatively few asymmetric crises that mediation has its greatest impact. The parties to mediated asymmetric crises tend to be more satisfied with the outcomes of these crises than negotiators in unmediated symmetric crises, most likely due to the fact that, under these circumstances, they can confirm that the outcomes are aligned with their relative capabilities, largely through the terms of agreements reached. Combining the joint effects of mediator style and relative power relations, we find that while manipulative mediation continues to have the greatest positive effect on crisis processes and outcomes in general, this style of mediation is particularly effective in achieving higher overall payoffs for the weaker parties in asymmetric crises. Furthermore, asymmetric crises involving manipulative mediation tended to terminate more quickly than did other asymmetric negotiations. Manipulators are more successful in preventing stronger party domination and weaker party insecurities, thus helping to ensure that hostilities do not escalate. However, while parties to asymmetric crises exhibiting manipulative mediation are more satisfied with the outcomes, they are not necessarily satisfied with the activities of the mediators themselves. We also find some evidence that, when mediators restrict their activities to formulation, they are highly successful at producing formal agreements in symmetric crises.

This study has also addressed the difficult question of how the concept of conflict ripeness, discussed widely in the theoretical literature on resolving international conflicts and crises, can be evaluated in the context of efforts at crisis mediation. After developing a measure of ripeness based on zones of agreement (ZOA) among the parties to a crisis both before and during the course of a negotiation, we were able to track the impact of this factor, along with that of mediation style, on the outcomes of crises. Our central finding is that the size of the ZOA that exists between the parties as crisis negotiations begin has a significant and positive effect on the likelihood of the crisis terminating in agreement as opposed to violence/war. Furthermore, the most intrusive form of mediation – manipulation – was found to have a significant positive impact on the expansion of the zone of agreement during negotiations, while facilitation had no impact on the breadth of the ZOA. These results support the notion that mediators with leverage will more profoundly affect bargaining zones than those lacking such power. Finally, and quite unexpectedly, the experimental findings show that while larger zones of agreement produce more frequent agreements, greater expansion of this zone of agreement during the negotiation seems to actually *decrease* the probability of agreement. We speculate that an expansion of the ZOA, and the accompanying proliferation of options available to negotiators on both sides of the conflict, may actually lead to an inability to coordinate on one specific outcome in circumstances in which time pressures are building. One drawback to our study, though, is that, due to the small number of crises that were initially *unripe* in our universe of analysis, we were unable to effectively investigate the effect of mediation, and changing bargaining zones, on such initially unripe crises. Mediation and especially manipulative mediation may have a positive impact on the probability of a crisis terminating in agreement when it can *create* ZOAs. Future studies are encouraged to examine this issue in more detail.

Taken together, our findings point to the importance of foreign policy choice, within certain constraints, in determining the outcome of international crises. The decision to mediate is one taken by both large and small states using significantly different approaches to the process of mediation. The choice to mediate and the style chosen can have significant repercussions for the level of violence in crises and the potential for further violence in the future. Mediators who push and who sanction may not win friends but they do have a positive impact on the international relations of states involved in these dangerous situations. Even when accounting for the power discrepancy between parties and the ripeness of a conflict, mediation is on average a successful method of crisis management, and aggressive mediation is a best choice for lessening of the chance of violence or future crises. Our endorsement of manipulation must be tempered, though, by at least two factors that need to be explored more rigorously in the future. First, our experimental analysis has only looked at the two extreme styles of mediation – facilitation and manipulation. It may be the case that formulative mediation, which falls between these two extreme styles, is an even more effective management tool under certain circumstances. For instance, formulation may be the most effective approach for helping negotiators focus in on desirable outcomes in the presence of an expansive zone of agreement.

A second concern with manipulative mediation relates to both the short- and long-term implications of solutions developed and sometimes even forced upon parties by an outsider. Such situations can lead to feelings of alienation and resentment of the mediator, of the process of negotiation, and even of the other parties involved in the negotiation (Princen 1992; Kelman 1992; Keashly and Fisher 1996). In view of this, it is not surprising that we discovered evidence that formulation and facilitation are generally more likely than manipulation to lead to a post-crisis reduction in tensions between actors. While our findings on negotiator satisfaction do not reveal more resentment of manipulation vis-à-vis facilitation, greater consideration of the unintended consequences that could accompany the adoption of manipulative mediation as a crisis management tool is necessary before we can conclude that manipulation is an appropriate – or perhaps the most appropriate – means of managing international crises. Our current findings, though, do indicate that manipulation shows potential as a key approach to mitigating the violence and instability associated with international crises.

We believe that our findings have particular weight because we have made an effort to triangulate our research using both empirical and experimental methods. This successful approach points out the value of combining methods in the social sciences and underlines the importance of using experimental methods which have often received short shrift. While experimentation remains largely outside the mainstream of international relations research, and of political science in general, this book illustrates the importance of bringing experimental methods into the fold. Experimentation allows researchers to isolate crucial independent variables to control for extraneous factors, and it provides an opportunity to observe sometimes stark contrasts between control groups and subject groups. (Campbell and Stanley 1963; see also Laponce 1972; Bositis 1990; McGraw 1993).

In this case we compared the outcomes of simulated crises between groups that had mediators and those that did not. This comparison allowed us to provide a precise view of a certain phenomenon, a certain relationship – between mediator style (and the involvement of a mediator, in general) and the outcome of crises. Experimentation has provided us with important support for our empirical analysis of crisis using the International Crisis Behavior (ICB) dataset. In addition, the experimental approach allowed us to explore dynamics of crisis mediation in new and distinct ways. Reliance on crisis simulations provided us with a means for exploring ripeness, an objective that had proven to be elusive through reliance on historical data. Furthermore, we had better access to and could collect more reliable data from participants in simulations – particularly regarding their perception of the mediator – more efficiently than would ever be possible in exploring historical crises.

We should of course attach two caveats. First, the transition from simulation environment, whose primary application in political science is for instruction and training, to the experimental laboratory, is not a simple one. Even with the prospects of great advancements in knowledge seemingly at our fingertips, too few of us venture into the unknown terrain of the experimental laboratory. Second, college students are not international leaders and on any given day they may have a host of distracting issues on their minds. That is not to say that real-world decision makers do not have extraneous things on their minds, but at least we know that some of their attention is focused on policy issues.

Even if these two problems could somehow be neutralized, the issue of the simulation itself remains. We know from the simulation literature that a model should be detailed enough to represent the important aspects of the reality it is meant to represent, but not so detailed as to overwhelm the participant with information (even though we know that that is exactly what happens to real-world decision makers, particularly in crisis). This turns out to be an extremely difficult undertaking. In our own case, we have some evidence to suggest that in a previous round of experiments involving a model of a fishing dispute roughly resembling the dispute between Canada and Spain in 1995, we not only packed the model with excessive detail, but then superimposed an elaborate mediation process, and the results showed that the subjects were not coping, and were therefore making decisions based on only partial use of the decision support tools they had available to them. If you add to all of this the expense and time involved in the design and execution of a series of experiments, it is not surprising that relatively few political scientists venture into this domain.

Despite these challenges, we believe that our research on mediation indicates the important contribution that experimental methods can make to political science. Important questions that confront both social scientists and policy makers are inherently bounded by subjective issues of perception, and mediation in crisis is but one example. Experimentation, carefully done, can help us to better understand choices made by decision makers to use force or to abstain from the use of force. We do not argue that experimentation should replace analysis using historical data, but political science is poorer for not employing the experimental tools. And, to successfully employ these experimental tools, we must begin to properly train the next generation of political scientists in simulation and experimental techniques.

That being said, there remain questions – including questions related to crisis mediation – that will be best answered by exploring the trends and patterns of diplomatic history. One of the key considerations omitted from this analysis of crisis mediation but essential for a more complete understanding of this phenomenon relates to the multiple and perhaps conflicting motivations and interests of a mediator at the time of intervention. As Touval (2003) notes, given the variety of foreign policy goals of states and organizations in the international system, it may not be the case that a mediator's sole or primary goal in intervening is crisis management or resolution. Such goals will no doubt influence the nature of the mediator's impact on the trajectory of a crisis. Similarly, despite our evidence of the merits of manipulative mediation, states may be unwilling or unable to adopt these tactics given other concerns or policy calculations. Insights into the motivations of states and organizations as crisis mediators can best be achieved not through experimentation but, rather, through an examination of data from historians, policy makers, and observers of international relations. We encourage additional analyses into the factors that determine which mediation strategy a third party employs in an international crisis, and we hope that the findings presented here serve to foster additional rigorous analyses of crisis management approaches, towards the goal of determining how crises of the future may be most successfully controlled.

Appendix A: Mediated international crises, 1918–2001

[1]In this column, the crisis name is listed in all caps, followed by a listing of the crisis actors underneath. If the same actor is listed more than once, this indicates that the actor experienced two or more separate, discrete crisis incidents throughout the course of the crisis as a whole.

[2]For both trigger and termination dates, if the month and year were known, but the day was unknown, only the month and year are listed here. If the specific day was unknown but could be approximated, the following convention was followed: "Early" = day 1 to day 10; "Mid" = day 11 to day 20; and "Late" = day 21 to the end of the month.

[3]The primary mediator was determined by which mediator or mediation team was the most active in the crisis, temporally speaking. Thus, if several actors are listed here, these actors worked as a mediation team. If coders were able to determine which actor assumed the role of the "head" of this mediation team, that actor's name is listed in italics. For cases involving international or regional organizations, if coders were able to determine which organizational bodies (whether permanent or temporarily created to handle a specific crisis or conflict) were used to conduct the mediation efforts, those bodies are identified here. Similarly, if coders were able to determine the specific state actors that were involved in the mediation efforts under the auspices of an international or regional organization, those state actors are listed in parentheses next to the name of the organization.

[4]In the October–Yom Kippur War crisis, the United States is coded as the primary mediator even though it is a crisis actor because it was only in crisis with the Soviet Union. In this case, the United States mediated after its crisis with the Soviet Union ended.

CRISIS NAME (and Crisis Actors)[1]	TRIGGER DATE[2]	TERMINATION DATE	PRIMARY MEDIATOR[3]	GOAL OF MEDIATOR	HIGHEST FORM OF MEDIATION	EFFECT OF MEDIATION ON CRISIS ABATEMENT
AALAND ISLANDS Sweden Finland	5 June 1920	20 Oct. 1921	League of Nations Council and Commission of Inquiry	Conflict resolution	Formulation	Most important factor in easing tensions
VILNA I Poland Lithuania	12 July 1920	29 Nov. 1920	League of Nations Council	Crisis management	Formulation	Important factor in easing tensions
BURGENLAND DISPUTE Hungary Austria	28 Aug. 1921	28 Dec. 1921	*Italy*, France, United Kingdom	Conflict resolution	Manipulation	Most important factor in easing tensions
RUHR II Germany France	29 Apr. 1924	30 Aug. 1924	United Kingdom, United States	Conflict resolution	Manipulation	Most important factor in easing tensions
NICARAGUA CIVIL WAR I Nicaragua	17 Aug. 1926	15 May 1927	United States	Crisis management	Formulation	Important factor in easing tensions
VILNA II Poland Lithuania	Mid Oct. 1927	10 Dec. 1927	League of Nations Council	Crisis management	Missing data	Most important factor in easing tensions

CHACO I Bolivia Paraguay	5 Dec. 1928	12 Sept. 1929	Conference of the Pan-American Organization (*United States*, Mexico, Cuba, Colombia, Uruguay)	Crisis management	Formulation	Most important factor in easing tensions
SHANGHAI China Japan	24 Jan. 1932	5 May 1932	*United Kingdom*, United States, France	Crisis management	Formulation	Most important factor in easing tensions
CHACO II Paraguay Bolivia	18 June 1932	12 June 1935	Argentina, Brazil, Chile, Peru, United States, Uruguay	Conflict resolution	Manipulation	Important factor in easing tensions
LETICIA Colombia Peru	8 Sept. 1932	25 May 1933	League of Nations Council and Advisory/ Monitoring Commission (Brazil, Spain, United States)	Conflict resolution	Manipulation	Important factor in easing tensions
ETHIOPIAN WAR Ethiopia United Kingdom France Italy	6 Dec. 1932	5 May 1936	League of Nations (Three Power Conference, Committee of Five, and Committee of Thirteen to Mediate)	Crisis management	Formulation	No effect
ALEXANDRETTA Turkey France	9 Sept. 1936	23 June 1939	League of Nations Council	Conflict resolution	Formulation	Important factor in easing tensions

CRISIS NAME (and Crisis Actors)[1]	TRIGGER DATE[2]	TERMINATION DATE	PRIMARY MEDIATOR[3]	GOAL OF MEDIATOR	HIGHEST FORM OF MEDIATION	EFFECT OF MEDIATION ON CRISIS ABATEMENT
MARCO POLO BRIDGE China Japan	8 July 1937	16 Jan. 1938	Germany, United Kingdom	Conflict resolution	Formulation	No effect
POSTAGE STAMP CRISIS Honduras Nicaragua	Mid Aug. 1937	10 Dec. 1937	Costa Rica, United States, Venezuela	Crisis management	Formulation	Most important factor in easing tensions
DOMINICAN REPUBLIC/HAITI I Haiti	5 Oct. 1937	31 Jan. 1938	Cuba, Mexico, United States, Pan-American Union (Argentina, Guatemala, Peru)	Crisis management	Formulation	Most important factor in easing tensions
ITALY THREAT/ FRANCE France	30 Nov. 1938	31 Mar. 1939	United Kingdom	Crisis management	Facilitation	Marginal factor in easing tensions
ECUADOR/PERU BORDER II Ecuador Peru	5 July 1941	29 Jan. 1942	Argentina, Brazil, United States	Conflict resolution	Manipulation	Most important factor in easing tensions

INDONESIA INDEPENDENCE I Netherlands Indonesia	29 Sept. 1945	25 Mar. 1947	United Kingdom	Crisis management	Facilitation	Important factor in easing tensions
INDONESIA INDEPENDENCE II Indonesia Netherlands	21 July 1947	17 Jan. 1948	United Nations Good Offices Committee (Australia, Belgium, United States)	Conflict resolution	Formulation	Most important factor in easing tensions
KASHMIR I India Pakistan	24 Oct. 1947	1 Jan. 1949	United Nations Commission for India and Pakistan (*Czechoslovakia*, Argentina, Belgium, Colombia, United States)	Conflict resolution	Manipulation	Most important factor in easing tensions
PALESTINE PARTITION/ISRAEL INDEPENDENCE Iraq Egypt Lebanon Jordan Syria Israel	29 Nov. 1947	20 July 1949	United Nations General Assembly mediator (i.e., Count Folke Bernadotte) and Under-Secretary General	Crisis management	Manipulation	Most important factor in easing tensions
BERLIN BLOCKADE Soviet Union France United Kingdom United States	7 June 1948	12 May 1949	United Nations Security Council (the neutral members only: *Argentina*, Belgium, Canada, Colombia, China, Syria)	Conflict resolution	Formulation	No effect

CRISIS NAME (and Crisis Actors)[1]	TRIGGER DATE[2]	TERMINATION DATE	PRIMARY MEDIATOR[3]	GOAL OF MEDIATOR	HIGHEST FORM OF MEDIATION	EFFECT OF MEDIATION ON CRISIS ABATEMENT
COSTA RICA/ NICARAGUA I Costa Rica	11 Dec. 1948	21 Feb. 1949	Organization of American States Committee of Information (*Mexico*, Brazil, Colombia, Peru, United States)	Conflict resolution	Formulation	Important factor in easing tensions
INDONESIA INDEPENDENCE III Indonesia Netherlands	19 Dec. 1948	27 Dec. 1949	United Nations Commission for Indonesia (Australia, Belgium, United States)	Conflict resolution	Formulation	Most important factor in easing tensions
HULA DRAINAGE Syria Israel	12 Feb. 1951	15 May 1951	United Nations Mixed Armistice Commission	Crisis management	Formulation	Important factor in easing tensions
PUNJAB WAR SCARE I India Pakistan	7 July 1951	Aug. 1951	United Nations Representative for India and Pakistan	Conflict resolution	Manipulation	No effect
BURMA INFILTRATION Burma	8 Feb. 1953	15 Oct. 1954	United Nations-sponsored Joint Military Commission (the non-disputants only: United States and Thailand)	Crisis management	Formulation	Marginal factor in easing tensions

TRIESTE II Yugoslavia Italy	8 Oct. 1953	5 Dec. 1953	*United States*, United Kingdom	Conflict resolution	Manipulation	Most important factor in easing tensions
DIEN BIEN PHU France United States United Kingdom	13 Mar. 1954	21 July 1954	Soviet Union, China (i.e., the non-crisis actors at Geneva Conference, where mediation took place)	Conflict resolution	Formulation	Most important factor in easing tensions
COSTA RICA/ NICARAGUA II Costa Rica Nicaragua	8 Jan. 1955	20 Jan. 1955	Organization of American States Committee of Investigation (*Mexico*, Brazil, Ecuador, Paraguay, United States)	Conflict resolution	Manipulation	Most important factor in easing tensions
GAZA RAID – CZECHOSLOVAKIA ARMS Egypt Israel	28 Feb. 1955	23 June 1956	United Nations Secretary General	Crisis management	Formulation	No effect
PUSHTUNISTAN II Afghanistan Pakistan	27 Mar. 1955	Nov. 1955	Iran, Iraq, Turkey	Crisis management	Manipulation	Most important factor in easing tensions
MOCORON INCIDENT Nicaragua Honduras	26 Feb. 1957	9 May 1957	Organization of American States Committee of Investigation (*Mexico*, Brazil, Ecuador, Paraguay, United States)	Crisis management	Formulation	Important factor in easing tensions

CRISIS NAME (and Crisis Actors)[1]	TRIGGER DATE[2]	TERMINATION DATE	PRIMARY MEDIATOR[3]	GOAL OF MEDIATOR	HIGHEST FORM OF MEDIATION	EFFECT OF MEDIATION ON CRISIS ABATEMENT
IFNI Spain	23 Nov. 1957	Apr. 1958	United States	Missing data	Missing data	Missing data
EGYPT/SUDAN BORDER I Sudan	9 Feb. 1958	25 Feb. 1958	Arab League Secretary General	Conflict resolution	Missing data	Missing data
CAMBODIA/ THAILAND Thailand Cambodia	24 July 1958	6 Feb. 1959	United Nations (personal envoy of the Secretary General)	Crisis management	Missing data	Most important factor in easing tensions
PATHET LAO OFFENSIVE United States Thailand	9 Mar. 1961	16 May 1961	United Kingdom	Crisis management	Formulation	Important factor in easing tensions
PUSHTUNISTAN III Pakistan Afghanistan	19 May 1961	29 Jan. 1962	United States	Crisis management	Facilitation	No effect
WEST IRIAN II Indonesia Netherlands	26 Sept. 1961	15 Oct. 1962	United Nations (the United States Ambassador)	Conflict resolution	Manipulation	Important factor in easing tensions

CHINA/INDIA BORDER II India China (PRC)	8 Sept. 1962	23 Jan. 1963	Burma, Cambodia, Ceylon, Ghana, Indonesia, Egypt (i.e., the six non-aligned states at the Colombo Conference, where mediation took place)	Conflict resolution	Formulation	Marginal factor in easing tensions
YEMEN WAR I Jordan Saudi Arabia Egypt Yemen	26 Sept. 1962	15 Apr. 1963	United States	Crisis management	Manipulation	Most important factor in easing tensions
MALAYSIA FEDERATION Malaysia Indonesia	11 Feb. 1963	9 Aug. 1965	United States	Crisis management	Facilitation	Marginal factor in easing tensions
DOMINICAN REPUBLIC/HAITI II Dominican Republic Haiti	26 Apr. 1963	3 June 1963	Organization of American States Mediation Commission (Bolivia, Chile, Colombia, Ecuador, El Salvador) and Committee of Investigation	Crisis management	Formulation	No effect

CRISIS NAME (and Crisis Actors)[1]	TRIGGER DATE[2]	TERMINATION DATE	PRIMARY MEDIATOR[3]	GOAL OF MEDIATOR	HIGHEST FORM OF MEDIATION	EFFECT OF MEDIATION ON CRISIS ABATEMENT
ALGERIA/ MOROCCO BORDER Algeria Morocco	1 Oct. 1963	4 Nov. 1963	Ethiopia, Mali	Crisis management	Formulation	Important factor in easing tensions
CYPRUS I Turkey Cyprus Greece	30 Nov. 1963	10 Aug. 1964	United Nations Security Council	Conflict resolution	Manipulation	Marginal factor in easing tensions
DAHOMEY/NIGER Niger Dahomey	21 Dec. 1963	4 Jan. 1964	Afro-Malagasy Union for Economic Cooperation, Gabon, Nigeria, Togo	Crisis management	Missing data	Missing data
YEMEN WAR II Yemen Egypt Saudi Arabia	Mid May 1964	8 Nov. 1964	Algeria, Iraq	Crisis management	Missing data	Important factor in easing tensions
YEMEN WAR III Egypt Yemen Saudi Arabia	3 Dec. 1964	25 Aug. 1965	Algeria, Jordan, Kuwait	Conflict resolution	Missing data	No effect

RANN OF KUTCH India Pakistan	8 Apr. 1965	30 June 1965	United Kingdom	Crisis management	Manipulation	Important factor in easing tensions
DOMINICAN INTERVENTION United States	24 Apr. 1965	31 Aug. 1965	Organization of American States Secretary General	Conflict resolution	Formulation	Most important factor in easing tensions
KASHMIR II India Pakistan India	5 Aug. 1965	10 Jan. 1966	Soviet Union	Crisis management	Manipulation	Most important factor in easing tensions
YEMEN WAR IV Saudi Arabia Egypt Yemen	14 Oct. 1966	26 Sept. 1967	Sudan	Conflict resolution	Formulation	Important factor in easing tensions
CYPRUS II Turkey Greece Cyprus	15 Nov. 1967	4 Dec. 1967	*United States*, North Atlantic Treaty Organization, United Nations	Crisis management	Manipulation	Most important factor in easing tensions
ESSEQUIBO I Guyana	9 July 1968	Aug. 1968	United Nations Secretary General	Conflict resolution	Facilitation	No effect
WAR OF ATTRITION Israel Egypt Soviet Union Israel Egypt	8 Mar. 1969	7 Aug. 1970	United States	Crisis management	Manipulation	Important factor in easing tensions

CRISIS NAME (and Crisis Actors)[1]	TRIGGER DATE[2]	TERMINATION DATE	PRIMARY MEDIATOR[3]	GOAL OF MEDIATOR	HIGHEST FORM OF MEDIATION	EFFECT OF MEDIATION ON CRISIS ABATEMENT
FOOTBALL WAR El Salvador Honduras	15 June 1969	30 July 1969	Organization of American States Secretary General	Conflict resolution	Manipulation	Important factor in easing tensions
CAIRO AGREEMENT – PLO Lebanon	22 Oct. 1969	3 Nov. 1969	Egypt	Conflict resolution	Missing data	Important factor in easing tensions
BLACK SEPTEMBER Syria United States Israel Jordan	15 Sept. 1970	29 Sept. 1970	League of Arab States	Conflict resolution	Manipulation	Most important factor in easing tensions
CHAD/LIBYA I Libya Chad	24 May 1971	17 Apr. 1972	Niger	Conflict resolution	Facilitation	Most important factor in easing tensions
TANZANIA/ UGANDA II Uganda Tanzania	17 Sept. 1972	5 Oct. 1972	Somalia	Crisis management	Manipulation	Most important factor in easing tensions
NORTH/SOUTH YEMEN I North Yemen South Yemen	26 Sept. 1972	28 Nov. 1972	Libya	Conflict resolution	Manipulation	Important factor in easing tensions

IRAQ INVASION/ KUWAIT Kuwait	20 Mar. 1973	8 June 1973	Yasser Arafat	Crisis management	Missing data	Important factor in easing tensions
OCTOBER – YOM KIPPUR WAR Israel Syria United States Egypt Soviet Union Israel	5 Oct. 1973	31 May 1974	United States[4]	Crisis management	Manipulation	Important factor in easing tensions
OMAN/SOUTH YEMEN Oman	18 Nov. 1973	11 Mar. 1976	Saudi Arabia	Conflict resolution	Manipulation	Most important factor in easing tensions
CYPRUS III Cyprus Turkey Greece	15 July 1974	24 Feb. 1975	*United Kingdom*, United States	Crisis management	Manipulation	No effect
WAR IN ANGOLA Zambia Zaire South Africa Angola Cuba Soviet Union United States	12 July 1975	27 Mar. 1976	Organization of African Unity Secretary General	Conflict resolution	Formulation	No effect

CRISIS NAME (and Crisis Actors)[1]	TRIGGER DATE[2]	TERMINATION DATE	PRIMARY MEDIATOR[3]	GOAL OF MEDIATOR	HIGHEST FORM OF MEDIATION	EFFECT OF MEDIATION ON CRISIS ABATEMENT
MOROCCAN MARCH Spain Morocco Algeria Mauritania	16 Oct. 1975	14 Apr. 1976	United Nations Security Council and Secretary General	Crisis management	Formulation	No effect
COD WAR II United Kingdom Iceland	23 Nov. 1975	1 June 1976	United Nations Security Council	Crisis management	Formulation	Marginal factor in easing tensions
AEGEAN SEA I Greece Turkey	6 Aug. 1976	25 Sept. 1976	United Nations Security Council	Crisis management	Formulation	Important factor in easing tensions
SHABA Zaire Angola	8 Mar. 1977	26 May 1977	Nigeria	Crisis management	Missing data	Marginal factor in easing tensions
BELIZE II United Kingdom	25 June 1977	28 July 1977	United States	Crisis management	Formulation	Important factor in easing tensions
EGYPT/LIBYA CLASHES Libya Egypt	14 July 1977	10 Sept. 1977	*Palestine Liberation Organization*, Algeria, Kuwait, Togo	Conflict resolution	Formulation	Most important factor in easing tensions

OGADEN II Ethiopia Somalia	22 July 1977	14 Mar. 1978	Organization of African Unity Mediation Committee (*Gabon*, Cameroon, Lesotho, Liberia, Mauritania, Nigeria, Senegal, Tanzania)	Crisis management	Facilitation	No effect
FRENCH HOSTAGES IN MAURITANIA France Algeria	25 Oct. 1977	23 Dec. 1977	United Nations Secretary General	Crisis management	Facilitation	Important factor in easing tensions
CHAD/LIBYA II Libya Chad	22 Jan. 1978	27 Mar. 1978	Niger, Sudan	Crisis management	Missing data	Most important factor in easing tensions
SHABA II Zaire Angola Belgium United States France	11 May 1978	30 July 1978	Congo, United States (mediation conducted at the Brazzaville Conference)	Crisis management	Formulation	Important factor in easing tensions
NICARAGUA CIVIL WAR II Nicaragua Costa Rica Nicaragua	10 Sept. 1978	17 July 1979	Organization of American States (Dominican Republic, Guatemala, United States)	Crisis management	Formulation	No effect

CRISIS NAME (and Crisis Actors)[1]	TRIGGER DATE[2]	TERMINATION DATE	PRIMARY MEDIATOR[3]	GOAL OF MEDIATOR	HIGHEST FORM OF MEDIATION	EFFECT OF MEDIATION ON CRISIS ABATEMENT
BEAGLE CHANNEL II Chile Argentina	16 Oct. 1978	9 Jan. 1979	Catholic Church (i.e., Pope John Paul II)	Conflict resolution	Manipulation	Most important factor in easing tensions
FALL OF AMIN Tanzania Uganda Libya	30 Oct. 1978	10 Apr. 1979	Organization of African Unity Mediation Committee	Crisis management	Formulation	No effect
NORTH/SOUTH YEMEN II North Yemen South Yemen	24 Feb. 1979	30 Mar. 1979	Missing data	Conflict resolution	Missing data	Most important factor in easing tensions
CHAD/LIBYA IV Libya Chad France	12 Apr. 1979	10 Nov. 1979	Nigeria	Conflict resolution	Manipulation	Marginal factor in easing tensions
RHODESIA SETTLEMENT Rhodesia Botswana Mozambique Zambia	15 July 1979	4 Mar. 1980	United Kingdom	Conflict resolution	Manipulation	Most important factor in easing tensions

US HOSTAGES IN IRAN United States Iran	4 Nov. 1979	20 Jan. 1981	Algeria	Crisis management	Manipulation	Most important factor in easing tensions
RAID ON GAFSA Tunisia Libya	27 Jan. 1980	30 Apr. 1980	Arab League (*Iraq*, Jordan, Kuwait, Syria)	Crisis management	Missing data	No effect
JORDAN/SYRIA CONFRONTATION Jordan	25 Nov. 1980	14 Dec. 1980	Saudi Arabia	Crisis management	Manipulation	Important factor in easing tensions
CHAD/LIBYA V France Libya	6 Jan. 1981	16 Nov. 1981	Nigeria	Conflict resolution	Formulation	Important factor in easing tensions
ECUADOR/PERU BORDER III Ecuador Peru	22 Jan. 1981	2 Apr. 1981	Argentina, Brazil, Chile, United States (i.e., the guarantor states of the Rio Protocol)	Conflict resolution	Manipulation	Important factor in easing tensions
ESSEQUIBO II Guyana Venezuela	4 Apr. 1981	Mar. 1983	United Nations Secretary General	Missing data	Missing data	Missing data
AL-BIQA MISSILES I Syria Israel	28 Apr. 1981	24 July 1981	*United States*, Saudi Arabia	Crisis management	Formulation	Marginal factor in easing tensions

CRISIS NAME (and Crisis Actors)[1]	TRIGGER DATE[2]	TERMINATION DATE	PRIMARY MEDIATOR[3]	GOAL OF MEDIATOR	HIGHEST FORM OF MEDIATION	EFFECT OF MEDIATION ON CRISIS ABATEMENT
CAMEROON/ NIGERIA I Nigeria Cameroon	15 May 1981	24 July 1981	Organization of African Unity Secretary General	Crisis management	Missing data	Important factor in easing tensions
GALTAT ZEMMOUR I Morocco	13 Oct. 1981	9 Nov. 1981	Organization of African Unity Secretary General	Conflict resolution	Formulation	No effect
KHORRAMSHAHR Iraq	22 Mar. 1982	30 July 1982	Gulf Cooperation Council (Bahrain, Kuwait, Oman, Qatar, Saudi Arabia, United Arab Emirates)	Conflict resolution	Manipulation	No effect
FALKLANDS/ MALVINAS United Kingdom Argentina	31 Mar. 1982	14 June 1982	United States	Crisis management	Manipulation	No effect
WAR IN LEBANON Lebanon Syria Israel	5 June 1982	17 May 1983	*United States*, United Nations	Crisis management	Manipulation	Important factor in easing tensions
CHAD/LIBYA VI Chad France Libya	24 June 1983	11 Dec. 1984	Congo	Conflict resolution	Facilitation	No effect

OPERATION ASKARI Angola	6 Dec. 1983	16 Feb. 1984	*United States*, Zambia	Crisis management	Manipulation	Important factor in easing tensions
BASRA-KHARG ISLAND Iraq Iran Kuwait Saudi Arabia	21 Feb. 1984	11 July 1984	United Nations Secretary General	Conflict resolution	Formulation	Important factor in easing tensions
EXPULSION OF TUNISIANS Tunisia	21 Aug. 1985	26 Sept. 1985	Arab League, Kuwait, Morocco, United States	Crisis management	Facilitation	Marginal factor in easing tensions
AL-BIQA MISSILES II Syria Israel	19 Nov. 1985	15 Jan. 1986	United States	Crisis management	Manipulation	Important factor in easing tensions
BURKINA FASO/ MALI BORDER Mali Burkina Faso	20 Dec. 1985	18 Jan. 1986	Libya, Nigeria	Conflict resolution	Facilitation	Important factor in easing tensions
AL-DIBAL INCIDENT Bahrain	26 Apr. 1986	15 June 1986	Kuwait, Oman, Saudi Arabia, United Arab Emirates	Conflict resolution	Formulation	Most important factor in easing tensions
ATTEMPTED COUP IN TOGO Togo	23 Sept. 1986	5 Feb. 1987	Organization of African Unity Fact-Finding Mission and Secretary General	Crisis management	Facilitation	Missing data

CRISIS NAME (and Crisis Actors)[1]	TRIGGER DATE[2]	TERMINATION DATE	PRIMARY MEDIATOR[3]	GOAL OF MEDIATOR	HIGHEST FORM OF MEDIATION	EFFECT OF MEDIATION ON CRISIS ABATEMENT
CHAD/LIBYA VIII Chad Libya	12 Dec. 1986	11 Nov. 1987	Organization of African Unity Chairman	Crisis management	Facilitation	Most important factor in easing tensions
SAND WALL Morocco Mauritania Algeria	25 Feb. 1987	4 May 1987	Saudi Arabia	Crisis management	Formulation	Most important factor in easing tensions
SOUTH AFRICA INTERVENTION IN ANGOLA Angola South Africa	3 Oct. 1987	22 Aug. 1988	United States	Conflict resolution	Manipulation	Most important factor in easing tensions
IRAQ RECAPTURE OF AL-FAW Iran	18 Apr. 1988	8 Aug. 1988	United Nations Security Council	Conflict resolution	Facilitation	Important factor in easing tensions
MAURITANIA/ SENEGAL Senegal Mauritania	21 Aug. 1989	18 July 1991	Organization of African Unity Chairman	Conflict resolution	Formulation	Marginal factor in easing tensions
CAMBODIA PEACE CONFERENCE Cambodia Vietnam	30 Aug. 1989	27 Jan. 1990	Australia	Conflict resolution	Formulation	Most important factor in easing tensions

KASHMIR III: INDIA/PAKISTAN NUCLEAR CRISIS India Pakistan	14 Jan. 1990	Late June 1990	United States	Crisis management	Facilitation	Important factor in easing tensions
GULF WAR Kuwait United States Bahrain Egypt France Iraq Israel Oman Qatar Saudi Arabia Syria United Arab Emirates United Kingdom	2 Aug. 1990	12 Apr. 1991	Soviet Union	Crisis management	Formulation	Marginal factor in easing tensions
RWANDA/UGANDA Rwanda	30 Sept. 1990	29 Mar. 1991	*Zaire*, Burundi, Kenya, Tanzania	Conflict resolution	Formulation	Most important factor in easing tensions
LIBERIA/SIERRA LEONE Sierra Leone	23 Mar. 1991	31 Oct. 1991	Economic Community of West African States	Conflict resolution	Formulation	Most important factor in easing tensions

CRISIS NAME (and Crisis Actors)[1]	TRIGGER DATE[2]	TERMINATION DATE	PRIMARY MEDIATOR[3]	GOAL OF MEDIATOR	HIGHEST FORM OF MEDIATION	EFFECT OF MEDIATION ON CRISIS ABATEMENT
YUGOSLAVIA I: CROATIA/ SLOVENIA Yugoslavia Slovenia Croatia	25 June 1991	3 Jan. 1992	United Nations Security Council	Crisis management	Manipulation	Most important factor in easing tensions
NAGORNYY – KARABAKH Armenia Azerbaijan	27 Nov. 1991	Mid Aug. 1992	Conference on Security and Cooperation in Europe (Belarus, Czechoslovakia, France, Germany, Italy, Sweden, Russia, Turkey, United States)	Crisis management	Formulation	Marginal factor in easing tensions
YUGOSLAVIA II: BOSNIA Serbia Bosnia Croatia	3 Mar. 1992	21 Nov. 1995	United States	Conflict resolution	Manipulation	Most important factor in easing tensions
NORTH KOREA NUCLEAR CRISIS North Korea South Korea United States	Early Mar. 1993	21 Oct. 1994	Jimmy Carter (i.e., former United States President acting independently)	Conflict resolution	Formulation	Important factor in easing tensions

OPERATION ACCOUNTABILITY Israel Lebanon	10 July 1993	31 July 1993	*United States*, Syria	Crisis management	Manipulation	Important factor in easing tensions
CAMEROON/ NIGERIA III Nigeria Cameroon	Late Dec. 1993	Late Nov. 1994	Organization of African Unity Deputy Secretary General	Crisis management	Facilitation	No effect
ECUADOR/PERU V Ecuador Peru	9 Jan. 1995	1 Mar. 1995	Argentina, Brazil, Chile, United States (i.e., the guarantor states of the Rio Protocol)	Conflict resolution	Formulation	Most important factor in easing tensions
RED SEA ISLANDS Eritrea Yemen	15 Dec. 1995	31 Dec. 1995	United Nations Secretary General	Missing data	Formulation	Important factor in easing tensions
AEGEAN SEA IV Turkey Greece	26 Jan. 1996	31 Jan. 1996	United States	Crisis management	Formulation	Important factor in easing tensions
OPERATION GRAPES OF WRATH Israel Lebanon	9 Apr. 1996	27 Apr. 1996	United States	Crisis management	Formulation	Most important factor in easing tensions
NORTH KOREAN SUBMARINE South Korea North Korea	18 Sept. 1996	29 Dec. 1996	United States	Crisis management	Formulation	Most important factor in easing tensions

CRISIS NAME (and Crisis Actors)[1]	TRIGGER DATE[2]	TERMINATION DATE	PRIMARY MEDIATOR[3]	GOAL OF MEDIATOR	HIGHEST FORM OF MEDIATION	EFFECT OF MEDIATION ON CRISIS ABATEMENT
ZAIRE CIVIL WAR Zaire Rwanda	8 Oct. 1996	16 May 1997	United Nations	Crisis management	Formulation	Important factor in easing tensions
UNSCOM I United States Iraq	13 Nov. 1997	23 Feb. 1998	United Nations Secretary General	Crisis management	Manipulation	Most important factor in easing tensions
ERITREA/ETHIOPIA Eritrea Ethiopia	6 May 1998	12 Dec. 2000	Organization of African Unity (*Algeria*)	Conflict resolution	Manipulation	Important factor in easing tensions
DEMOCRATIC REPUBLIC OF CONGO (DRC) CIVIL WAR Rwanda Angola Chad DRC Namibia Zimbabwe Uganda	29 July 1998	30 July 2002	Zambia	Crisis management	Formulation	Marginal factor in easing tensions

KOSOVO Albania Belgium Canada France Germany Italy Netherlands Portugal Spain United Kingdom United States Yugoslavia	20 Feb. 1999	10 June 1999	United States	Crisis management	Manipulation	Marginal factor in easing tensions

Appendix B: Ecuador-Peru simulation crisis scenarios

The following pages contain the text of the Ecuador-Peru border crisis simulation scenario that was developed for the experimental analyses conducted in this book and provided to the student negotiators. The left-hand column below contains the "base" scenario described in Chapters 2 and 4 and used for the analyses in Chapters 4 and 6.

The "base" scenario involves a situation in which the crisis was asymmetric, wherein Peru has greater aggregate and issue-specific power. For the analyses contained in Chapter 5, we altered this base design in order to make possible a comparison of asymmetric and symmetric crises. The right-hand column below contains the text of the symmetric version of this scenario, wherein the parties are roughly equal in terms of relative power. Italics are used to indicate the specific sections of the scenario text that differed from version to version.[1]

POWER ASYMMETRY

(analyses in Chapters 4 and 6)

In January 1981, fighting broke out between the military forces of Peru and Ecuador along the border between the two states in a region known as Cordillera del Condor. Ecuador alleged that a Peruvian helicopter attacked an Ecuadorian military outpost near the Ecuadorian town of Paquisha. Peru denied this allegation, stating that Ecuadorian forces had fired on a plane en route to Peruvian border posts with supplies.

Widespread fighting followed this initial clash. On January 28, Peru announced that Ecuador was conducting military operations within Peruvian territory. Ecuador, on the other hand, stated that its military was operating within Ecuador but was under attack by Peruvian planes. The states disagreed about which party triggered the crisis, but *both countries mobilized forces in the border region.* Peru claimed that Ecuadorian troops had moved eight to 12 kilometers within Peruvian territory, and deadly fighting broke out between the two sides.

This crisis was the latest in a long chain of conflicts between Peru and Ecuador stemming from a disagreement about where the border between these two countries falls, but this 1981 crisis represented the most violent flare-up in the region since the 1940s.

Background

Peru and Ecuador are neighboring countries in northwestern South America. The geography of each country is dominated by the Andes Mountains, and both countries border the Pacific Ocean. The countries share a common history, each having been colonized by Spain in the 1500s, and both have struggled to overcome the political and economic legacies of this

POWER SYMMETRY

(analyses in Chapter 5)

In January 1981, fighting broke out between the military forces of Peru and Ecuador along the border between the two states in a region known as Cordillera del Condor. Ecuador alleged that a Peruvian helicopter attacked an Ecuadorian military outpost near the Ecuadorian town of Paquisha. Peru denied this allegation, stating that Ecuadorian forces had fired on a plane en route to Peruvian border posts with supplies.

Widespread fighting followed this initial clash. On January 28, Peru announced that Ecuador was conducting military operations within Peruvian territory. Ecuador, on the other hand, stated that its military was operating within Ecuador but was under attack by Peruvian planes. The states disagreed about which party triggered the crisis, but *Ecuador had mobilized forces in the border region and Peru was threatening to do the same.* Peru claimed that Ecuadorian troops had moved eight to 12 kilometers within Peruvian territory, and deadly fighting broke out between the two sides.

This crisis was the latest in a long chain of conflicts between Peru and Ecuador stemming from a disagreement about where the border between these two countries falls, but this 1981 crisis represented the most violent flare-up in the region since the 1940s.

Background

Peru and Ecuador are neighboring countries in northwestern South America. The geography of each country is dominated by the Andes Mountains, and both countries border the Pacific Ocean. The countries share a common history, each having been colonized by Spain in the 1500s, and both have struggled to overcome the political and economic legacies of this

POWER ASYMMETRY

(analyses in Chapters 4 and 6)

colonization. The shared characteristics of these countries, though, do not mean that the people or the leaders of Peru and Ecuador share a similar perspective on all issues. Rather, relations between these two countries have been tense – often turning violent – since the 1800s. The main source of conflict between the two countries has been persistent disagreement about the border between the two countries.

The question of where Peruvian territory ends and Ecuadorian territory begins is rooted in the colonial era. As Spain's South American empire began to break apart, little effort was made to clarify or specify official territorial divisions. Peru and Ecuador both lay claim to some of the same tracts of territory in northern Peru and southern Ecuador. These conflicting territorial claims have led to more than thirty violent clashes between the two countries.

Until 1941, fighting between Peruvian and Ecuadorian forces, resulting from their conflicting claims, had been troubling, but each violent flare-up was relatively short-lived. In 1941, this trend changed: The more-powerful Peru invaded Ecuadorian territory. The occupation by Peruvian forces led to four months of brutal fighting between the two states.

As the fighting continued, the depth and complexity of the dispute between Peru and Ecuador became apparent to all parties, including the hemispheric neighbors of these two countries. Argentina, Brazil, Chile, and the United States were intent on securing peace within the Western Hemisphere as World War II raged in Europe and the Pacific, and the four powers drew up a plan to end the fighting by *dividing the disputed territory between Peru and Ecuador.* The leaders of both Peru and

POWER SYMMETRY

(analyses in Chapter 5)

colonization. The shared characteristics of these countries, though, do not mean that the people or the leaders of Peru and Ecuador share a similar perspective on all issues. Rather, relations between these two countries have been tense – often turning violent – since the 1800s. The main source of conflict between the two countries has been persistent disagreement about the border between the two countries.

The question of where Peruvian territory ends and Ecuadorian territory begins is rooted in the colonial era. As Spain's South American empire began to break apart, little effort was made to clarify or specify official territorial divisions. Peru and Ecuador both lay claim to some of the same tracts of territory in northern Peru and southern Ecuador. These conflicting territorial claims have led to more than thirty violent clashes between the two countries.

Fighting between Peruvian and Ecuadorian forces resulting from their conflicting claims had been troubling, but, until 1941, each violent flare-up was relatively short-lived. In 1941, this trend changed when Peru invaded Ecuadorian territory. The occupation by Peruvian forces led to four months of brutal fighting between the two states.

As the fighting continued, the depth and complexity of the dispute between Peru and Ecuador became apparent to all parties, including the hemispheric neighbors of these two countries. Argentina, Brazil, Chile, and the United States were intent on securing peace within the Western Hemisphere as World War II raged in Europe and the Pacific, and the four powers drew up a plan to end the fighting by *devising an arrangement, according to which neither Peru nor Ecuador had sovereign*

POWER ASYMMETRY	*POWER SYMMETRY*
(analyses in Chapters 4 and 6)	*(analyses in Chapter 5)*
Ecuador agreed to the conditions of this agreement, known as the Rio Protocol, and signed a treaty codifying the agreement in 1942, despite the fact that Ecuador lost about 5,000 square miles of territory. Argentina, Brazil, Chile, and the United States agreed to serve as the "guarantors" of the agreement. These four large powers agreed to watch over developments in the relationship between Peru and Ecuador. Any escalation of tensions between the two belligerent states would prompt involvement by guarantor states. Such a design was intended to insure that the parties would continue to recognize and support the conditions of the agreement.	*control of the region but citizens from both countries could continue to live in the region. Under pressure from these world powers,* the leaders of both Peru and Ecuador agreed to the conditions of this agreement, known as the Rio Protocol, and signed a treaty codifying the agreement in 1942. Argentina, Brazil, Chile, and the United States agreed to serve as the "guarantors" of the agreement. These four large powers agreed to watch over developments in the relationship between Peru and Ecuador. Any escalation of tensions between the two belligerent states would prompt involvement by guarantor states. Such a design was intended to insure that the parties would continue to recognize and support the conditions of the agreement.
For years, Ecuadorian officials voiced displeasure with the agreement, claiming that they had been unfairly forced to sign the Protocol. After all, they noted, Ecuador was under Peruvian occupation when the agreement was proposed. This vulnerable position made it almost impossible for Ecuador's leaders to question the agreement. Subsequent discoveries about the location of historical Ecuadorian settlements intensified Ecuador's objections to the settlement detailed in the Rio Protocol. In short, Ecuador believed that huge tracts of its territory had been stolen from the country in 1942. Leaders and the public alike considered this to be a national embarrassment for Ecuador. But the consequences of the division went beyond just national pride. The Rio Protocol division denied Ecuador any access to tributaries of the Amazon River. Lack of access to the Amazon, which would in turn provide access to the Atlantic Ocean, frustrated Ecuadorian efforts to improve its own economic conditions.	*For years, Ecuadorian and Peruvian officials voiced displeasure with the agreement, claiming that they had been unfairly forced to sign the Protocol in 1942. Though neither Peru nor Ecuador had legal control over the disputed territory, both countries claimed the right to it. While citizens of both Ecuador and Peru continued to live throughout the disputed region, Peruvians were concentrated in the portion of the disputed territory that included a tributary of the Amazon River, thus limiting safe Ecuadorian access to this waterway and their ability to use it as a way to increase international trade.*

POWER ASYMMETRY

(analyses in Chapters 4 and 6)

In 1960, Ecuador officially renounced the Rio Protocol and demanded *renewed consideration of the division of the border between Peru and Ecuador. Peruvian leaders responded by re-stating their faith in and commitment to the 1942 agreement. Peru refused to recognize that any territorial dispute existed between the two countries, arguing that the dispute was resolved with the Rio Protocol.*

The settlement defined in the Rio Protocol remained the recognized international border between Peru and Ecuador, but this region persisted as an international "hot-spot." Peruvian and Ecuadorian forces sporadically clashed in the region, and relations between the two countries – both on official levels and among their general publics – deteriorated. In the late 1970s, both Peru and Ecuador experienced shifts from totalitarian rule towards democratic governance, but these regime changes neither altered the fundamental disagreements nor reduced the intense animosity between the two states. It came as little surprise, then, when fighting broke out between the Peruvian and Ecuadorian forces in January 1981. What was surprising, however, was the intensity of the fighting and the resistance of both sides to make any concessions. It was difficult to foresee an end to the fighting after it began in 1981.

The Negotiations

Peru believes that the division of territory between the two countries that occurred in 1942 was a fair and objective settlement, a view historically shared by the international community. Peru believes that Ecuador disregarded this agreement and violated Peru's sovereignty first by shooting on supply planes flying in Peruvian airspace and, subsequently, by sending troops eight to 12 kilometers into Peruvian territory.

POWER SYMMETRY

(analyses in Chapter 5)

In 1960, Ecuador officially renounced the Rio Protocol and demanded *that a new border between the two countries be drawn which would indicate that the disputed territory belonged wholly to Ecuador. Peruvian leaders responded in turn by also expressing a lack of faith in and commitment to the 1942 agreement but refusing to accept the conditions put forth by Ecuador.*

The somewhat unsatisfying settlement defined in the Rio Protocol remained in place despite objections from the two countries, and this region persisted as an international "hot-spot." Peruvian and Ecuadorian forces sporadically clashed in the region, and relations between the two countries – both on official levels and among their general publics – deteriorated. In the late 1970s, both Peru and Ecuador experienced shifts from totalitarian rule towards democratic governance, but these regime changes neither altered the fundamental disagreements nor reduced the intense animosity between the two states. It came as little surprise, then, when fighting broke out between the Peruvian and Ecuadorian forces in January 1981. What was surprising, however, was the intensity of the fighting and the resistance of both sides to make any concessions. It was difficult to foresee an end to the fighting after it began in 1981.

The Negotiations

Peru believes that Ecuador poses a threat to Peruvians in the disputed territory as well as to Peru in general, especially given Ecuador's recent use of force in the region. Ecuador shot at supply planes flying in Peruvian airspace and, subsequently, sent troops eight to 12 kilometers into a section of the disputed territory occupied by Peruvians. Peru feels its military actions against Ecuadorian forces are justified,

POWER ASYMMETRY	*POWER SYMMETRY*
(analyses in Chapters 4 and 6)	*(analyses in Chapter 5)*
Peru feels its military actions against Ecuadorian forces are justified, stating that, "We are simply throwing out invaders as soon as possible."	stating that, "We are simply throwing out invaders as soon as possible."
Ecuador has demanded reconsideration of the location of the border between the two states but maintains that it was merely defending itself against Peruvian challenges by bringing military forces into the disputed region in January 1981. Ecuador's president argued that as long as Ecuador was denied control of the large tracts of land to which it was historically entitled, Peru would continue to exploit and pose a threat to Ecuador.	*Ecuador maintains that it was merely defending itself against Peruvian challenges by bringing military forces into the disputed region in January 1981. Ecuador's president argued that as long as Ecuador was denied control of the large tracts of land to which he believes are a rightful part of the Ecuadorian country, Peru would continue to pose a threat to Ecuador.*
Despite the deep tensions between the governments of Peru and Ecuador, the two agreed to negotiate with one another after fighting broke out in 1981. These negotiations were intended as a venue for consideration and discussion of both short-term and long-term problems between Peru and Ecuador.	Despite the deep tensions between the governments of Peru and Ecuador, the two agreed to negotiate with one another after fighting broke out in 1981. These negotiations were intended as a venue for consideration and discussion of both short-term and long-term problems between Peru and Ecuador.
Agreement Options The negotiators could pursue a short-term solution to stop the current violence in the border region, or the negotiators could try to find a long-term solution that would address the fundamental disagreement about which country controls what portions of the border region. While considering agreements about the fate of the border region, each negotiator could also offer concessions to the other country on a group of issues of concern to both countries.	**Agreement Options** The negotiators could pursue a short-term solution to stop the current violence in the border region, or the negotiators could try to find a long-term solution that would address the fundamental disagreement about which country controls what portions of the border region. While considering agreements about the fate of the border region, each negotiator could also offer concessions to the other country on a group of issues of concern to both countries.
Either negotiator can propose any of these agreements, but the other country has to accept the agreement in order for it to be implemented. Negotiators cannot choose to pursue a combination of these agreements; each side needs to agree to one and only one of the following options in order to conclude	Either negotiator can propose any of these agreements, but the other country has to accept the agreement in order for it to be implemented. Negotiators cannot choose to pursue a combination of these agreements; each side needs to agree to one and only one of the following options in order to conclude

POWER ASYMMETRY

(analyses in Chapters 4 and 6)

the negotiations. (The order in which these are listed in no way reflects the desirability or the likelihood of the outcomes.)

1. Status Quo (terminate negotiations): If the negotiators both believe that the negotiations have come to a deadlock, they may agree to terminate the negotiation, even if there is still time left in the session.

If both sides agree to terminate the negotiation, the existing state of conditions between the two states would continue. Neither side would stop its forces from fighting in the border region, and *the division of territory would remain as it has been since 1942.*

2. Territorial Division: This option represents an agreement by both sides to change the settlement agreed upon in the Rio Protocol. Either side can propose a *new* division of the territory within the 200,000 square-kilometer border region. This region has been divided into ten sectors or districts of 20,000 square kilometers each, and the negotiators must agree on how *many of these sectors – now controlled by Peru – should be granted to Ecuador.* Agreement to a division of territory also includes agreement to a ceasefire.

Peru would like to maintain control of as much of this territory as possible, while Ecuador wants to expand its territory as much as possible.
(Note: During these talks, negotiators are not tasked with deciding which sectors should be controlled by which country.)

3. Ceasefire: This option represents an agreement by both sides to demand that Peruvian and Ecuadorian military forces in the border region both stop the fighting that erupted in January.

POWER SYMMETRY

(analyses in Chapter 5)

the negotiations. (The order in which these are listed in no way reflects the desirability or the likelihood of the outcomes.)

1. Status Quo (terminate negotiations): If the negotiators both believe that the negotiations have come to a deadlock, they may agree to terminate the negotiation, even if there is still time left in the session.

If both sides agree to terminate the negotiation, the existing state of conditions between the two states would continue. Neither side would stop its forces from fighting in the border region, and *no settlement regarding a division of the disputed territory would be reached.*

2. Territorial Division: This option represents an agreement by both sides to change the settlement agreed upon in the Rio Protocol. Either side can propose a division of the territory within the 200,000 square-kilometer border region. This region has been divided into ten sectors or districts of 20,000 square kilometers each, and the negotiators must agree on how *these sectors should be divided up between the two countries.* Agreement to a division of territory also includes agreement to a ceasefire.

Both sides would like to gain control over as much of this territory as possible.
(Note: During these talks, negotiators are not tasked with deciding which sectors should be controlled by which country.)

3. Ceasefire: This option represents an agreement by both sides to demand that Peruvian and Ecuadorian military forces in the border region both stop the fighting that erupted in January.

POWER ASYMMETRY

(analyses in Chapters 4 and 6)

This agreement leaves unresolved the issue of territorial division and only addresses the short-term issue of this particular crisis.

4. Accept Arbitration: This decision represents an agreement by both sides to let a third party (another country or an international institution) *evaluate the existing division of the disputed border territory.* If the parties agree to arbitration, both states will be obligated to accept the findings of the arbitrator – be it to *allow Peru to retain control of all of its territory* (as Peru would want), to grant Ecuador control over the whole disputed region (as Ecuador would want), or to divide the territory between the two states. The arbitrator – not the state's negotiators – will serve as the final determinant of which state controls what.

Opt-Out Options

The governments of both Peru and Ecuador have granted their negotiators a significant amount of power. If either negotiator believes that it would be necessary or desirable to do so, each has the power to forego the pursuit of an agreement between the countries. Such a move does not require the agreement of the other side, but once one negotiator decides to pursue this course of action, that side "opts out" of the negotiation, and the negotiations are terminated.

1. Peruvian Military Action: The Peruvian government has agreed that it will launch an all-out war against Ecuador if the Peruvian negotiator believes this to be the best course of action. *Given the superiority of Peru's military capacity, the damage to Ecuador could be severe, but Peru could face significant losses of its own and is not guaranteed victory in such a war.*

POWER SYMMETRY

(analyses in Chapter 5)

This agreement leaves unresolved the issue of territorial division and only addresses the short-term issue of this particular crisis.

4. Accept Arbitration: This decision represents an agreement by both sides to let a third party (another country or an international institution) *decide upon the final status of the disputed territory that runs between the two countries.* If the parties agree to arbitration, both states will be obligated to accept the findings of the arbitrator – be it to *grant Peru control over the entirety of the territory* (as Peru would want), to grant Ecuador control over the whole disputed region (as Ecuador would want), or to divide the territory between the two states. The arbitrator – not the state's negotiators – will serve as the final determinant of which state controls what.

Opt-Out Options

The governments of both Peru and Ecuador have granted their negotiators a significant amount of power. If either negotiator believes that it would be necessary or desirable to do so, each has the power to forego the pursuit of an agreement between the countries. Such a move does not require the agreement of the other side, but once one negotiator decides to pursue this course of action, that side "opts out" of the negotiation, and the negotiations are terminated.

1. Peruvian Military Action: The Peruvian government has agreed that it will launch an all-out war against Ecuador if the Peruvian negotiator believes this to be the best course of action. *Peru and Ecuador are essentially equal in terms of military power: Peru's army is larger than Ecuador's, but Ecuador has more advanced weaponry. As such, it is difficult to predict whether a Peruvian military action would prove*

POWER ASYMMETRY

(analyses in Chapters 4 and 6)

2. Ecuadorian Military Action: The Ecuadorian government has agreed that it will launch an all-out war against Peru if the Ecuadorian negotiator believes this to be the best course of action. *Ecuador's military is overmatched versus Peru's military, but Ecuador could manage to defeat its more powerful rival. Such an outcome would likely require a significant investment of national resources by Ecuador.*

World State Parameters
Each negotiator may change the policies of its country on a limited number of issues. Changing the status of one or more of these world state parameters will have an effect on the other country, but changing these parameters is not a collective decision. Each state decides on its own whether to change any or all of its world state parameters. Each negotiator controls a distinct set of world state parameters.

Peru's World State Parameters
1. Border status with Ecuador: As the negotiations begin, your border with Ecuador is open. This means that Ecuadorians may enter your country and bring goods for sale into your country. This also means that commercial Ecuadorian planes can fly within your airspace. You have the authority to close this border. This would significantly limit Ecuadorians' ability to enter into Peru and to maintain trade relations with Peru, one of its main export markets. Exports represent the largest portion of Ecuador's gross domestic product (GDP). Closing the border, however, would also limit your country's access to Ecuadorian goods.

POWER SYMMETRY

(analyses in Chapter 5)

to be victorious. It is likely, though, that such a war would be bloody and costly to both sides.

2. Ecuadorian Military Action: The Ecuadorian government has agreed that it will launch an all-out war against Peru if the Ecuadorian negotiator believes this to be the best course of action. *Ecuador and Peru are essentially equal in terms of military power: Peru's army is larger than Ecuador's, but Ecuador has more advanced weaponry. As such, it is difficult to predict whether an Ecuadorian military action would prove to be victorious. It is likely, though, that such a war would be bloody and costly to both sides.*

World State Parameters
Each negotiator may change the policies of its country on a limited number of issues. Changing the status of one or more of these world state parameters will have an effect on the other country, but changing these parameters is not a collective decision. Each state decides on its own whether to change any or all of its world state parameters. Each negotiator controls a distinct set of world state parameters.

Peru's World State Parameters
1. Border status with Ecuador: As the negotiations begin, your border with Ecuador is open. This means that Ecuadorians may enter your country and bring goods for sale into your country. This also means that commercial Ecuadorian planes can fly within your airspace. You have the authority to close this border. This would significantly limit Ecuadorians' ability to enter into Peru and to maintain trade relations with Peru, one of its main export markets. Exports represent the largest portion of Ecuador's gross domestic product (GDP). Closing the border, however, would also limit your country's access to Ecuadorian goods.

POWER ASYMMETRY	*POWER SYMMETRY*
(analyses in Chapters 4 and 6)	*(analyses in Chapter 5)*
2. Mobilization of troops: As the negotiations begin, Peru has troops stationed *and operating within the contentious border region.* You have the authority to mobilize *more* Peruvian forces in order to get them better prepared to fight on short notice, and you have the power to order that these troops be moved into the disputed region. This dedication of resources would be expensive for Peru but might encourage Ecuador to resolve the dispute rather than face a Peruvian military offensive attack.	**2. Mobilization of troops:** As the negotiations begin, Peru has troops stationed *near the contentious border region, but they are not yet mobilized.* You have the authority to mobilize *these* Peruvian forces in order to get them better prepared to fight on short notice, and you have the power to order that these troops be moved into the disputed region. This dedication of resources would be expensive for Peru but might encourage Ecuador to resolve the dispute rather than face a Peruvian military offensive attack.
3. Navigation rights to the Amazon: *As the negotiations begin, your country has sovereign control over the Marañón River, which is a tributary of the great Amazon River. Parts of this river are contained within the border region. The Marañón River provides your country access to the Amazon River, which – in turn – provides Peru with direct access to both Brazil and the Atlantic Ocean. This access makes widespread trade easier and more efficient for Peru. Ecuador has no access to the Amazon River and believes that access to the river would greatly bolster its economy.*	**3. Safe access to the Amazon:** *As the negotiations begin, Peruvians are living in the portion of the disputed territory that includes a tributary of the Amazon River. This tributary provides your country access to the Amazon River, which – in turn – provides Peru with direct access to both Brazil and the Atlantic Ocean. The concentration of Peruvians along this waterway makes trade easier and more efficient for Peru. Trade is more difficult for the people of Ecuador because it has no safe access to the Amazon River given the distribution of population in the border region.*
The Peruvian government has the authority to grant to Ecuador the right to navigate the Marañón. This would provide Ecuador its much sought-after, indirect access to the Amazon River. Peru would not lose access to the river by granting these rights to Ecuador.	*The Peruvian government has the option of granting the government and people of Ecuador secure access to this waterway.* Peru would not lose access to the river by granting these rights to Ecuador.
Ecuador's World State Parameters **1. Troop presence in the border region:** As the negotiations begin, Ecuador has sent troops into parts of the disputed border *controlled by Peru.* Ecuador claims that the troop presence is a defensive one to guard against a Peruvian invasion of Ecuador. You have the authority to order the withdrawal of these troops *from Peruvian territory.* Withdrawal would	**Ecuador's World State Parameters** **1. Troop presence in the border region:** As the negotiations begin, Ecuador has sent troops into parts of the disputed border *region.* Ecuador claims that the troop presence is a defensive one to guard against a Peruvian invasion of Ecuador. You have the authority to order the withdrawal of these troops. Withdrawal would help to conserve Ecuador's limited resources but would

POWER ASYMMETRY

(analyses in Chapters 4 and 6)

help to conserve Ecuador's limited resources but would leave Ecuador less prepared if an all-out war broke out between the two countries.

2. Border status with Peru: As the negotiations begin, your border with Peru is open. This means that Peruvians may continue to enter your country and bring goods for sale into your country. This also means that commercial Peruvian planes can fly within your airspace. You have the authority to close this border. Closing the border would pose a threat to Peru because Peru is not agriculturally self-sufficient; given the large portion of its territory that cannot be cultivated, Peru must rely on trade with other countries to ensure an adequate food supply. Sealing the country's northwest border would threaten the flow of this supply of food. Closing the border, however, would also choke off the supply of Peruvian goods which are available to Ecuadorians.

Third-Party Involvement

Argentina, Brazil, Chile, and the United States have remained involved with this conflict since they each put forth efforts in 1942 to secure a settlement between Peru and Ecuador and to ensure that that settlement was in fact implemented. These guarantor states have attempted to deal with escalating tensions between the two belligerent states on a number of occasions, and the nature of their reactions has varied from situation to situation.

Within days of the violent military exchanges between Peru and Ecuador in 1981, the guarantor states issued a statement urging the foes to find a peaceful settlement to their dispute. Both Peruvian and Ecuadorian leaders requested that officials from the guarantor states investigate the

POWER SYMMETRY

(analyses in Chapter 5)

leave Ecuador less prepared if an all-out war broke out between the two countries.

2. Border status with Peru: As the negotiations begin, your border with Peru is open. This means that Peruvians may continue to enter your country and bring goods for sale into your country. This also means that commercial Peruvian planes can fly within your airspace. You have the authority to close this border. Closing the border would pose a threat to Peru because Peru is not agriculturally self-sufficient; given the large portion of its territory that cannot be cultivated, Peru must rely on trade with other countries to ensure an adequate food supply. Sealing the country's northwest border would threaten the flow of this supply of food. Closing the border, however, would also choke off the supply of Peruvian goods which are available to Ecuadorians.

Third-Party Involvement

Argentina, Brazil, Chile, and the United States have remained involved with this conflict since they each put forth efforts in 1942 to secure a settlement between Peru and Ecuador and to ensure that that settlement was in fact implemented. These guarantor states have attempted to deal with escalating tensions between the two belligerent states on a number of occasions, and the nature of their reactions has varied from situation to situation.

Within days of the violent military exchanges between Peru and Ecuador in 1981, the guarantor states issued a statement urging the foes to find a peaceful settlement to their dispute. Both Peruvian and Ecuadorian leaders requested that officials from the guarantor states investigate the

POWER ASYMMETRY

(analyses in Chapters 4 and 6)

circumstances surrounding the events which ignited this round of violence. The Organization of American States (OAS) noted that representatives from Argentina, Brazil, Chile, and the U.S. would have to play a key role if any resolution to the border conflict was to be found. (Each of these states is a member of the OAS.)

The Mediator in the Negotiations
A group comprised of representatives from the guarantor states agrees to serve as the mediating body during negotiations between Peru and Ecuador. [Note: Only some of the negotiations in this simulation will involve a mediator. You will find out whether a mediator is involved in your negotiation once the simulation begins.] The mediation group is objective and sides with neither party in this conflict. The mediator will attempt to facilitate discussion between the Peruvian negotiator and the Ecuadorian negotiator. You may use the mediator as a sounding board for proposals you are considering offering or as a messenger of proposals to the other negotiator. You can accept or ignore suggestions made by the mediator. The mediator knows the nature of the conflict between Ecuador and Peru and the general position of each country but does not have access to the detailed information which each negotiator will be using to assist him/her in assessing the costs and benefits of different proposals.

It is no accident that the mediation group is made up of representatives from the most powerful countries in the Western Hemisphere. These states were encouraged to step forward in the 1940s because they would have the leverage to compel Peru and Ecuador – relatively weak states in the region – to accept the suggested settlement. In 1981, the guarantor states remain vastly

POWER SYMMETRY

(analyses in Chapter 5)

circumstances surrounding the events which ignited this round of violence. The Organization of American States (OAS) noted that representatives from Argentina, Brazil, Chile, and the U.S. would have to play a key role if any resolution to the border conflict was to be found. (Each of these states is a member of the OAS.)

The Mediator in the Negotiations
A group comprised of representatives from the guarantor states agrees to serve as the mediating body during negotiations between Peru and Ecuador. [Note: Only some of the negotiations in this simulation will involve a mediator. You will find out whether a mediator is involved in your negotiation once the simulation begins.] The mediation group is objective and sides with neither party in this conflict. The mediator will attempt to facilitate discussion between the Peruvian negotiator and the Ecuadorian negotiator. You may use the mediator as a sounding board for proposals you are considering offering or as a messenger of proposals to the other negotiator. You can accept or ignore suggestions made by the mediator. The mediator knows the nature of the conflict between Ecuador and Peru and the general position of each country but does not have access to the detailed information which each negotiator will be using to assist him/her in assessing the costs and benefits of different proposals.

It is no accident that the mediation group is made up of representatives from the most powerful countries in the Western Hemisphere. These states were encouraged to step forward in the 1940s because they would have the leverage to compel Peru and Ecuador – relatively weak states in the region – to accept the suggested settlement. In 1981, the guarantor states remain vastly

POWER ASYMMETRY

(analyses in Chapters 4 and 6)

more powerful than either Peru or Ecuador. In fact, both Peru and Ecuador rely significantly on these states for assistance in their efforts to pursue democracy and to hasten their economic development. [*NOTE TO READER: The following material was provided only to participants working with a manipulative mediator.] The mediator may try to use its leverage to encourage the states to agree to a settlement more rapidly.

Mediator's World State Parameters
1. Mediator's trade relations with Peru: As negotiations begin, free and active trade occurs between the mediating states and Peru. About 30 percent of Peru's imports come from the United States, while almost *25* percent of Peru's total exports are sold to the United States. The mediator has the authority to impose trade sanctions on Peru that would prohibit Peruvians from either buying goods from the guarantor countries or selling goods to the significant markets in those countries.

2. Mediator's trade relations with Ecuador: As negotiations begin, free and active trade occurs between the mediating states and Ecuador. Thirty-two percent of Ecuador's imports come from the United States, while 38 percent of Ecuador's total exports are sold to the United States. The mediator has the authority to impose trade sanctions on Ecuador that would prohibit Ecuadorians from buying goods from either the guarantor countries or selling goods to the significant markets in those countries.

3. Mediator's stance on weapons sales to Ecuador: As negotiations begin, the United States – one of the guarantors – is holding up the conclusion of a weapon sales agreement between Ecuador and Israel because the U.S.

POWER SYMMETRY

(analyses in Chapter 5)

more powerful than either Peru or Ecuador. In fact, both Peru and Ecuador rely significantly on these states for assistance in their efforts to pursue democracy and to hasten their economic development. [*NOTE TO READER: The following material was provided only to participants working with a manipulative mediator.] The mediator may try to use its leverage to encourage the states to agree to a settlement more rapidly.

Mediator's World State Parameters
1. Mediator's trade relations with Peru: As negotiations begin, free and active trade occurs between the mediating states and Peru. About 30 percent of Peru's imports come from the United States, while almost *35* percent of Peru's total exports are sold to the United States. The mediator has the authority to impose trade sanctions on Peru that would prohibit Peruvians from either buying goods from the guarantor countries or selling goods to the significant markets in those countries.

2. Mediator's trade relations with Ecuador: As negotiations begin, free and active trade occurs between the mediating states and Ecuador. Thirty-two percent of Ecuador's imports come from the United States, while 38 percent of Ecuador's total exports are sold to the United States. The mediator has the authority to impose trade sanctions on Ecuador that would prohibit Ecuadorians from buying goods from either the guarantor countries or selling goods to the significant markets in those countries.

3. Mediator's stance on weapons sales to Ecuador: As negotiations begin, the United States – one of the guarantors – is holding up the conclusion of a weapon sales agreement between Ecuador and Israel because the U.S.

POWER ASYMMETRY (*analyses in Chapters 4 and 6*)	*POWER SYMMETRY* (*analyses in Chapter 5*)
believes that Ecuador's acquisition of new fighter jets could be a destabilizing force in South America. (The weapons contain American parts, so the U.S. is within its rights to block this sale.) Despite these reservations, the mediator has the authority to lift the block on the sale of the fighter jets to Ecuador.	believes that Ecuador's acquisition of new fighter jets could be a destabilizing force in South America. (The weapons contain American parts, so the U.S. is within its rights to block this sale.) Despite these reservations, the mediator has the authority to lift the block on the sale of the fighter jets to Ecuador.
4. U.S. aid to Peru: As negotiations begin, 15 percent of the external aid that Peru receives each year to help with its political and economic development comes from United States. The mediator has the authority to reduce or cut off this aid to Peru.	**4. U.S. aid to Peru:** As negotiations begin, 15 percent of the external aid that Peru receives each year to help with its political and economic development comes from United States. The mediator has the authority to reduce or cut off this aid to Peru.
5. U.S. aid to Ecuador: As negotiations begin, *5* percent of the external aid that Ecuador receives each year to help with its political and economic development comes from the United States. The mediator has the authority to reduce or cut off this aid to Ecuador.	**5. U.S. aid to Ecuador:** As negotiations begin, *12* percent of the external aid that Ecuador receives each year to help with its political and economic development comes from the United States. The mediator has the authority to reduce or cut off this aid to Ecuador.

[1]Modifications consistent with the symmetric scenario were also made to the decision-support system (DSS) made available to crisis negotiators. For the symmetric scenario, changes were made to reflect equivalent probabilities of Peru and Ecuador winning a war compared to each other; under asymmetric conditions, in comparison, Peru was more likely than Ecuador to prove successful if it launched a military attack against the other. The impact of time on the simulation was also altered. In the power symmetry model, the effect of time on the probability of a successful attack was the same for both parties, whereas time had a differential effect on each party's probabilities of a successful attack in the power asymmetry model, with Ecuador's probability decreasing at a faster rate.

Bibliography

African Union (2002) "The Constitutive Act: Article 3 – Objectives," 9 July. Online. Available at http://www.africa-union.org//about_AU/AbConstitutive_Act.htm#Article3 (accessed 25 July, 2004).

Aldrich, J.H. and Nelson, F.D. (1984) *Linear Probability, Logit, and Probit Models*, Sage University Paper Series on Quantitative Applications in the Social Sciences, series no. 07-045, Beverly Hills, CA: Sage.

Allison, G.T. (1971) *The Essence of Decision: Explaining the Cuban Missile Crisis*, Boston: Little, Brown, and Co.

Asal, V., Wilkenfeld, J., Young, K., Quinn, D., Pate, A., and Beardsley, K. (2002) "Mediating Ripeness: The Impact of Mediation on Negotiators' Zones of Agreement," paper presented at the Annual Meeting of the American Political Science Association, Boston, MA, 28 August–1 September.

Azar, E.E., Jureidini, P., and McLaurin, R. (1978) "Protracted Social Conflict: Theory and Practice in the Middle East," *Journal of Palestine Studies*, 8: 41–60.

Balakrishnan, P.V. (S.) and Eliashberg, J. (1995) "An Analytical Process Model of Two-party Negotiations," *Management Science*, 41: 226–43.

Beardsley, K., Quinn, D., Biswas, B., and Wilkenfeld, J. (2004) "Mediation Style and Crisis Outcomes in the Twentieth Century," paper presented at the Annual Meeting of the International Studies Association, Montreal, Quebec, Canada, 17–20 March.

Beer, F. (1993) "Validities: A Political Science Perspective," *Social Epistemology*, 7: 85–105.

Bell, C. (1971) *The Conventions of Crisis: A Study in Diplomatic Management*, London: Oxford University Press.

Bercovitch, J. (1985) "Third Parties in Conflict Management: The Structure and Conditions of Effective Mediation in International Relations," *International Journal*, 40: 736–52.

—— (1986) "International Mediation: A Study of the Incidence, Strategies and Conditions of Successful Outcomes," *Cooperation and Conflict*, 21: 155–68.

—— (1991) "International Mediation and Dispute Settlement: Evaluating the Conditions for Successful Mediation," *Negotiation Journal*, 7: 17–30.

—— (1992) "The Structure and Diversity of Mediation in International Relations," in J. Bercovitch and J.Z. Rubin (eds) *Mediation in International Relations: Multiple Approaches to Conflict Management*, New York: St. Martin's Press.

—— (1996) "Understanding Mediation's Role in Preventive Diplomacy," *Negotiation Journal*, 12: 241–58.

—— (1997) "Mediation in International Conflict: An Overview of Theory, a Review of Practice," in I.W. Zartman and J.L. Rasmussen (eds) *Peacemaking in International Conflict: Methods and Techniques*, Washington, DC: United States Institute of Peace Press.

Bercovitch, J. and Houston, A. (1996) "The Study of International Mediation: Theoretical Issues and Empirical Evidence," in J. Bercovitch (ed.) *Resolving International Conflicts: The Theory and Practice of Mediation*, Boulder, CO: Lynne Rienner.

—— (2000) "Why Do They Do It Like This?: An Analysis of Factors Influencing Mediation Behavior in International Conflicts," *Journal of Conflict Resolution*, 44: 170–202.

Bercovitch, J. and Jackson, R. (2001) "Negotiation or Mediation?: An Exploration of Factors Affecting the Choice of Conflict Management in International Conflict," *Negotiation Journal*, 17: 59–77.

Bercovitch, J. and Langley, J. (1993) "The Nature of the Dispute and the Effectiveness of International Mediation," *Journal of Conflict Resolution*, 37: 670–99.

Bercovitch, J. and Regan, P.M. (1997) "Managing Risks in International Relations: The Mediation of Enduring Rivalries," in G. Schneider and P.A. Weitsman (eds) *Enforcing Cooperation*, New York: St. Martin's Press.

Bercovitch, J., Anagnoson, J.T., and Wille, D.L. (1991) "Some Conceptual Issues and Empirical Trends in the Study of Successful Mediation in International Relations," *Journal of Peace Research*, 28: 7–17.

Berridge, G.R. (2002) *Diplomacy: Theory and Practice*, 2nd edn, London: Palgrave.

Bidwell, R. (1983) *The Two Yemens*, Boulder, CO: Westview Press.

Blainey, G. (1973) *The Causes of War*, New York: The Free Press.

Bloomfield, D., Nupen, C., and Harris, P. (1998) "Negotiation Processes," in P. Harris and B. Reilly (eds) *Democracy and Deep-rooted Conflict: Options for Negotiators*, Stockholm, Sweden: International Institute for Democracy and Electoral Assistance (IDEA).

Bositis, D.A. (1990) *Research Designs for Political Science: Contrivance and Demonstration in Theory and Practice*, Carbondale, IL: Southern Illinois University Press.

Brecher, M. (1993) *Crises in World Politics: Theory and Reality*, Oxford: Pergamon Press.

Brecher, M. and Wilkenfeld, J. (1989) *Crisis, Conflict and Instability*, Oxford: Pergamon Press.

—— (2000) *A Study of Crisis*, 2nd edn (with CD-Rom), Ann Arbor, MI: University of Michigan Press.

Brecher, M., Wilkenfeld, J., and Moser, S. (1988) *Crises in the Twentieth Century: Vol. 1 – Handbook of International Crises*, Oxford: Pergamon Press.

Brody, R.A. (1969) "The Study of International Politics *qua* Science: The Emphasis on Methods and Techniques," in K. Knorr and J.N. Rosenau (eds) *Contending Approaches to International Politics*, Princeton, NJ: Princeton University Press.

Brookmire, D.A. and Sistrunk, F. (1980) "The Effects of Perceived Ability and Impartiality of Mediators and Time Pressure on Negotiation," *Journal of Conflict Resolution*, 24: 311–27.

Burton, J.W. (1969) *Conflict and Communication: The Use of Controlled Communication in International Relations*, New York: The Free Press.

—— (1972) "The Resolution of Conflict," *International Studies Quarterly*, 16: 5–29.

—— (1984) *Global Conflict: The Domestic Sources of International Crisis*, Brighton, England: Wheatsheaf Books.

—— (1987) *Resolving Deep-rooted Conflict: A Handbook*, Lanham, MD: University Press of America.

—— (1990) *Conflict: Resolution and Prevention*, New York: St. Martin's Press.

Campbell, D.T. (1969) "Ethnocentrism of Disciplines and the Fish-scale Model of Omniscience," in M. Sherif and C.W. Sherif (eds) *Interdisciplinary Relationships in the Social Sciences*, Chicago: Aldine.

Campbell, D.T. and Stanley, J.C. (1963) *Experimental and Quasi-experimental Designs for Research*, Chicago: Rand-McNally.

Carnevale, P.J.D. and Arad, S. (1996) "Bias and Impartiality in International Mediation," in J. Bercovitch (ed.) *Resolving International Conflicts: The Theory and Practice of Mediation*, Boulder, CO: Lynne Rienner.

Carnevale, P.J.D. and Conlon, D.E. (1988) "Time Pressure and Strategic Choice in Mediation," *Organizational Behavior and Human Decision Processes*, 42: 111–33.

Carnevale, P.J.D. and Lawler, E.J. (1986) "Time Pressure and the Development of Integrative Agreements in Bilateral Negotiations," *Journal of Conflict Resolution*, 30: 636–59.

Carnevale, P.J.D. and Pegnetter, R. (1985) "The Selection of Mediation Tactics in Public-Sector Disputes: A Contingency Analysis," *Journal of Social Issues*, 41: 65–81.

Carnevale, P.J.D., O'Connor, K., and McCusker, C. (1993) "Time Pressure in Negotiation and Mediation," in O. Svenson and A.J. Maule (eds) *Time Pressure and Stress in Human Judgment and Decision Making*, New York: Plenum Press.

Claude, I. (1962) *Power and International Relations*, New York: Random House.

CNN (1996) "Holbrooke: Greece, Turkey were on the Verge of Battle," 31 January. Online. Available at http://www.cnn.com/world/9601/turkey_greece_dispute/01-31/ (accessed 22 July, 2004).

Coleman, P.T. (1997) "Redefining Ripeness: A Social-psychological Perspective," *Peace and Conflict*, 3: 81–103.

Collier, P. and Hoeffler, A. (2002) "Greed and Grievance in Civil War," World Bank Working Paper, 1 March. Online. Available at http://econ.worldbank.org/programs/conflict/library/doc?id=12205 (accessed 5 September, 2002).

Conlon, D.E., Carnevale, P.J.D., and Murnighan, J.K. (1994) "Intravention: Third-party Intervention with Clout," *Organizational Behavior and Human Decision Processes*, 57: 387–410.

Craig, G.A. and George, A.L. (1983) *Force and Statecraft: Diplomatic Problems of Our Time*, New York: Oxford University Press.

Crocker, C.A., Hampson, F.O., and Aall, P. (eds) (1999) *Herding Cats: Multiparty Mediation in a Complex World*, Washington, DC: United States Institute of Peace Press.

Deutsch, M. (1973) *The Resolution of Conflict: Constructive and Destructive Processes*, New Haven, CT: Yale University Press.

Dixon, W.J. (1993) "Democracy and the Management of International Conflict," *Journal of Conflict Resolution*, 37: 42–68.

—— (1994) "Democracy and the Peaceful Settlement of International Conflict," *American Political Science Review*, 88: 14–32.

—— (1996) "Third-party Techniques for Preventing Conflict Escalation and Promoting Peaceful Settlement," *International Organization*, 50 (4): 653–81.

Donohue, W.A. (1989) "Communicative Competence in Mediators," in K. Kressel and D.G. Pruitt (eds) *Mediation Research: The Process and Effectiveness of Third-party Intervention*, San Francisco: Jossey-Bass.

Druckman, D. (1993) "The Situational Levers of Negotiating Flexibility," *Journal of Conflict Resolution*, 37: 236–76.

—— (1994a) "Determinants of Compromising Behavior in Negotiation: A Meta-analysis," *Journal of Conflict Resolution*, 38: 507–56.

—— (1994b) "Tools for Discovery: Experimenting with Simulations," *Simulation & Gaming*, 25: 446–55.

Edmead, F. (1977) "Analysis and Prediction in International Mediation," in K.V. Raman (ed.) *Dispute Settlement through the United Nations*, Dobbs Ferry, NY: Oceana.

Evans, G. and Newnham, J. (1998) *The Penguin Dictionary of International Relations*, London: Penguin Books.

Fearon, J.D. (1994) "Signaling versus the Balance of Power and Interests: An Empirical Test of a Crisis Bargaining Model," *Journal of Conflict Resolution*, 38: 236–69.

—— (1995) "Rationalist Explanations for War," *International Organization*, 49: 379–414.

Fisher, R.J. (1972) "Third Party Consultation: A Method for the Study and Resolution of Conflict," *Journal of Conflict Resolution*, 16: 67–94.

Fisher, R.J. and Keashly, L. (1988) "Distinguishing Third Party Interventions in Intergroup Conflict: Consultation is not Mediation," *Negotiation Journal*, 4: 381–93.

Fisher, R. and Ury, W. (1981) *Getting to Yes: Negotiating Agreement Without Giving In*, Boston: Houghton Mifflin.

Fisher, R., Schneider, A.K., Borgwardt, E., and Ganson, B. (1997) *Coping with International Conflict: A Systematic Approach to Influence in International Negotiation*, Upper Saddle River, NJ: Prentice Hall.

Franklin, A. (1996) *Experiment, Right or Wrong*, New York: Cambridge University Press.

Garnett, J. (1975) "The Role of Military Power," in J. Baylis, K. Booth, J. Garnett, and P. Williams (eds) *Contemporary Strategy: Theories and Policies*, New York: Holmes and Meier Publishers.

George, A.L. (1984) "Crisis Management: The Interaction of Political and Military Considerations," *Survival*, 26: 223–34.

—— (ed.) (1991) *Avoiding War: Problems of Crisis Management*, Boulder, CO: Westview Press.

George, A.L., Hall, D.K., and Simons, W.E. (1971) *The Limits of Coercive Diplomacy: Laos, Cuba, Vietnam*, Boston: Little, Brown.

Gilbert, A.N. and Lauren, P.G. (1980) "Crisis Management: An Assessment and Critique," *Journal of Conflict Resolution*, 24: 641–64.

Glasl, F. (1982) "The Process of Conflict Escalation and Roles of Third Parties," in G.B.J. Bomers and R.B. Peterson (eds) *Conflict Management and Industrial Relations*, Boston: Kluwer-Nijhoff.

Gochman, C.S. and Maoz, Z. (1984) "Militarized Interstate Disputes, 1816–1976: Procedures, Patterns, and Insights," *Journal of Conflict Resolution*, 28: 585–616.

Green, D.P. and Gerber, A.S. (2002) "Reclaiming the Experimental Tradition in Political Science," in H. Milner and I. Katznelson (eds) *Political Science: State of the Discipline III*, Washington, DC: American Political Science Association.

Greenberg, M.C., Barton, J.H., and McGuiness, M.E. (2000) *Words over War: Mediation and Arbitration to Prevent Deadly Conflict*, Lanham, MD: Rowman and Littlefield.

Greig, J.M. (2001) "Moments of Opportunity: Recognizing Conditions of Ripeness for International Mediation," *Journal of Conflict Resolution*, 45: 691–718.

Grieco, J. (1988) "Anarchy and the Limits of Cooperation: A Realist Critique of the Newest Liberal Institutionalism," *International Organization*, 42: 485–507.

Groom, A.J.R. and Webb, K. (1987) "Injustice, Empowerment, and Facilitation in Conflict," *International Interactions*, 13: 236–80.

Gurr, T.R. (2000) *Peoples versus States: Minorities at Risk in the New Century*, Washington, DC: United States Institute of Peace Press.

Haass, R.N. (1990) *Conflicts Unending*, New Haven, CT: Yale University Press.

Habeeb, W.M. (1988) *Power and Tactics in International Negotiations: How Weak Nations Bargain with Strong Nations*, Baltimore, MD: Johns Hopkins University Press.

Hancock, L.E. (2001) "To act or to Wait: A Two Stage View of Ripeness," *International Studies Perspectives*, 2: 195–205.

Hermann, C.F. (1969) "International Crisis as a Situational Variable," in J.N. Rosenau (ed.) *International Politics and Foreign Policy*, 2nd edn, New York: Free Press.

Hiltrop, J.-M. (1985) "Mediator Behavior and the Settlement of Collective Bargaining Disputes in Britain," *Journal of Social Issues*, 41: 83–99.

—— (1989) "Factors Associated with Successful Mediation," in K. Kressel and D.G. Pruitt (eds) *Mediation Research: The Process and Effectiveness of Third Party Intervention*, San Francisco: Jossey-Bass.

Holsti, O.R. (1972) *Crisis, Escalation, War*, Montreal, Quebec, Canada: McGill-Queen's University Press.

—— (1989) "Crisis Decision Making," in P.E. Tetlock, J.L. Husbands, R. Jervis, P.C. Stern, and C. Tilly (eds) *Behavior, Society, and Nuclear War, Vol. 1*, New York: Oxford University Press.

Hopmann, P.T. (1996) *The Negotiation Process and the Resolution of International Conflicts*, Columbia, SC: University of South Carolina Press.

—— (2001) "Bargaining and Problem Solving: Two Perspectives on International Negotiation," in C.A. Crocker, F.O. Hampson and P. Aall (eds) *Turbulent Peace: The Challenges of Managing International Conflict*, Washington, DC: United States Institute of Peace Press.

Hughes, B.B. (1999) *International Futures: Choices in the Face of Uncertainty*, 3rd edn, Boulder, CO: Westview Press.

International Crisis Group (2003) "Ethiopia and Eritrea: War or Peace?," in *International Crisis Group Africa Report*, 68 (24 September).

Jabri, V. (1996) *Discourse on Violence: Conflict Analysis Reconsidered*, Manchester, England: Manchester University Press.

Jones, D.L. (2000) "Mediation, Conflict Resolution and Critical Theory," *Review of International Studies*, 26: 647–62.

Jones, D.M., Bremer S.A., and Singer, J.D. (1996) "Militarized Interstate Disputes, 1816–1992: Rationale, Coding Rules, and Empirical Patterns," *Conflict Management and Peace Science*, 15: 163–213.

Kanazawa, S. (1999) "Using Laboratory Experiments to Test Theories of Corporate Behavior," *Rationality & Society*, 11: 443–62.

Keashly, L. and Fisher, R.J. (1996) "A Contingency Perspective on Conflict Interventions: Theoretical and Practical Considerations," in J. Bercovitch (ed.) *Resolving International Conflicts: The Theory and Practice of Mediation*, Boulder, CO: Lynne Rienner.

Kelman, H.C. (1972) "The Problem-solving Workshop: A Social-psychological Contribution to the Resolution of International Conflicts," in R.L. Merritt (ed.) *Communication in International Politics*, Urbana, IL: University of Illinois Press.

—— (1992) "Informal Mediation by the Scholar/Practitioner," in J. Bercovitch and J.Z. Rubin *Mediation in International Relations: Multiple Approaches to Conflict Management*, New York: St. Martin's Press.

Keohane, R.O. and Nye, J.S. (1977) *Power and Interdependence: World Politics in Transition*, Boston: Little, Brown, and Co.

Kersten, G.E. and Noronha, S.J. (1999) "WWW-based Negotiation Support: Design, Implementation, and Use," *Decision Support Systems*, 25: 135–54.

Kinder, D. and Palfrey, T. (1993) "On Behalf of an Experimental Political Science," in D. Kinder and T. Palfrey (eds) *Experimental Foundations of Political Science*, Ann Arbor, MI: University of Michigan Press.

Kintner, W.R. and Schwarz, D.C. (1965) *A Study on Crisis Management*, Philadelphia: University of Pennsylvania Policy Research Institute.

Kissinger, H. (1999) *Years of Renewal*, New York: Simon & Schuster.

Kleiboer, M. (1994) "Ripeness of Conflict: A Fruitful Notion?," *Journal of Peace Research*, 31: 109–16.

—— (1996) "Understanding Success and Failure of International Mediation," *Journal of Conflict Resolution*, 40: 360–90.

—— (1998) *The Multiple Realities of International Mediation*, Boulder, CO: Lynne Rienner.

—— (2002) "Great Power Mediation: Using Leverage to Make Peace?," in J. Bercovitch (ed.) *Studies in International Mediation: Essays in Honor of Jeffrey Z. Rubin*, Houndsmills, Basingstoke, Hampshire, UK: Palgrave MacMillan.

Kolb, D.M. and Babbitt, E.F. (1995) "Mediation Practice on the Home Front: Implications for Global Conflict Resolution," in J.A. Vasquez, J.T. Johnson, S. Jaffee, and L. Stamato (eds) *Beyond Confrontation: Learning Conflict Resolution in the Post-Cold War Era*, Ann Arbor, MI: University of Michigan Press.

Krasner, S.D. (1991) "Global Communications and National Power: Life on the Pareto Frontier," *World Politics*, 43: 336–66.

Kraus, S. (2001) *Strategic Negotiation in Multiagent Environments*, Cambridge, MA: MIT Press.

Kraus, S., Wilkenfeld, J., and Zlotkin, G. (1995) "Multi-agent Negotiation Under Time Constraints," *Artificial Intelligence Journal*, 75: 297–345.

Kressel, K. and Pruitt, D.G. (eds) (1989) *Mediation Research: The Process and Effectiveness of Third Party Intervention*, San Francisco: Jossey-Bass.

Kriesberg, L. (1996) "Varieties of Mediating Activities and Mediators in International Relations," in J. Bercovitch (ed.) *Resolving International Conflicts: The Theory and Practice of Mediation*, Boulder, CO: Lynne Rienner.

Kugler, J. and Lemke, D. (eds) (1996) *Parity and War: Evaluations and Extensions of The War Ledger*, Ann Arbor, MI: University of Michigan Press.

Kugler, J. and Organski, A.F.K. (1989) "The Power Transition: A Retrospective and Prospective Evaluation," in M.I. Midlarsky (ed.) *Handbook of War Studies*, Boston: Unwin Hyman.

Laponce, J.A. (1972) "Experimenting: A Two-person Game between Man and Nature," in J.A. Laponce and P. Smoker (eds) *Experimentation and Simulation in Political Science*, Toronto, Ontario, Canada: University of Toronto Press.

Lebow, R.N. (1981) *Between Peace and War: The Nature of International Crisis*, Baltimore, MD: Johns Hopkins University Press.

—— (1996) *The Art of Bargaining*, Baltimore, MD: Johns Hopkins University Press.

Leng, R.J. (1983) "Will They Ever Learn?: Coercive Bargaining in Recurrent Crises," *Journal of Conflict Resolution*, 27: 379–419.

—— (1988) "Crisis Learning Games," *The American Political Science Review*, 82: 179–94.

—— (1993) *Interstate Crisis Behavior, 1816–1980: Realism vs. Reciprocity*, Cambridge, MA: Cambridge University Press.

—— (2000) *Bargaining and Learning in Recurring Crises: The Soviet-American, Egyptian-Israeli, and Indo-Pakistani Rivalries*, Ann Arbor, MI: University of Michigan Press.

Leng, R.J. and Singer, J.D. (1988) "Militarized International Crises: The BCOW Typology and its Applications," *International Studies Quarterly*, 32: 155–73.

Lim, R.G. and Carnevale, P.J.D. (1990) "Contingencies in the Mediation of Disputes," *Journal of Personality and Social Psychology*, 58: 259–72.

Lipson, L. (1966) "Crisis Management or Crisis Prevention," in *NATO Letter* (August–September).

Lockhart, C. (1979) *Bargaining in International Conflicts*, New York: Columbia University Press.

McDermott, R. (2002) "Experimental Methods in Political Science," *Annual Review of Political Science*, 5: 31–61.

McGraw, K. (1993) "Political Methodology: Research Design and Experimental Methods," in R.E. Goodin and H.-D. Klingemann (eds) *A New Handbook of Political Science*, New York: Oxford University Press.

Mandell, B.S. and Tomlin, B.W. (1991) "Mediation in the Development of Norms to Manage Conflict: Kissinger in the Middle East," *Journal of Peace Research*, 28: 43–55.

Maoz, Z. (1990) *National Choices and International Processes*, Cambridge, MA: Cambridge University Press.

—— (2004) "Conflict Management and Conflict Resolution: A Conceptual and Methodological Introduction," in Z. Maoz, A. Mintz, T.C. Morgan, G. Palmer, and R.J. Stoll (eds) *Multiple Paths to Knowledge in International Relations: Methodology in the Study of Conflict Management and Conflict Resolution*, Lanham, MD: Lexington Books.

Maoz, Z., Mintz, A., Morgan T.C., Palmer, G., and Stoll, R.J. (eds) (2004) *Multiple Paths to Knowledge in International Relations: Methodology in the Study of Conflict Management and Conflict Resolution*, Lanham, MD: Lexington Books.

Merrills, J.G. (1998) *International Dispute Settlement*, 3rd edn, Cambridge, UK: Cambridge University Press.

Miall, H. (1992) *The Peacemakers: Peaceful Settlement of Disputes since 1945*, New York: St. Martin's Press.

Milburn, T.W. (1972) "The Management of Crisis," in C.F. Hermann (ed.) *International Crises: Insights from Behavioral Research*, New York: The Free Press.

Mintz, A. (2004) "How Do Leaders Make Decisions?: A Poliheuristic Perspective," *Journal of Conflict Resolution*, 48: 3–13.

Mintz, A. and Geva, N. (1993) "Why Don't Democracies Fight Each Other?: An Experimental Study," *Journal of Conflict Resolution*, 37: 484 –503.

Mintz, A., Geva, N., Redd, S.B., and Carnes, A. (1997) "The Effect of Dynamic and Static Choice Sets on Political Decision Making: An Analysis using the Decision Board Platform," *American Political Science Review*, 91: 553–66.

Mitchell, C.R. (1981) *Peacemaking and the Consultant's Role*, New York: Nichols.

—— (1993) "The Process and Stages of Mediation: Two Sudanese Cases," in D.R. Smock (ed.) *Making War and Waging Peace*, Washington, DC: United States Institute of Peace Press.

Mitchell, C.R. and Webb, K. (eds) (1988) *New Approaches to International Mediation*, New York: Greenwood Press.

Modelski, G. (1964) "International Settlement of Internal Wars," in J.N. Rosenau (ed.) *International Aspects of Civil Strife*, Princeton, NJ: Princeton University Press.

Mooradian, M. and Druckman, D. (1999) "Hurting Stalemate or Mediation?: The Conflict over Nagorno-Karabakh, 1990–1995," *Journal of Peace Research*, 36: 709–27.

Morgan, T.C. (1984) "A Spatial Model of Crisis Bargaining," *International Studies Quarterly*, 28: 407–26.

—— (1994) *Untying the Knot of War: A Bargaining Theory of International Crises*, Ann Arbor, MI: University of Michigan Press.

Morrow, J.D. (1989) "Capabilities, Uncertainty, and Resolve: A Limited Information Model of Crisis Bargaining," *American Journal of Political Science*, 33: 941–72.

—— (1992) "Signaling Difficulties with Linkage in Crisis Bargaining," *International Studies Quarterly*, 36: 153–72.

Mosterd, I. and Rutte, C.G. (2000) "Effects of Time Pressure and Accountability to Constituents on Negotiation," *International Journal of Conflict Management*, 11: 227–47.

Nickles, R.W. and Hedgespeth, J. (1991) "A Generic Model for Divorce Mediation," *Journal of Divorce and Remarriage*, 17: 157–69.

Northedge, F.S. and Donelan, M.D. (1971) *International Disputes: The Political Aspects*, New York: St. Martin's Press.

Organski, A.F.K. (1960) *World Politics*, New York: Knopf.

Ostowani, M. (1998) "Yemen Celebrates Court Victory," *Al-Ahram Weekly Online*, issue no. 399, 15–21 October. Online. Available at http://weekly.ahram.org.eg/1998/399/re6.htm (accessed 4 August, 2004).

Ott, M.C. (1972) "Mediation as a Method of Conflict Resolution: Two Cases," *International Organization*, 26: 595–618.

Peterson, S. (1996) *Crisis Bargaining and the State: The Domestic Politics of International Conflict*, Ann Arbor, MI: University of Michigan Press.

Princen, T. (1992) *Intermediaries in International Conflict*, Princeton, NJ: Princeton University Press.

Pruitt, D.G. (1981) *Negotiation Behavior*, New York: Academic Press.

Pruitt, D.G. and Carnevale, P.J.D. (1993) *Negotiation in Social Conflict*, Pacific Grove, CA: Brooks/Cole Publishing Co.

Quinn, D., Wilkenfeld, J., Young, K., and Asal, V. (2003) "Factors in Crisis

Mediation: Style of Mediation, Relative Power of Crisis Actors, and Zones of Agreement," paper presented at CEEISA/International Studies Association International Convention, Budapest, Hungary, 26–28 June.

Raiffa, H. (2002) *The Art and Science of Negotiation*, 2nd edn, Cambridge, MA: Belknap Press of Harvard University Press.

Raymond, G.A. and Kegley, C.W., Jr (1985) "Third Party Mediation and International Norms: A Test of Two Models," *Conflict Management and Peace Science*, 9: 33–51.

Regan, P.M. and Stam, A.C. (2000) "In the Nick of Time: Conflict Management, Mediation Timing, and the Duration of International Disputes," *International Studies Quarterly*, 44: 239–60.

Rogan, R.G., Hammer, M.R., and Van Zandt, C.R. (eds) (1997) *Dynamic Processes of Crisis Negotiation: Theory, Research, and Practice*, Westport, CT: Praeger.

Ross, W.H. and Wieland, C. (1996) "Effects of Interpersonal Trust and Time Pressure on Managerial Mediation Strategy in a Simulated Organizational Dispute," *Journal of Applied Psychology*, 81: 228–48.

Rothman, J. (1992) *From Confrontation to Cooperation: Resolving Ethnic and Regional Conflict*, Newbury Park, CA: Sage Publications.

Rubin, J.Z. (1980) "Experimental Research on Third-party Intervention in Conflict: Toward Some Generalizations," *Psychological Bulletin*, 87: 379–91.

—— (1991) "The Timing of Ripeness and the Ripeness of Timing," in L. Kriesberg and S.J. Thorson (eds) *Timing the De-escalation of International Conflicts*, Syracuse, NY: Syracuse University Press.

Rubin, J.Z. and Zartman, I.W. (1995) "Asymmetrical Negotiations: Some Survey Results that may Surprise," *Negotiation Journal*, 11: 349–64.

Rupesinghe, K. (1996) "Mediation in Internal Conflicts: Lessons from Sri Lanka," in J. Bercovitch (ed.) *Resolving International Conflicts: The Theory and Practice of Mediation*, Boulder, CO: Lynne Rienner.

Sacks, M.A., Reichert, K.S., and Proffitt, W.T., Jr (1999) "Broadening the Evaluation of Dispute Resolution: Context and Relationships over Time," *Negotiation Journal*, 15: 339–45.

Santmire, T.E., Wilkenfeld, J., Kraus, S., Holley, K.M., Santmire, T.E., and Gleditsch, K.S. (1998) "The Impact of Cognitive Diversity on Crisis Negotiations," *Political Psychology*, 19: 721–48.

Schelling, T.C. (1960) *The Strategy of Conflict*, Cambridge, MA: President and Fellows of Harvard College.

Schrodt, P.A. and Gerner, D.J. (2004) "An Event Analysis of Third-Party Mediation in the Middle East and Balkans," *Journal of Conflict Resolution*, 48: 310–30.

Schroeder, P.W. (1974) "*Crisis, Escalation, War*, by O.R. Holsti." Reviewed in: *Journal of Modern History*, 46: 537–40.

Schwarzer, G. (1998) "The Peaceful Settlement of Interstate Conflict: Saar, Austria, and Berlin," *Journal of Peace Research*, 35: 743–57.

Sears, D.O. (1986) "College Sophomores in the Laboratory: Influences of a Narrow Data Base on Social Psychology's View of Human Nature," *Journal of Personality and Social Psychology*, 51: 515–30.

Sheffer, G. (2003) *Diaspora Politics: At Home Abroad*, Cambridge, UK: Cambridge University Press.

Shmueli, D. and Vranesky, A. (1996) "Environmental Mediation in International

Relations," in J. Bercovitch (ed.) *Resolving International Conflicts: The Theory and Practice of Mediation*, Boulder, CO: Lynne Rienner.

Simmons, B.A. (1999) *Territorial Disputes and Their Resolution: The Case of Peru and Ecuador*, Peaceworks Paper No. 27, Washington, DC: United States Institute of Peace Press.

Singer, J.D. (1963) "Inter-nation Influence: A Formal Model," *American Political Science Review*, 57: 420–30.

Skjelsbaek, K. (1986) "Peaceful Settlement of Disputes by the United Nations and Other Intergovernmental Bodies," *Cooperation and Conflict*, 21: 139–54.

Small, M. and Singer, J.D. (1982) *Resort to Arms: International and Civil Wars, 1816–1980*, Beverly Hills, CA: Sage.

Smith, D.L., Pruitt, D.G., and Carnevale, P.J.D. (1982) "Matching and Mismatching: The Effect of Own Limit, Other's Toughness, and Time Pressure on Concession Rate in Negotiation," *Journal of Personality and Social Psychology*, 42: 876–83.

Snyder, G.H. and Diesing, P. (1977) *Conflict Among Nations: Bargaining, Decision-making, and System Structure in International Crises*, Princeton, NJ: Princeton University Press.

Starke, K. and Rangaswamy, A. (1999) "Computer-mediated Negotiations: Review and Research Opportunities," *Encyclopedia of Microcomputers, Vol. 26*, New York: Marcel Inc.

Starkey, B., Boyer, M.A., and Wilkenfeld, J. (2005) *Negotiating a Complex World: An Introduction to International Negotiation*, 2nd edn, Lanham, MD: Rowman and Littlefield.

Stern, P.C. and Druckman, D. (2000) "Evaluating Interventions in History: The Case of International Conflict Resolution," *International Studies Review*, 2: 33–63.

Stevens, C.D. and Ash, R.A. (2001) "The Conscientiousness of Students in Subject Pools: Implications for 'Laboratory' Research," *Journal of Research in Personality*, 35: 91–7.

Stevens, C.M. (1963) *Strategy and Collective Bargaining Negotiation*, New York: McGraw-Hill.

Stuhlmacher, A.F., Gillespie, T.L., and Champagne, M.V. (1998) "The Impact of Time Pressure in Negotiation: a meta-analysis," *International Journal of Conflict Management*, 9: 97–116.

Susskind, L. and Babbitt, E.F. (1992) "Overcoming the Obstacles to Effective Mediation of International Disputes," in J. Bercovitch and J.Z. Rubin (eds) *Mediation in International Relations: Multiple Approaches to Conflict Management*, New York: St. Martin's Press.

Taras, R.C. and Ganguly, R. (2002) *Understanding Ethnic Conflict: The International Dimension*, 2nd edn, New York: Longman.

Terris, L. and Maoz, Z. (2001) "Rational Mediation: A Theory and a Test," paper presented at the Annual Meeting of the American Political Science Association, San Francisco, CA, 30 August–2 September.

Thoennes, N.A. and Pearson, J. (1985) "Predicting Outcomes in Divorce Mediation: The Influence of People and Process," *Journal of Social Issues*, 41: 115–26.

Touval, S. (1982) *The Peace Brokers: Mediators in the Arab-Israeli Conflict, 1948–1979*, Princeton, NJ: Princeton University Press.

—— (2003) "Mediation and Foreign Policy," *International Studies Review*, 5: 91–5.

Touval, S. and Zartman, I.W. (1985) "Introduction: Mediation in Theory," in S. Touval and I.W. Zartman (eds) *International Mediation in Theory and Practice*, Boulder, CO: Westview Press.

—— (2003) "International Mediation in the post-Cold War Era," in C.A. Crocker, F.O. Hampson and P. Aall (eds) *Turbulent Peace: The Challenges of Managing International Conflict*, Washington, DC: United States Institute of Peace Press.

United Nations (1992) *Handbook on the Peaceful Settlement of Disputes Between States*, New York: United Nations.

United Nations Department of Peacekeeping Operations (2004) "UNMEE: United Nations Mission in Ethiopia and Eritrea – background," Online. Available at http://www.un.org/Depts/dpko/missions/unmee/background.html (accessed 6 July, 2004).

United Nations Development Programme (2004) *Human Development Report 2004: Cultural Liberty in Today's Diverse World*, New York: Oxford University Press.

Wall, J.A., Jr. and Lynn, A. (1993) "Mediation: A Current Review," *Journal of Conflict Resolution*, 37: 160–94.

Wall, J.A., Jr., Stark, J.B., and Standifer, R.L. (2001) "Mediation: A Current Review and Theory Development," *Journal of Conflict Resolution*, 45: 370–91.

Watkins, M. (2002) *Breakthrough Business Negotiations: A Toolbox for Managers*, San Francisco: Jossey-Bass.

Wehr, P. (1979) *Conflict Regulation*, Boulder, CO: Westview Press.

Wehr, P. and Lederach, J.P. (1991) "Mediating Conflict in Central America," *Journal of Peace Research*, 28: 85–98.

—— (1996) "Mediating Conflict in Central America," in J. Bercovitch (ed.) *Resolving International Conflicts: The Theory and Practice of Mediation*, Boulder, CO: Lynne Rienner.

Wilkenfeld, J. (2002) "Simulation and Experimentation in Foreign Policy Analysis: Some Personal Observations on Problems and Prospects," in M. Brecher and F. Harvey (eds) *Millennium Reflections on International Studies: Conflict, Security, Foreign Policy, and International Political Economy*, Ann Arbor, MI: University of Michigan Press.

Wilkenfeld, J. and Brecher, M. (2000) "Interstate Crises and Violence: Twentieth-century Findings," in M.I. Midlarsky (ed.) *Handbook of War Studies II*, Ann Arbor, MI: University of Michigan Press.

Wilkenfeld, J., Brecher, M., and Moser, S. (1988) *Crises in the Twentieth Century: Vol. 2 – Handbook of Foreign Policy Crises*, Oxford: Pergamon Press.

Wilkenfeld, J., Kraus, S., Holley, K.M., and Harris, M.A. (1995) "GENIE: A Decision Support System for Crisis Negotiations, *Decision Support Systems*, 14: 369–91.

Wilkenfeld, J., Kraus, S., Santmire, T.E., and Frain C.K. (2004) "The Role of Mediation in Conflict Management: Conditions for Successful Resolution," in Z. Maoz, A. Mintz, T.C. Morgan, G. Palmer, and R.J. Stoll (eds) *Multiple Paths to Knowledge in International Relations: Methodology in the Study of Conflict Management and Conflict Resolution*, Lanham, MD: Lexington Books.

Wilkenfeld, J., Young, K., Asal, V., and Quinn, D. (2003) "Mediating International Crises: Cross-national and Experimental Perspectives," *Journal of Conflict Resolution*, 47: 279–301.

Wright, Q. (1965) *A Study of War*, 2nd edn, Chicago, IL: University of Chicago Press.

Yilmaz, Ö. and Gerner, D.J. (2003) "U.S. and British Mediation Efforts During the 1974 Crisis Over Cyprus," Pew Case Studies in International Affairs, case no. 269, Washington, DC: Institute for the Study of Diplomacy.

Young, K., Quinn, D., Asal, V., and Wilkenfeld, J. (2004) "Mediation and the Relative Power of Crisis Actors: An Experimental Analysis," paper presented at the Annual Meeting of the International Studies Association, Montreal, Quebec, Canada, 17–20 March.

Young, K., Wilkenfeld, J., Quinn, D., and Asal, V. (2002) "Power Play: An Evaluation of Mediation Efforts in Asymmetric Crises," paper presented at the Annual Meeting of the International Studies Association, New Orleans, LA, 24–27 March.

Young, O.R. (1967) *The Intermediaries: Third Parties in International Crises*, Princeton, NJ: Princeton University Press.

—— (1968) *The Politics of Force: Bargaining During International Crises*, Princeton, NJ: Princeton University Press.

Zartman, I.W. (1981) "Explaining Disengagement," in J.Z. Rubin (ed.) *Dynamics of Third Party Intervention: Kissinger in the Middle East*, New York: Praeger.

—— (1988) "Alternative Attempts at Crisis Management: Concepts and Processes," in G.R. Winham (ed.) *New Issues in International Crisis Management*, Boulder, CO: Westview Press.

—— (1989) *Ripe for Resolution: Conflict and Intervention in Africa*, updated edn, New York: Oxford University Press.

—— (ed.) (1995) *Elusive Peace: Negotiating an End to Civil Wars*, Washington, DC: Brookings Institution.

—— (1997) "Toward the Resolution of International Conflicts," in I.W. Zartman and J.L. Rasmussen (eds) *Peacemaking in International Conflict: Methods and Techniques*, Washington, DC: United States Institute of Peace Press.

—— (2000) "Ripeness: The Hurting Stalemate and Beyond," in P.C. Stern and D. Druckman (eds) *International Conflict Resolution after the Cold War*, Washington, DC: National Academy Press.

—— (2001) "The Timing of Peace Initiatives: Hurting Stalemates and Ripe Moments," *Global Review of Ethnopolitics*, 1: 8–18.

Zartman, I.W. and Touval, S. (1996) "International Mediation in the post-Cold War Era," in C.A. Crocker, F.O. Hampson, and P. Aall (eds) *Managing Global Chaos: Sources of and Responses to International Conflict*, Washington, DC: United States Institute of Peace Press.

Index

For Product Safety Concerns and Information please contact our EU representative GPSR@taylorandfrancis.com
Taylor & Francis Verlag GmbH, Kaufingerstraße 24, 80331 München, Germany

www.ingramcontent.com/pod-product-compliance
Ingram Content Group UK Ltd.
Pitfield, Milton Keynes, MK11 3LW, UK
UKHW011003180926
475701UK00004B/535